Private Metropolis

GLOBALIZATION AND COMMUNITY

Susan E. Clarke, Series Editor
Dennis R. Judd, Founding Editor

(continued on page 303)

Private Metropolis

The Eclipse of Local Democratic Governance

DENNIS R. JUDD
EVAN McKENZIE
ALBA ALEXANDER
EDITORS

GLOBALIZATION AND COMMUNITY, VOLUME 32

 University of Minnesota Press
Minneapolis
London

Published by the University of Minnesota Press
111 Third Avenue South, Suite 290
Minneapolis, MN 55401-2520
http://www.upress.umn.edu

ISBN 978-1-5179-1081-5 (hc)
ISBN 978-1-5179-1082-2 (pb)

Library of Congress record available at https://lccn.loc.gov/2020058446

Printed in the United States of America on acid-free paper

The University of Minnesota is an equal-opportunity educator and employer.

UMP BmB 2021

Contents

Acknowledgments

This volume originates from a conference in Chicago at the University of Illinois in May 2015, "Reconsidering the Politics of Urban Infrastructure." The conference was made possible largely through generous support from the Office of the Dean of the College of Arts and Sciences, UIC. The editors regret that they did not have space to include all contributions from that event. We are deeply grateful to Susan Clarke, series editor of Globalization and Community for the University of Minnesota Press, for guiding the project through the process to publication. We also thank the anonymous reviewer whose reflections on the manuscript improved it in final revisions. And we appreciate the sturdy assistance of Marcie Reynolds and Stephanie Whitaker in organizing the conference, as well as the crucial aid of Tingting Ding, Amy Schoenecker, and Marilyn Getzov at critical points along the way.

Introduction

Shadow Governments and the Remaking of the American Local State

Dennis R. Judd, Evan McKenzie, and Alba Alexander

The essays that compose this book trace the outlines of an evolving institutional structure that has thoroughly altered the governance of America's cities and urban regions. In the twenty-first century a "shadow local state" has emerged that is made up, on the one hand, of an extraordinarily complex mix of quasi-public and wholly privatized institutions that have assumed responsibility for many of the policy initiatives and public services provided within urban regions. A second aspect of this shadow state is the diminishing status of the American municipality, which has offloaded many of its historic responsibilities onto a bewildering variety of quasi-public institutions. The result of this historic development is far-reaching and rarely acknowledged: the municipality is no longer the privileged seat of governance in urban America. Much of the responsibility for governance, urban development, and the provision of public services is now located outside the municipality, in a local state made up of a multitude of institutions that exist largely beyond public awareness and accountability.

The institutional structure of local governance has been evolving for more than a century, but until recent decades it would have been appropriate to employ the term *the local state* to refer mainly to municipalities and their powers.[1] For much of the nation's history, such a singular focus on cities would have been justified; until the twentieth century, the only other consequential units of governments were counties. Beginning in the 1920s, local governance became at first gradually, and then by leaps and bounds, increasingly fragmented. By 2012 the Census Bureau listed 90,056 local governments in the United States. In addition to the federal government and the fifty states, there were 38,910 general-purpose governments: 3,031 counties and 35,879 subcounty governments, including 19,519 municipalities and 16,360 townships. The remainder, which formed over one-half of the total number, were "special purpose" local governments, including 12,880 school districts and 38,266 special districts.[2] By 2017 the number of local governments slightly increased to 90,126, when the census recorded an increase of "more than 1,500 special districts and removed roughly 1,260 that are no longer operating."[3]

Except in the case of school districts, these new governmental units mostly fit into a catch-all category, "special purpose government," that was so elastic it was virtually meaningless. The rather unsatisfactory adjective *special* was employed to describe everything from tiny development districts that financed single residential subdivisions to sprawling metropolitan-wide service agencies that managed sewers, ports, and transportation systems. The numbers of these entities continued to grow both because they provided a way of escaping the budgetary and statutory restraints imposed on general-purpose governments and because they offered a strategy for sharply separating policy expertise and project planning from the vicissitudes of electoral politics. These entities became, in effect, shadow governments because, although they had become a ubiquitous presence within urban regions, for the most part they were out of sight and out of mind. Today, although they "exist in the confines of state law, most states have not taken an active role in" their oversight; indeed, it is doubtful that even a single state in the United States would be able to provide a list of them.[4]

To the casual observer, special districts and special authorities may appear to be "postpolitical" in nature and intent because, as a corporatized and bureaucratized form of decision-making and service delivery, they exist outside the realm of electoral politics.[5] Even so, development politics in the New York and Los Angeles regions from the 1920s to the 1960s, as described vividly in Robert Caro's book about Robert Moses and in the films *Who Framed Roger Rabbit?* and *Chinatown* (and elsewhere), should have long ago alerted perceptive observers to the deeply political nature of special authorities.[6] Instead, even scholars who study local governments have only recently begun to appreciate the degree to which quasi-public institutions are insulated from democratic processes.[7] Beginning in the 1990s, a growing number of scholars have written about the increasingly elaborate architecture of the local state in both the United States and elsewhere. The contributors to this volume reference the various strands of this literature, which range from the Miliband–Poulantzas "theory of the state" through Cynthia Cockburn's *The Local State* and its spinoff debate to critical commentaries offered by Saskia Sassen and other urbanists.[8] The theme that binds these diverse works together is the shared agreement that the proliferation of quasi-public institutions insulates much of the policy apparatus of urban regions from the "political"—that is to say, the democratic—realm.[9] Municipal governments may remain as the principal formal venues for electoral democracy, but in the institutional landscape of the American metropolis, they possess a diminishing share of policy-making authority and capacity.

The ubiquitous presence of institutions that operate beyond the norms of public accountability raises important issues. The characteristics that are thought to make them efficient and effective also reduce the opportunities for influence and oversight by voters and the public officials who represent them. Quasi-governmental institutions generally operate more like private corporations than like public entities; by contrast, mayors and other elected public officials are obliged to answer to the local electorate; as a consequence, the municipal arena tends to provoke whatever Sturm und Drang there is left in the public life of urban governance. Increasingly, the urban electorate is left debating symbolic issues that may be only tangentially connected to some of the most important policies that affect people's lives. Recognizing this fact, a writer in *Governing* magazine in 2003 wondered if city councils were becoming "relics of the political past, poorly adapted to making the decisions of twenty-first century urban life."[10] It is our hope that the essays in this volume will equip the reader to render an independent judgment on whether that is so, and, if so, stir some thought as to what to do about it.

"Special" Governments as Political Institutions

A merely descriptive history of special authorities and special districts and the dizzying variety of their relations and kin would likely give no hint that they might evolve into governance institutions capable of playing a powerful role in local political affairs. Originally, it appears that special districts arose strictly to serve presumably limited pragmatic ends. In the United States, by the mid-nineteenth century, special assessment or special taxing districts were commonly employed as a means of charging urban residents for public services.[11] Rather than following any kind of coherent design, they merely reflected the infinite variety of state charter and incorporation laws that brought them into being, and for that reason they have defied easy explanation. Scholarly discussions have not always clarified things. Jerry Mitchell, for example, has argued that "there is probably no such thing as a typical government corporation."[12]

In the United States, many doubts have been expressed about the Census Bureau's methods for counting quasi-governmental and special district entities. The U.S. Census of Governments count of special districts is virtually useless because these governmental oddities are not even registered in most states, and no distinction is made between the tiny Davids and the giant Goliaths among them. Frequently, in fact, the biggest of them do not even appear on the census tallies.[13] For instance, Jameson Doig found that almost seven thousand large public authorities and corporations were left out of the Census Bureau's 1981 count.[14] For these and other reasons, most of these institutions fly under the radar.

Special authorities may appear to be entirely dependent upon the state and general-purpose governments that bring them into existence, but their subordinate status is often not much more than a legal technicality. Kathryn Foster found that they "ordinarily operate under appointed rather than elected boards, with most appointments made by officials of the parent government [generally

a state or a municipality] . . . that created the district."[15] This structure confers a formal extent of external control, but in practice the
degree to which that is exercised depends upon the attention, interest, and political skills of the officials who run general-purpose
governments. The Metropolitan Pier and Exposition Authority
in Chicago provides an instructive example of how effective oversight sometimes works. By 2010 McPier, as it was locally dubbed,
had more than five hundred staff positions and more than a billion
dollars in bonding authority. The mayor of Chicago and the governor of Illinois each appointed three of the six board members, while
the mayor appointed the board chair. During his six terms in office, from 1989 to 2011, Mayor Richard M. Daley relied heavily upon
McPier to finance an aggressive program of construction along the
city's lakefront. Daley was, at the time, probably America's most
powerful mayor, which set the terms for his relationship with the
members of the McPier's board.[16]

By contrast, anyone who has read Robert Caro's biography of
Robert Moses knows that in the New York region, for decades the tail
wagged the dog. From the 1920s to the 1960s, Moses presided over
a vast empire that guided urban development throughout a sprawling multistate region. Moses derived much of his power from the
extraordinary reach of the Triborough Bridge and Tunnel Authority, which stretched over a vast geographic region. Moses became
adept at broadly interpreting the rather ambiguous powers granted
to the Authority to his own advantage. For instance, the Authority
was granted the power to build bridges as well as their "approaches."
Robert Moses interpreted this to mean that he had the legal purview
to build roads throughout the boroughs of New York as well as all
roads that indirectly led to his bridges. Officials in the towns and
cities that lay in the path of his projects found it nearly impossible
to influence his plans.[17]

The broader an authority's power, the more ambitious development officials can be. What determines the breadth of an authority's room for maneuver is typically contained in its enabling
legislation—that is, the powers laid out in legislative language by
the general-purpose governments, local or state, that create them.
In some cases, the power of authorities may be very specific—aimed
at enabling an institution to carry out one task within a very limited

geographic space (a mosquito or subdivision district, for example). However, an authority's powers may be also be quite ambiguous; when that is the case, it gives those who operate it a "wider canvas" for pursuing their visions.[18] If given the opportunity, officials and administrators within these organizations tend to take an expansive view. In their classic 1960s study of power and patronage in the New York metropolitan region, Wallace S. Sayre and Herbert Kaufman concluded that "the leaders of the authorities [became] major figures in the decisions and actions that distribute the prizes of politics."[19]

Alan Altshuler and David Luberoff have noted that "mega-projects are usually constructed by regional and state agencies" and not by municipal governments.[20] However, this does not mean that all the regional authorities in the country flex as much political muscle as they do in New York. In the early twentieth century, for example, Los Angeles limited the autonomy (but certainly not the political influence) of its infrastructure agencies. Rather than turning to independent regional authorities for infrastructure development, as did New York, Los Angeles kept the departments of water and power, harbor, and airports within the city government. In doing so, the city kept them "under the nominal control of mayors and city councils," where they could "serve as coherent instruments of municipal policies involving central-city development, regional dominion, and global competitiveness."[21] In 1996–97 the proprietary agencies claimed nearly half the city's budget and made up more than three-fourths of city-issued debt.[22]

Other cities across the Sunbelt, however, went in the opposite direction; as Amy Bridges has shown, beginning as early as the 1920s, progrowth regimes in the Southwest created infrastructure authorities designed explicitly to insulate large development projects from both electoral politics and municipal authority. As in New York, development agencies thereby became some of the most powerful and resource-rich institutions within their regions.[23]

The proliferation of quasi-public institutions has gradually moved the center of gravity in the American local state away from municipalities; still, it would be premature to announce the imminent death of municipal governance. To a considerable degree, municipal officials have learned the fine art of using special authorities to access vast public resources that would otherwise be beyond their reach. To serve their own ends, adept mayors forge alliances with independent authorities, but it is a dangerous game. Such mayors, or their less savvy replacements, run the risk of becoming marginalized players in the increasingly complex local state that they have had a hand in creating.

The complicated dance of power between municipal officials and independent governmental and quasi-public entities took off in earnest in the second half of the twentieth century. Although the basic template for the special purpose authority had been established decades before, most of the countless variations on the theme we see today began to appear in the years just before and after World War II, when the federal government became interested in treating the social problems of the central cities. The Public Housing Act of 1937 specified that federal housing funds would be distributed through grants-in-aid to local housing authorities; a few years later, the 1949 Housing Act required cities to establish urban renewal authorities to receive the federal dollars allocated for clearance, renewal, and housing projects. The lure of federal dollars thus provided the catalyst for the formation of formidable public–private partnerships in cities from coast to coast, although these entities were supposed to be open to public scrutiny and accountability.

Though the precise combination of actors varied from one city to the next, typically, broad-based coalitions formed that brought together mayors and other political leaders, civic elites, labor-union executives, universities, and the local media. Robert Salisbury referred to the alliance that formed around urban renewal in cities all over the country as "the new convergence of power."[24] The urban renewal program catalyzed the formation of civic coalitions in cities across the country. With the backing of such a powerful alliance, the administrators of local renewal agencies, such as M. Justin Herman in San Francisco, wielded extraordinary power because they were able to make use of vast fiscal and political resources offered by local civic coalitions and federal administrators.[25] Until neighborhood protests against clearance projects ("urban removal") began to gather sufficient momentum in the 1960s, these agencies asserted nearly complete control over the land-use and economic development policies of local communities.

In the 1960s a second generation of institutions devoted to helping the cities came into being, with federal funds being directed through Community Action Agencies, Model Cities programs, neighborhood associations, and nonprofits of all kinds. At first mayors were delighted that more federal dollars were flowing from federal sources, but their delight soon turned to dismay when activists intent on challenging city hall captured control of local programs. Rather than strengthening mayoral authority and the downtown business elite, the infusion of federal funds provided a base for countervailing power that permanently shook up local power structures by bringing a generation of new leaders into the public realm.[26] "Social radicalism is not a civil service calling," as Daniel P. Moynihan in *Maximum Feasible Misunderstanding* put the lesson he derived at the time.[27] Moynihan's complaint revealed the essential truth that many of the 1960s-era institutions served as powerful mechanisms for opening up new spaces for participation and influence within local political structures. Many of the community and neighborhood programs that exist today got their start in that era.

Things changed quickly in the 1970s when a generation of mayors were forced to accept that they could no longer count on federal help to deal with their economic problems. Even when the fiscal crunch subsided, the federal spigots stayed at a trickle afterward.[28] To compensate, these mayors pioneered the creation of institutions they hoped were capable of financing and administering projects to revitalize the urban core. An administrative device once reserved mainly for regional megaprojects had filtered down to development projects of almost every conceivable size. Rather than encouraging participation, this new generation of institutions tended to hide development projects behind a veil; development professionals now worked in a close collaboration with investors and private sector entrepreneurs. A similar process unfolded in Europe for similar reasons. Special authorities provided a means of bypassing restrictions on local borrowing and raising the substantial public resources needed for infrastructure and economic development projects, especially for older manufacturing cities hit hardest by economic restructuring and offshoring.[29]

A generation of aggressive mayors began to cast about for creative ways to raise the capital needed for the redevelopment districts, waterfronts, marketplaces, festival malls, cultural facilities, and open spaces that made up an emerging economy based on tourism, consumption, and urban amenities. The funds for development projects were now raised not primarily through the issuance of general obligation bonds but by development authorities empowered to issue revenue bonds, which did not require approval by voters.

Baltimore shows how a skillful mayor, William Donald Schaefer, used special authorities to circumvent the slow-moving bureaucratic and democratic processes of city government. Schaefer relied on a network of twenty-four quasi-public development corporations (which grew to more than thirty by 2002) that contracted with city government to direct and implement local redevelopment efforts. Proponents portrayed these agencies as an "apolitical means for improving the city's development potential by infusing speed, flexibility, and technical expertise into the policy-making process."[30] In actuality, they not only were embedded within the political process but also became the means of establishing a new process altogether—one that put Schaefer at the center. In Baltimore and other cities across the country, urban development occurred not through the kind of large-scale public planning that, for example, characterized the urban renewal era but through the behind-the-scenes, day-to-day negotiations among city administrators, the staff of special purpose agencies, and private developers. In this way public officials were able to avoid some of the public controversies that might have erupted when local priorities were shifted in favor of tourists' and middle-class users' entertainment spaces.[31] The deals that public officials negotiated with private developers to assemble land, provide public amenities, and guarantee sufficient profits became so complicated that participants involved in the process tried very hard to avoid involving the public, which, they believed could be spared the arcane details.[32]

As instruments of development, the new institutions seemed to work miracles. Special authorities and special districts, in their many variations (such as tax incentive finance districts), became essential instruments for raising and managing huge volumes of public debt. This arrangement moved some of the most important policy decisions affecting urban residents effectively beyond the reach of democratic processes, and over time, development decisions began to elude the grasp of municipal authorities too. As these institutions matured, their administrators and staff inevitably began to pursue their own interests and agendas. They were free to do so because they were not obliged to answer to electorates; perhaps even more importantly, they were not necessarily "bound by the spatial limits of the municipality."[33]

Professionals within special purpose authorities became adept at forging linkages with specialists outside the metropolitan areas within which they resided. Before long, the staffs of convention centers became closely allied and identified with a vast and sprawling meetings industry, and they learned to turn to this industry for information and political support when proposing new or expanded convention and meetings facilities.[34] Other special purpose authorities followed a similar trajectory by forging ties to national and international groups that shared their interests and expertise. These connections became crucial for preserving and augmenting a degree of autonomy from local officials and administrators. Sports authorities worked closely with national sports organizations; likewise, mall developers participated in national and international organizations devoted to development issues. Local development officials also forged connections to bond underwriters, banks, financial consultants, and investors. All of these relationships helped the professionals in quasi-governmental organizations to become powerful players in local politics.

Local Democracy in a Postpolitical Era

In today's metropolitan regions, important public policy decisions are made within a constellation of quasi-governmental institutions that operate within their own spheres of power. Within this amorphous system, the style of politics normally associated with democratic governance occurs alongside a process of decision-making that, by outward appearances, seems to constitute a kind of postpolitical regime. This impression is reinforced by the fact that so many of the institutions of the local state are able to avoid public controversy merely by keeping their operations from public view.[35] Momentous issues of equity and social justice may be debated within the public space of municipal politics, but in the everyday business of city building, the values that prevail are efficiency and speed, not equity.[36] Even within the realm of municipal governance, the space for democratic engagement has shrunk. In recent decades, a large share of the responsibilities once shouldered by municipalities have been offloaded to privatized residential developments run by homeowner associations. Generally chartered as Common Interest Developments (CIDs), private residential developments numbered only about 500 in 1964, but by 2015, sixty-eight million people lived in 338,000 housing developments governed by homeowner and condominium associations.[37] The shuffling of urban residents into privatized spaces has been encouraged by municipal officials. Faced with severe fiscal constraints, local governments now regularly require that a range of services be provided by CIDs. Developers borrow the funds needed to build roads, sewer and water systems, and other infrastructure; pay off the loans from the sale of new homes; and incorporate a CID governed by a residential association. The boards of these associations assume the responsibility for maintaining infrastructure and providing services in perpetuity. This arrangement is advantageous for municipalities because CID residents continue to pay a full share of property taxes to the local general-purpose government. In this way, municipalities are able to treat CIDs like "cash cows."

One of the points made by Evan McKenzie in his groundbreaking book *Privatopia*, is that these communities facilitate a "gradual secession" of the affluent from the political and social life of cities, potentially making them "financially untenable for the many and socially unnecessary for the few."[38] One consequence is that citizens who have less need for the public services offered beyond their walls come to resent and resist efforts to make them pay for those services because, as Sheryll Cashin has observed, they "tend to view themselves as taxpayers rather than citizens, and they often perceive local property taxes as a fee for services they should receive rather than their contribution to services local government must provide to the community as a whole."[39] CIDs, in effect, excuse municipalities from offering services to entire neighborhoods, but in the process, they have planted the seeds for a mindset stirring taxpayer revolts against what remains of municipal authority.

Municipal officials have engaged in more ambitious strategies for offloading their responsibilities as well. Multiple-function special districts that can perform nearly all the functions of a municipality are an increasingly popular vehicle for assuming risk. These districts, which have proliferated in Florida, California, Colorado, and several other states, strive to make municipal incorporation unnecessary. They can issue tax-exempt municipal bonds. District property owners must pay what they owe the district as a line item on their property tax bill. Districts are often free from tax and expenditure limits that hamper local governments. They are separate entities that have their own bond rating; they are largely invisible and their charges relatively unnoticed and mysterious. Local government officials are not held electorally accountable for all the costs these districts impose on residents. Such districts are in many cases controlled by developers rather than voters during their critical early years, and they can be established in a form that offers incredible financial windfalls to real estate developers.[40] These multiple-function districts deploy the powers of municipalities but operate as if they were special purpose districts.

The proliferation of special purpose and privatized government clearly has significant consequences for regional governance. Just as the intense competition among cities makes it difficult to achieve meaningful cooperation on the regional level, the entrepreneurial activities of special purpose authorities fracture urban regions. The literature in public policy has shown that policy-making at the national level tends to fragment into constellations of actors interested in particular issues and problems.[41] These constellations may typically begin with an exchange of information between state actors and groups. As the policy community becomes firmly established it attempts to police its ranks, keep out unwanted interlopers, and institutionalize its privileged status through the creation of administrative mechanisms of policy implementation.[42]

Stephen Graham and Simon Marvin have described the emergence of such networks in the building of urban infrastructure. In water and waste management, energy provision, telecommunications, and transport, specialized participants have sought to "unbundle" infrastructure development from local power structures by establishing closed policy communities composed of local participants and actors embedded within globalized circuits of infrastructure development.[43] In a similar vein, with respect to megaprojects for highways, airports, and rail transit, "local interests gained leverage in national politics during the 1940s and 1950s by joining national industry-based coalitions with much broader agendas."[44] As earlier noted, linkages to extralocal constituencies are important to the agencies involved in central-city development as well.

Writing in 1981, Paul Peterson praised the increasing autonomy granted to special authorities because, he said, it allowed them to operate more efficiently than general-purpose governments were able to:

> Operating like private firms, these independent authorities see little point in public discussion. Because it is in the city's interest to develop self-financing projects that enhance the productivity of the community, there can be no place for the contentious group conflict that may characterize another policy arena.[45]

People may dispute Peterson's judgment about the value of public debate in the policy arena, but his observation about the impact of independent authorities is largely correct: moving public decisions outside the realm of municipal politics reduces public input and conflict, at least so long as residents do not feel the pinch of acute adverse financial consequences. Even when general-purpose governments create independent authorities and special districts, their influence over them is uncertain and variable. The professional staffs and policy entrepreneurs that work within "special" governments now supply and control many of the critical information and fiscal resources required for major policy initiatives within urban regions. Can a space for a democratic politics be preserved, or reestablished, in the sprawling institutional maze of the twenty-first-century American metropolis? Is the American local state morphing into a nearly impenetrable labyrinth of shadow governments and quasi-governmental organizations? We anticipate that the essays in this volume may shed light on these important questions. Several of the essays rely upon case studies from Chicago and its metropolitan region. Although this method may have some limitations, the empirical findings and the lessons drawn by the authors confirm the disturbing trend often noted by the scholarship that has come before: the place for democratic politics in America's urban regions is shrinking. In our concluding chapter, we argue for an expanded democratic space and present some suggestions about how this might be accomplished.

Notes

1. Our conception of the local state is prefigured in Geiger and Wolch (1986), Wolch (1989, 1990), Kodras (1997), Lake and Newman (2002), and Trudeau (2008, 2012), who depict a changing relationship between government and nonprofit sectors, where the latter provides social services formerly offered by public agencies; in Brenner (2004), Swyngedouw (2004), Storper (2016), and Sassen (1996), who focus on reconfigurations of state power in the context of globalization; and especially in Cockburn (1977) who examines political processes through which local authorities insulate public decision-making from democratic oversight and engagement. For various discussions of the "shadow" state, see Robert K. Geiger and Jennifer R. Wolch, "A Shadow State? Voluntarism in Metropolitan Los Angeles, *Environment and Planning D: Society and Space* 4 (1986): 351–66; Jennifer Wolch, "The Shadow State: Transformations in the Voluntary Sector," in *The Power of Geography*, ed. Jennifer R. Wolch and Michael J. Dear (Winchester, Mass.: Unwin Hyman, 1989), 197–219; Jennifer R. Wolch, *The Shadow State: Government and the Voluntary Sector in Transition* (New York: The Foundation Center, 1990); Janet Kodras, "Restructuring the State: Devolution, Privatization, and the Geographic Redistribution of Power and Capacity in Governance," in *State Devolution in America: Implications for a Diverse Society*, ed. Janet Kodras, Lynn A. Staeheli, and Colin Flint (New York: Sage, 1997); Robert Lake and Kathe Newman, "Differential Citizenship in the Shadow State," *GeoJournal* 58, no. 2/3 (2002): 109–20; Daniel Trudeau, "Towards a Relational View of the Shadow State," *Political Geography* 27 (2008): 669–90; and Daniel Trudeau, "Constructing Citizenship in the Shadow State," *Geoforum* 43, no. 3 (2012): 442–52. For recent scholarship on the multi-institutional structure of the local state, see Neil Brenner, *New State Spaces: Urban Governance and the Rescaling of Statehood* (New York: Oxford University Press, 2004); Erik Swyngedouw, "Globalisation or 'Glocalisation'? Networks, Territories, and Rescaling," *Cambridge Review of International Affairs* 17, no. 1 (2004): 25–48; Michael Storper, "The Neo-liberal City as Idea and Reality," *Territory, Politics, Governance* 4, no. 2 (2016): 241–63; and Saskia Sassen, *Losing Control? Sovereignty in the Age of Globalization* (New York: Columbia University Press, 1996); also on insulating strategies, see Cynthia Cockburn, *The Local State: Management of Cities and People* (London: Pluto Press, 1977).

2. U.S. Bureau of the Census, 2012 Census of Governments.

3. U.S. Bureau of the Census, 2017 Census of Governments.

4. Anne O'M. Bowen and Richard Kearney, *State and Local Governance*, 10th ed. (Boston: Cengage Learning, 2017), 321.

5. Japhy Wilson and Erik Swyngedouw, ed., *The Post-Political and Its Discontents: Spaces of Depoliticisation, Spectres of Radical Politics* (Edinburgh, Scotland: Edinburgh University Press, 2014), 31; Ross Beveridge and Philippe Koch, "The Post-Political Trap? Reflections on Politics, Agency, and the City," *Urban Studies* 51, no. 1 (January 2017): 31–43. In 1998 Žižek wrote, "We are dealing with another form of the degeneration of the political, postmodern post-politics, which no longer merely 'represses' the political [but rather] more effectively 'forecloses' it." He went on to say that "in post-politics, the conflict of global ideological visions embodied in different parties which compete for power is replaced by the collaboration of enlightened technocrats . . . [and] via the process of negotiation of interests, a compromise is reached in the guides of a more or less universal consensus." Slavoj Žižek, *The Ticklish Subject: The Absent Centre of Political Ontology* (London: Verso, 1999), 198. The term is not new; preceding Žižek, for example, there was Alexandre Kojeve, "Note to the Second Edition," in *Introduction to the Reading of Hegel: Lectures on the Phenomenology of Spirit* (New York: Basic Books, 1969), 159.

6. Robert A. Caro, *The Power Broker* (New York: Vintage Books, 1975).

7. Nancy Burns, *The Formation of American Local Governments: Private Values in Public Institutions* (New York: Oxford University Press, 1994); Kathryn Foster, *The Political Economy of Special-Purpose Government* (Washington, D.C.: Georgetown University Press, 1997); and Megan Mullin, *Governing the Tap: Special District Governance and the New Local Politics of Water* (Cambridge, Mass.: MIT Press, 2009).

8. For an overview of the Miliband–Poulantzas debate, see Martin Carnoy, *The State and Political Theory* (Princeton, N.J.: Princeton University Press, 1984).

9. On the theme of insulation, see Leon Lindberg, Robert Alford, Colin Crouch, and Claus Offe, eds., *Stress and Contradiction in Modern Capitalism* (Lexington, Mass.: Lexington Books, 1976.)

10. Rob Gurwitt, "Are City Councils a Relic of the Past?" *Governing* (April 2003): 22.

11. Gurwitt, 22.

12. Jerry Mitchell, *The American Experiment with Government Corporations* (Armonk, N.Y.: M. E. Sharpe, 1999), 12.

13. James Leigland, "The Census Bureau's Role in Research on Special Districts: A Critique," *The Western Political Quarterly* 43, no. 2 (June 1990): 367–80.

14. Jameson Doig, "If I See a Murderous Fellow Sharpening a Knife

Cleverly . . . : The Wilsonian Dichotomy and the Public Authority Tradition," *Public Administration Review* 43, no. 4 (July–August 1983): 294–95.

15. Foster, *Political Economy*, 7.

16. Costas Spirou and Dennis R. Judd, *Building the City of Spectacle: Mayor Richard M. Daley and the Remaking of Chicago* (Ithaca, N.Y.: Cornell University Press, 2016).

17. Caro, *Power Broker*.

18. Jameson Doig, *Empire on the Hudson: Entrepreneurial Vision and Political Power at the Port of New York Authority* (New York: Columbia University Press, 2001), 298.

19. Wallace S. Sayre and Herbert Kaufman, *Governing New York City: Politics in the Metropolis* (New York: W. W. Norton, 1960), 337.

20. Alan Altshuler and David Luberoff, *Mega-Projects: The Changing Politics of Urban Public Investment* (Washington, D.C., and Cambridge, Mass.: Brookings Institution Press and Lincoln Institute of Land Policy, 2003).

21. Steven P. Erie, "Los Angeles as a Developmental City-State," in *From Chicago to L.A.: Making Sense of Urban Theory*, ed. Michael J. Dear (Thousand Oaks, Calif.: Sage, 2002), 139.

22. Erie, 139.

23. Amy Bridges, *Morning Glories: Municipal Reform in the Southwest* (Princeton, N.J.: Princeton University Press, 1996).

24. Robert H. Salisbury, "The New Convergence of Power in Urban Politics," *Journal of Politics* 26 (1964): 775–97; also, see Susan S. Fainstein and Norman I. Fainstein, *Restructuring the City: The Political Economy of Urban Redevelopment*, rev. ed. (New York: Longman, 1986), chapter 1.

25. See Chester Hartman, *Yerba Buena: Land Grab and Community Resistance in San Francisco* (San Francisco: Glide, 1974).

26. Frances Fox Piven and Richard A. Cloward, *Regulating the Poor: The Functions of Public Welfare* (New York: Pantheon, 1971).

27. Daniel P. Moynihan, *Maximum Feasible Misunderstanding: Community Action in the War on Poverty* (New York: Free Press, 1969), 187.

28. See, for example, Peter Eisinger, "City Politics in an Era of Devolution," *Urban Affairs Review* 33, no. 3 (January 1998): 308–25.

29. Neil Brenner, *New State Spaces: Urban Governance and the Rescaling of Statehood* (New York: Oxford University Press, 2004), 194.

30. Robert P. Stoker, "Baltimore: The Self-Evaluating City?," in *The Politics of Urban Development*, ed. Clarence N. Stone and Heywood T. Sanders (Lawrence: University Press of Kansas, 1987), 248.

31. Peter Eisinger, "The Politics of Bread and Circuses: Building the City for the Visitor Class," *Urban Affairs Review* 35, no. 3 (January 2000): 316–31.

32. Bernard J. Frieden and Lynne B. Sagalyn, *Downtown, Inc.: How America Rebuilds Cities* (Cambridge, Mass.: MIT Press, 1989).

33. Frieden and Sagalyn, 89.

34. David Laslo and Dennis R. Judd, "Convention Center Wars and the Decline of Local Democracy," *Journal of Convention and Event Tourism* 6 (Summer 2004): 1235–56.

35. Susan S. Fainstein, *The City Builders* (Lawrence: University Press of Kansas, 2001).

36. Paul Kantor, "The End of American Urban Policy—Or a Beginning," *Urban Affairs Review* 52, no. 6 (November 2016): 895.

37. Community Associations Institute, *National and State Statistical Review for 2015* (2015), https://bit.ly/2rts1UD.

38. Community Associations Institute, *National and State Statistical Review for 2015*.

39. Evan McKenzie, *Privatopia: Homeowner Associations and the Rise of Residential Private Government* (New Haven, Conn.: Yale University Press, 1994).

40. Sheryll D. Cashin, "Privatized Communities and the 'Secession of the Successful': Democracy and Fairness Beyond the Gate," *Fordham Urban Law Journal* 28 (2001): 1679.

41. Martin J. Smith, *Pressure Power and Policy: State Autonomy and Policy Networks in Britain and the United States* (Pittsburgh: University of Pittsburgh Press, 1993).

42. Deborah G. Martin, "Reconstructing Urban Politics: Neighborhood Activism in Land-Use Change," *Urban Affairs Review* 39, no. 2 (May 2004): 592.

43. Stephen Graham and Simon Marvin, *Splintering Urbanism: Networked Infrastructures, Technological Mobilities, and the Urban Condition* (New York: Routledge, 2001), 172–73.

44. Altshuler and Luberoff, *Mega-projects*, 285.

45. Paul E. Peterson, *City Limits* (Chicago: University of Chicago Press, 1981), 134.

PART I

The Eclipse of the Municipal State

1

City-Building Capacity and Special-Purpose Authorities

Institutions, Interests, and the Local State

James M. Smith

Scholarship on urban development and governance in twentieth-century U.S. cities has used, for the most part, an agency-based approach, focusing on informal governing coalitions. It is becoming increasingly clear, however, that a more institutional focus will characterize many emerging studies of urban power and decision-making. This scholarly turn reflects several changes in the actual governance of cities, and, specifically, the shifting nature of institutions managing development projects. While much of the recent research and theorizing on urban institutions looks at institutional change over eras, scholars must also consider the immediate impact of institutions on city governance and capacity.[1] One such governing institution that urban policy makers are utilizing with growing regularity (and for more diverse purposes) is the special-purpose urban development authority.

The creation and maintenance of special-purpose authorities is directly and significantly affecting the ways that U.S. cities are governed and managed. Although such institutions are often created with a very specific mission and charge, their reach often goes beyond basic management of infrastructure. One striking example is the Maryland Stadium Authority (MSA), the institution created to manage and finance new professional sports stadiums in Baltimore. In addition to completing stadium projects for professional sports teams in the National Football League (NFL) and Major League Baseball (MLB) in the 1990s, the MSA has more recently undertaken projects modernizing Baltimore's public school structures and building affordable housing.[2] As the influence of such institutions and the interests they represent grows, scholarly conceptions of urban development processes must adjust in the way they approach the character of urban governance.

In this chapter I present a model for analyzing urban development processes that focuses directly on the institutions involved. This more structural approach suggests that institutional design of the local state is a key explanatory factor for cities' capacity to reach development goals. As discussed in this volume's Introduction, the range of institutions created to manage contemporary urban development has displaced municipal government as the epicenter of decision-making and implementation for policies shaping cities. Such institutions, whether they be special-purpose authorities, tax increment finance districts, or public–private partnerships, were created in the name of ensuring that economic development in cities would not stall, or be entirely interrupted, by the day-to-day politics or fiscal limitations of city government. In this sense, the interests woven into these institutions represent an embrace of a prodevelopment consensus—the basis of which is that cities must pursue, finance, and maintain certain types of development in order to remain competitive and relevant.[3]

The physical manifestation of this consensus can be witnessed while walking through the central areas of world cities; patterns of growth have emerged in which cities are clearly pursuing similar strategies rooted in the construction of spaces for global capital firms, spaces of entertainment and tourism, and new—or newly renovated—residential districts aimed at attracting and retaining a fresh wave of urban residents, as well as visitors. This politics of consensus does not just relate to the built environment. In many cities, the institutional arrangements through which such projects are completed and financed also share many characteristics. In most cases, projects are managed by quasi-governmental authorities or specially created development authorities.[4]

While the collection of institutions capable of carrying out such development is growing, the special-purpose authority has been a key player due to the institution's ability to pursue plans without obtaining direct public approval and authorities' access to (or creation of) independent revenue streams. This chapter focuses on the case of Chicago and one institution in particular, the Metropolitan Pier and Exposition Authority (MPEA), a special-purpose authority created to fund and manage the redevelopment of the festival marketplace Navy Pier, in 1989, and to manage the McCormick Place Convention Center. The evolution of the MPEA demonstrates the ways in which the restructuring of the local state has shaped Chicago's governance, and specifically, created a venue where consensus politics are the norm.

Special-Purpose Authorities on the Rise

While there is a wide array of new institutions changing the character of the local state in contemporary cities (business improvement districts, tax increment finance districts, public–private partnerships), this chapter considers the special-purpose government, or development, authority because of its significant impact on the character of urban governance. Special-purpose authorities began to emerge around the turn of the twentieth century as part of the reform movement to bring business practices and technical expertise to municipal management.[5] As opposed to traditional, elected, branches of municipal government, these special-purpose authorities were structured like businesses, with appointed boards and, in some cases, chief executives. Most special-purpose authority-managed projects are infrastructure-related and focused on policies that are highly technical: transportation (such as major metropolitan airports, bridges, and transit systems), energy, water, and waste management, for example. While most projects of concern for this chapter are large scale, special-purpose governmental units have also been used to deliver infrastructure and water to suburban areas developing in unincorporated areas.[6]

Speaking of authorities generally, however, is misguided; the literature on authorities is littered with definitions, and scholars might agree only on the fact that institutions vary across states,

cities, and countries.[7] In the United States, special-purpose governments, like all local governments, are created and regulated by state
governments. Their structure and powers are described in state- or
local-level enabling legislation, and there is wide variation across
states, counties, and cities. The enabling legislation passed by parent governments (state or local) dictates the jurisdiction, fiscal powers, and governing structure for the special-purpose government in
question.

Some special-purpose districts (e.g., water districts) may have
very specific charges and small governing boards or executives
elected by constituents. Other special-purpose authorities will have
broader, more diverse powers; such authorities have large bureaucratic staffs to run day-to-day operations and are governed by appointed boards nominated by executives within their jurisdiction.
Appointment powers for these boards are usually shared by executives in other government units—for example, a mayor of the city in
which the authority operates, the governor of the state, or a county-
level executive. Take the Indiana Stadium and Convention Building
Authority, which was created by the Indiana legislature to manage
stadium and convention-center development and expansion; it has
a seven-member board of directors with four members appointed by
Indiana's governor, two appointed by Indianapolis's mayor, and one
nominated by the surrounding county, Marion (where Indianapolis
is located) who is then formally appointed by the governor.[8] This
is a representative example of larger authorities. It is also the case
that most members of governing boards are selected on the basis
of their expertise or experience in fields relating to the authority's
jurisdiction. Other members may be selected to represent constituencies affected by authority decisions or involved in work related to
the authority—for example, a union representative.

Authority revenue sources also vary; in some cases, states grant
authorities the power to borrow money via revenue bonds; expanded borrowing limits may function as a measure for escaping
debt limits or as a method for financing development beyond the
means of general-purpose municipal governments constrained by
balanced-budget requirements. Other sources of authority revenue
are access to state or local taxes related to their development projects; an example would be a state hotel and motel tax that generates

revenue used to pay down debt generated by building a convention center or sports stadium. Fees can also be a source of revenue for special-purpose governments.[9] A well-known example would be the bridge tolls generated to finance Robert Moses's Triborough Bridge and Tunnel Authority in New York.[10] Fees, however, can come from diverse sources; the MPEA, for example, draws funds from a fee on taxi fares to and from Chicago airports.

Special-purpose authorities have three primary effects on the governance of U.S. cities. First, they increase the fiscal capacity of cities because of their ability to help municipal policy makers find new sources of funding for critical projects; second, they alter the ecology of local governance by bringing state governments and private interests into formal decisions regarding urban policy; and, third, they reshape the democratic nature of local governance by contributing to a "postpolitical" politics of consensus in contemporary cities.[11] Although special-purpose authorities may produce a less publicly-contested politics of development than the post–World War II urban renewal era did, such institutions may at the same time perpetuate the tightly knit, and sometimes corrupt, urban politics of earlier eras. This paradox leaves the question of whether a contemporary politics of development managed by special-purpose authorities is truly new in its character or merely business as usual.

While special-purpose authorities are very connected with the building of a broader traditional infrastructure of a city, they have also been used widely by state and local officials in the recent wave of tourism-related infrastructure development.[12] To some extent, this is a result of timing; extensive tourism development took place in the decades after federal funding to cities began to decline, and city governments were experiencing severe fiscal stress. Thus, cities were building at a time when funds were scarce and needed to find a revenue source independent of their line-item budgets. While urban renewal funding had been a revenue source for large-scale development in preceding decades, it was no longer an option, and cities were also looking to avoid the political turmoil that resulted from urban renewal projects. In this sense, the special-purpose authority served two roles: it was a site of fiscal independence as well as political autonomy. It could provide funding in ways that shielded officials from political scrutiny originating within government, and the walled-off, technical politics of special-purpose authorities provided protection from neighborhood-based constituencies and voters who might defeat such plans in a referendum.[13]

Specifically, authorities have been used as aids to build and finance centrally located festival marketplaces, convention centers, sports stadiums, and waterfront development in U.S. cities. These megaprojects fit the bill of projects that needed large amounts of funding and low-conflict venues for implementing the projects themselves. Descriptive data in Figures 1.1 through 1.3 present the character of managing institutions with regard to three common components of the tourist infrastructure across all cities containing the infrastructure in question. It's clear that special-purpose authorities are the dominant management institution for convention centers, as well as NFL and MLB stadiums.

Figure 1.1. National Football League Stadium Management, 2015

Management Institution	Number of Stadiums
State-created special-purpose authority	16
Municipal government	7
Private company	4
County government	3
Public–private organization	1

Source: Author's research

Figure 1.2. Major League Baseball Stadium Management, 2015

Management Institution	Number of Stadiums
State-created special-purpose authority	11
Private company (publicly financed stadium)	4
Public–private partnership	2
Municipal government	3
Private company	3
County government	3
Municipal special authority	1
City–county stadium authority	1
City–county general-purpose government	1

Source: Author's research

In addition to looking at all cities with a stadium, I have also collected data on the twenty largest cities in the United States to look for patterns of authority use within cities. Here, patterns can be observed within individual states regarding infrastructure management. For example, in California and Texas, convention centers are mostly managed at the municipal level. We also see that certain cities use special-purpose authorities more often in these categories: Chicago and Houston. Indianapolis fits this category as well— there is no Major League Baseball stadium in Indianapolis; however, the Capital Improvement Board, which manages the convention center, also owns the Bankers Life Fieldhouse (home of the National Basketball Association's Pacers). Detroit is also emerging as a city reliant upon special-purpose authorities, with the recent creation of a regional special-purpose authority to manage the TCF Center.

Convention centers have the highest number of state-created authorities managing their policy area. In eight of the largest twenty cities, special-purpose authorities are managing or financing, or both, conventions. All cities considered had convention centers, and so the rate of centers being managed by special-purpose authorities was 40 percent. Municipal governments managed ten of the centers considered, and county governments, two. One other way of looking at this is not from the perspective of city size but from the perspective of leading convention cities (which is not necessarily correlated with population). Figure 1.3 presents the leading convention cities in 2019 on the basis of numerous metrics. Again, special-purpose authorities are the most common form of convention-center management.

In serving as a key institutional player in building tourist infrastructure, special-purpose authorities have also been tapped for more general development. In Chicago, for example, special-purpose authorities such as the MPEA and the Illinois Sports Facilities Authority have become go-to institutions when public financing is needed for large projects. For example, when Chicago was bidding to host the 2016 Olympics, the MPEA was quickly enlisted by the organizing committee to finance portions of the construction by selling air space above MPEA-owned property to private developers and transferring those funds to the city.[14]

In New York, the Port Authority of New York and New Jersey

Figure 1.3. Top 10 Convention Centers' Managing Institutions, 2019

City	Managing or Ownership Institution	Type of Institution
Orlando	Orange County, Florida	County government
Las Vegas	Las Vegas Convention and Visitors Authority	Special-purpose authority
Chicago	Metropolitan Pier and Exposition Authority	Special-purpose authority
Atlanta	Georgia World Congress Center Authority	Special-purpose authority
Dallas	City of Dallas	City government
Nashville	Nashville Metropolitan Development and Housing Agency	City government
San Diego	San Diego Convention Center Corporation	City government
New York	N.Y. Convention Center Development Corporation	Special-purpose authority
Miami	Greater Miami Convention and Visitors Bureau	County government
Washington, D.C.	Events DC	Special-purpose authority

Source: Cvent (2019) and author's research

Source information for Cvent: "Cvent Unveils Lists of Top Meeting Destinations Worldwide for 2019," July 16, 2019 (accessed February 4, 2020), www.cvent.com/en/press-release/cvent-unveils-lists-top-meeting-destinations-worldwide-2019.

has been a leading financier of real estate development in Lower Manhattan—particularly the World Trade Center site, where it has contributed around $7.7 billion in funding—and in 2014 was considering financing up to $1.2 billion to build the privately developed 3 World Trade Center building.[15] Because of pushback from a group of Port Authority commissioners, the deal was reconsidered and the developer received around $159 million in funding, only around one-tenth of the amount requested, but certainly significant public financing for a private real estate venture.[16]

The examples from Chicago and New York suggest that special-purpose authorities' role as developer continues to grow. Authorities may begin as institutions with very specific charges, but they have the potential to grow into diverse urban development institutions.[17] This is not a new phenomenon either; Heywood Sanders recounts New York's Triborough Bridge and Tunnel Authority's role in developing the New York Coliseum convention site.[18] Authorities also serve as models for public officials' experiments with new institutional forms. An example is the now-defunct Chicago Infrastructure Trust (CIT). CIT, which was a municipally created body, mimicked the shape of a classic public authority or special-purpose agency with a five-member board of directors and administrative staff. The CIT also resembled a special-purpose government in its ability to bypass the public-bonding process by directly financing infrastructure projects with private capital issued by banks looking to make a return on cost savings produced by the developments.[19]

These shifts in institutional structure and the expanding role of special-purpose authorities have implications for the governance of contemporary cities. As more functions are offloaded to new institutions of government, numerous dynamics within the city are affected. So, too, is the way that scholars think about power and governance in the city. Studying an institution, or institutions, created to manage tourism infrastructure may seem an indirect way to enhance the validity of urban theory, but in the case of urban development, tourism infrastructure has been at the heart of city building over the past forty years. Many of the megaprojects that cities pursue relate to tourism infrastructure, and if one wants to build theory for explaining urban development processes, studies must focus on the types of development currently taking place in the city. Studying the ways in which local governments plan for, and in some cases accomplish, ambitious and expensive projects tells us much about the ways in which local governance operates in the contemporary setting. This is especially true when these institutions are charged with taking on development projects only tangentially related to their original policy areas, such as the MSA's entrance into local education policy discussed at the opening of this chapter.

Urban Development Theory and Special-Purpose Authorities

Urban scholars and most governance theory tend to overlook institutional effects and actors in studies of large-scale development.

Most recent studies of urban power have focused on informal coalitions and municipal capacity instead. Clarence Stone's influential study of Atlanta identified a tightly knit public–private coalition that had guided decision-making and governing in the city for decades.[20] Studies of other cities followed suit, identifying regimes across the United States; in line with the growth machine theory of sociologists, regime theory demonstrated capital interests' stake in local governing decisions and their willingness to interject in such decisions when necessary. According to regime theorists, the public and private sectors were partners in governance, one providing the vision for central areas, the other providing the resources. However, as Stone and others have suggested, city governments during this time were quite reliant on a steady stream of funding from the federal government.[21]

The "convergence of power" that constituted urban regimes was of a certain period in the history of urban governance, what Stone recently called the "redevelopment period"—one of several "urban political orders" in U.S. cities.[22] The study of regimes, and scholars' adherence to the paradigm, however, continued in studies of central-city redevelopment in the 1990s, a time when the public side of the regime partnership turned to a more managerial approach.[23]

Recently, the focus of scholars has turned to determine what concepts, if any, might replace regime theory. In a 2013 paper, Stone argues that the time has come to develop approaches more suited to address what is occurring in contemporary cities, which feature what Stone refers to as a "piecemeal" approach to governing.[24] In this acknowledgment that regime theory may not be capable of explaining contemporary governing coalitions or outcomes, Stone suggests that development on a scale comparable to that of the "redevelopment era" is unlikely to reoccur:

> A governing initiative on the scale of yesteryear's redevelopment agenda would require an extraordinary mobilization of resources unlikely to be repeated. After all, the Salisbury-identified convergence of power involved not only resources from city hall and the business sector, but federal largesse poured into urban renewal and expressway construction in amounts not conceivable

in today's political climate. We are left with the question of what piecemeal governing looks like and whose concerns receive attention. I freely acknowledge that conventional regime analysis stands in need of modification, but I also maintain that modification needs to come without losing sight of the close link between resource capacity and the pursuit of policy aims.[25]

One approach to answering this challenge is to focus more closely on the *process* of project approval, governing decisions, and implementation to determine the key political actors.

Studies of large-scale redevelopment during the era of the 1980s and 1990s reveal that the process for approving and managing the central components of central-area megaproject development was often remarkably similar across cities and still involved the state or federal government.[26] City officials would lobby state government to finance capital projects outside the capacity of city budgets or borrowing. In return, state legislators, and perhaps more importantly, governors, expected shared jurisdictional control of the project in question. Thus, legislation approving funding would create the mechanism for delivering or borrowing that funding: a state-level special-purpose government authority with executives and board members appointed by the governor or state legislature. In an earlier study, I termed this cooperation among three institutional actors (city, state, and special-purpose authority) an "intergovernmental triad."[27]

The intergovernmental triad (IT) approach to governance has three significant effects on local development. First, it directly brings the state (especially a state's governor) into governing local decisions. Second, it formalizes the informal interactions of the private sector and public sector that Stone discusses as a key element of urban regimes via authorities' boards of directors. Third, it makes these changes long-standing or permanent—that is, it institutionalizes the interests of the regime on specific policies.[28] Once a special-purpose authority is created, it is likely to develop organizational interests of its own and pursue policies that will increase its power and longevity.[29] On a city level, it also has the capacity-increasing effect of enabling megaprojects to be pursued in the first place (at the time this approach to financing and governing megaprojects was being adopted, city governments did not necessarily have the fiscal capacity to support these projects).

Research on Chicago's central-area redevelopment in the 1980s and 1990s suggests that the IT approach was being used in the city during this time.[30] Although Chicago's "rebirth" and center-city revitalization are often discussed in terms of mayoral politics (with a focus on Richard M. Daley), the politics of megaproject financing were primarily at the state level.[31] The example of Navy Pier, an urban entertainment district and the state's leading tourist destination, is telling. Multiple mayors and city council members had worked to try to redevelop the Pier, meeting stifling public resistance and political gridlock on each occasion. Mayors Jane Byrne (1979–83), Harold Washington (1983–87), and Eugene Sawyer (1987–89) had each made attempts to revitalize the idle space into an urban festival marketplace similar to Baltimore's Harbor Place.[32] When Daley succeeded at redeveloping the Pier (it opened to much fanfare in 1995), it was a matter of being in office at the right time as much of the groundwork for redevelopment was already in place.[33] Governor James Thompson was another key political actor in this effort. In a last-minute legislative move in 1989, Thompson championed the redeveloped Pier and lobbied the state legislature to authorize $150 million in funding while also creating the MPEA to implement and manage the project.[34] The legislation creating the MPEA also gave it jurisdiction over Chicago's convention center, McCormick Place.

Rather than attributing the Pier's redevelopment to institutional creation or state-level politics, agency-based approaches might point out that the creation of the MPEA was a pragmatic act by a savvy mayor and thus bring the analysis back to the municipal level. For example, much recent scholarship has pointed to the pragmatic nature of city officials and particularly big city mayors.[35] From this perspective, again, the focus would remain local and would emphasize the managerial skills of "new mayors" such as Daley who are able to deliver the goods and services that their predecessors could not. Governor Thompson's role could also be characterized as a state-level official acting as part of the urban regime.[36]

A more institutional approach, such as the IT, suggests that scholars should focus not on the temporary entrance of governors

into local politics (as members of regimes) but on the long-term impact of special-purpose authorities once created. These institutions
are not short-term pragmatic solutions offering onetime money.
Instead, they are institutions that will continually pursue their own
interests in order to grow their jurisdictions and maintain their existence, thus altering the character of a city's governance.[37]

Institutional Longevity at Chicago's "McPier"

Of course, institutional approaches such as the IT are dependent
upon institutions' ability to sustain their power or adapt to changes.
The MPEA in Chicago demonstrates both the vulnerability and
strength of such a model. In 2010 the MPEA, a critical case in the
research that developed the triad approach, appeared to be on the
verge of disbanding. A debt crisis at the MPEA followed a political scandal, and Chicago was losing convention business to robust
competition in cities such as Orlando and Las Vegas, which had sur-
passed Chicago in terms of total convention business. At this time,
the MPEA was put on watch, and its board was all but stripped of
its power—the twelve-member board of directors was vacated and
replaced with a six-member board—and a trustee was appointed
to oversee a committee that would make suggestions aimed at restructuring the agency. Privatizing the convention center was one
option on the table.[38] The validity of the IT approach in Chicago
appeared to be breaking down; the organizational interests of the
MPEA, focused mainly on continual expansion, seemed not to be
strong enough to withhold the pressures of a recession and intercity
competition.

After a few tumultuous years, however, the MPEA reemerged as
a central player in megaproject development in Chicago. According
to media reports, Chicago wanted a basketball/multipurpose arena
for its central area. The prime tenant of the arena would be the De-
Paul University men's basketball team, which would play seventeen
home games there per season in addition to the women's team's ten
home games. In the offseason, the arena could host concerts and
other large events. Mirroring a failed development idea of the early
1990s, the arena would be attached to the McCormick Place Convention Center[39]—this time, however, the arena was completed and

the first DePaul games were played in 2017. The projected cost of the arena was $173 million.[40]

Suddenly, the MPEA, or "McPier" as the local press often refers to it, was back at the center stage of large-scale development planning. Initial reports of the financing package suggested it would be a public–private venture, with DePaul providing $70 million, the city providing $33 million in tax increment financing bonds, and the MPEA floating $70 million in bonds to cover the remainder.[41] This is notable because when the city needed to produce additional funds for a new piece of its tourist infrastructure, a special-purpose authority was the institution to which it turned. The planned arena would seat ten thousand and be connected to McCormick Place's West Building (the newest wing of the convention center, opened in 2007). Perhaps capitalizing on the timing, the MPEA announced it would also pursue development of two hotels in the vicinity of McCormick Place; then MPEA CEO Jim Reilly also did not rule out the possibility that the new "neighborhood" would contain an on-site casino.[42] One of the hotels described would contain 1,200 rooms and cost around $400 million—it would be owned by the MPEA.[43] When it opened in 2017, the *Chicago Tribune* deemed the Marriott Marquis a "mega hotel."[44]

With the additions of the new hotels and the arena, the MPEA began branding the area the "McCormick Place Entertainment District." The first steps toward establishing this district were reported in December 2012 when the MPEA purchased land two blocks from McCormick Place's West Building. Reilly said the purchase was part of the larger plan aimed at making "a more vibrant and interesting neighborhood for McCormick Place."[45] The MPEA now calls this development site, which is also in proximity to a newly opened Green Line Chicago Transit Authority stop, the "Collection at McCormick Square."[46] In an earlier online commercial, the MPEA described the area as "a one-stop shop" for visitors to Chicago.[47] A commercial for the new developments suggests that the multiple spaces included in the Collection are "all connected via walkways" and that "it's always seventy-two degrees" inside—presumably a rebuttal to Sun Belt cities that have been adept at sweeping away convention business over the past few decades.[48]

These ambitious, and expensive, plans were coupled with the

announcement that the Pier would undergo a major overhaul. The MPEA would finance up to $278 million for the renovations, which would be administered through the nonprofit corporation that took over the Pier's management in 2011—Navy Pier, Inc. The original bond issuing for the Pier's redevelopment (approved in 1989 and completed in 1995) was for $150 million (around $310 million in 2020 dollars). All these proposals were part of a larger proposal by Mayor Rahm Emanuel aimed at increasing the quality of Chicago's tourism infrastructure. The plan is called "Elevate Chicago."[49] The MPEA is clearly a, if not the, critical institution in implementing this vision.

Contrary to its usually supportive role in such discussions, the *Chicago Tribune* issued a wary editorial statement in response to the proposals in an editorial titled "The Missing Piece."[50] Calling McCormick Place and Navy Pier the "twin engines" of Chicago's tourist economy, the *Tribune* recognized the importance of investments in such infrastructure but saw the public financing of a private arena problematic. These were the exact sentiments that had halted the proposed dome for the NFL's Chicago Bears in 1991 and at least problematized the publicly financed renovation of Soldier Field in the mid-2000s. The editorial also asked the question of who would pay debt fees in the case that the MPEA came up short, as it had just before its restructuring.[51] In a more biting critique, reporter Ben Jorvasky of the *Chicago Reader*, a weekly independent newspaper in Chicago, described the proposed arena as a public handout to "well-off suburban kids" attending DePaul.[52] Jorvasky juxtaposed the announcement of the arena plans with the announcement that Chicago Public Schools would close fifty-four schools in primarily African American neighborhoods.[53]

In the mix of all these details on specific projects, the recent resurgence of the MPEA as an anchor for development in Chicago is built on two broader developments that came about during its "quiet period" of 2009–12. First, the *Chicago Tribune* reported in 2012 that labor negotiations at MPEA were complete—labor costs at McCormick Place had been a central concern for trade shows leading up to 2009.[54] By significantly lowering exhibitioner costs, the MPEA was attempting to compete more directly for the bigger shows it had lost to Orlando, Las Vegas, and other cities. Second, the legislation that restructured the MPEA in 2010 gave the authority greater capacity to borrow via new access to "expansion bonds."[55] After a period of apparent weakness, then, the MPEA emerged even stronger. This suggests again, that understanding the institutional components of large-scale urban development should take priority over understanding the individual politicians or policy actors involved at the time of the development's approval. The structural components of the MPEA, and its organizational interests, enhance its position as a shaper of governance and policy outcomes in Chicago over time. These shifts in the institutional power of the MPEA also make it a key site for a politics of consensus surrounding large-scale urban development.

Special-Purpose Authorities and the "New Politics" of Cities

The effects of special-purpose authorities' wider use in urban development in Chicago and beyond relates to what Erik Swyngedouw refers to as the "postpolitical condition" in contemporary cities.[56] While many studies of authorities focus on the concept of public accountability and authorities' role in reducing it, this does not fully capture the impact of authorities on governance. Indeed, authorities are accountable institutions, but mostly to their parent governments and the industries or policy communities, or both, that they work with regularly. And though they may be less accountable to the everyday citizen, there is some question of how accountable local governance in large cities is, generally, to the everyday citizen.

This is where Swyngedouw's theorization is useful. He views the current moment in cities as one that is "postpolitical" and focused on a politics of consensus regarding growth and globalization. In a study of environmental politics, Swyngedouw finds that a postpolitical city "reconfigures the act of governing to a stakeholder-based arrangement . . . in which the traditional state forms (national, regional or local government) partake together with experts, non-governmental organizations and other 'responsible' partners."[57] Thus, the political arrangement becomes one in which certain voices are recognized and others are excluded; the institutional design of special-purpose authorities intensifies this phenomenon. As Swyngedouw writes:

Consensual policymaking, in which the stakeholders (i.e. those with recognized speech) are known in advance and where disruption or dissent is reduced to debates over the institutional modalities of governing, the accountancy calculus of risk and the technologies of expert administration or management, announces the end of politics, annuls dissent from the consultative spaces of policymaking and evacuates the proper political from the public sphere.[58]

In the contemporary city, the special-purpose development authority is one manifestation of this politics.

Gordon MacLeod more directly connects Swyngedouw's postpolitical theory to the tourist infrastructure of contemporary cities. He suggests that the "mixed-use creative cultural quarters, buzzing economic districts, heritage and tourism villages and gentrified apartments" found in multiple cities across the globe "have been orchestrated by state-led coalitions and special-purpose agencies."[59] According to MacLeod, this set of institutions acts as a "safeguard" from criticism or electoral consequences.[60]

One challenge to the argument presented above, that authorities such as MPEA represent a new institutional politics for cities, or a postpolitical space, is that authorities often become a new housing for the politics that have dictated governance in cities for generations. The reasoning goes something like this: Capital interests will find ways to achieve development goals; the institutional form is irrelevant because development-based interests have no institutional preference so long as they achieve their goals. Additionally, one might frame the new institutions as protective institutions for entrenched political powers in a city. In other words, leadership positions at authorities, in some cases, may become a place for political allies who have previously served in more traditional government institutions. This pattern is evident at the MPEA, where Chicago mayors and Illinois governors have appointed close allies and former chiefs of staff to chairman or CEO positions.[61] One function of increased special-purpose authority use in one-party cities, then, could be to expand coalition influence into new sectors of both the government and the economy (the MPEA board also includes numerous individuals from finance, real estate, investment, and labor and is appointed by the mayor of Chicago and governor of Illinois, who could potentially reward political loyalty or support).

However, this is where the institutional interests and new politics of urban development become critical to the argument that something different is occurring regarding infrastructure and governance. As institutions persist, they develop independent interests that can be *as* influential in determining organizational operation as the political interests of appointees are. In other words, the new politics of development can exist *simultaneously* with the traditional political players in a city. Because institutions such as the MPEA are focused on economic growth that is directly tied to the city's overall political agenda, their politics and goals will rarely come into conflict with a mayoral administration or economic booster, but their goals may be driven as much by what is good for the institution, generally, as by what is good for the political agents who appointed the organization's current leadership.

By further considering the role of specific institutions in urban megaproject development, scholars can adjust theories and concepts to better address governing processes in the era of a reconstructed local state. The approach taken in this chapter focuses on the institutional dynamics of an authority charged with carrying out tourism-based development and the ways in which shifting institutional dynamics affect urban governance. While mayors, governors, and other elected officials certainly continue to influence local outcomes, this study suggests that cities could not pursue growth and infrastructure development at desired levels without the institutional creation and adaptation of bodies similar to the MPEA. Thus, by studying the specific character of institutions, and the ways in which they change over time, scholars can more closely assess cities' capacity to pursue development. Agency-based approaches that stress mayoral leadership or coalitions are not made redundant by a more institutional approach, but overrelying on existing models may lead scholars to focus on municipal-level debates that have limited impacts on the politics of development taking place in decision-making venues such as the MPEA.

By taking the more institutional approach, this chapter finds that special-purpose authorities in the United States are contributing to a "postpolitical" movement in urban development with a consensus for growth. As the case of the MPEA demonstrates, special-purpose authorities serve as a conducive venue for a politics of consensus regarding large-scale urban development. At the MPEA, the institutional interests of the organization are aimed at continual growth in the institution's respective policy areas (and sometimes beyond, as both the MPEA and MSA examples suggest). Thus, discussions regarding the politics of urban development, which were once characterized by conflict and intense political debate, are now more protected from many significant challenges or counterarguments within the party because of the use of special-purpose authorities as governing institutions.[62] Of course, the potential capacity of special-purpose governments, and the emerging politics of consensus at such institutions, should not be construed to suggest that all development wishes are granted, or occur automatically, as a result of authority officials drawing up plans. The long-standing characteristic of development plans shifting away from their original form, or in some cases not coming to fruition, can still play out with development managed by authorities.

And though looking at one type of institution within a broad array of arrangements that manage urban development in the United States might be viewed as a limitation, the expansion of special-purpose government into new policy areas should be a key focus for scholars. While the MPEA may focus on one policy area, as do most special-purpose authorities, the case data reviewed here reveal the ways in which authorities created for a specific purpose branch out as they age, particularly when public officials attempting to fund development projects reach out to authorities with fiscal and managerial tools that may be of critical importance. The postpolitical condition, or consensus politics, that exists around the decision of *whether* to move forward on development means that the politics surrounding decision-making is highly technical and takes place at the state level, or within special-purpose authorities, rather than primarily at the city and municipal level. Special-purpose authorities, then, play a key role in constructing a new local state, one in which economic-development politics are driven by consensus more than conflict.

Notes

1. See, for example, Richardson Dilworth, ed., *The City in American Political Development* (New York: Routledge, 2009); Clarence N. Stone, "Reflections on Regime Politics: From Governing Coalition to Urban Political Order," *Urban Affairs Review* 51, no. 1 (2015): 101–37; Joel Rast, "Why History (Still) Matters: Time and Temporality in Urban Political Analysis," *Urban Affairs Review* 48, no. 1 (2012): 3–36.

2. Maryland Stadium Authority, "Current Projects," https://bit.ly/2HYU310.

3. Erik Swyngedouw, "The Anatomies of the Postpolitical City: In Search of a Democratic Politics of Environmental Production," *International Journal of Urban and Regional Research* 33, no. 3 (2009): 601–20.

4. Gordon MacLeod, "Urban Politics Reconsidered: Growth Machine to Post-democratic City?," *Urban Studies* 48, no. 12 (2011): 2629–60.

5. Jameson W. Doig, "'If I See a Murderous Fellow Sharpening a Knife Cleverly . . .': The Wilsonian Dichotomy and the Public Authority Tradition," *Public Administration Review* (1983): 292–304.

6. Kathryn A. Foster, *The Political Economy of Special-Purpose Government* (Washington, D.C.: Georgetown University Press, 1974).

7. Jerry Mitchell, *The American Experiment with Government Corporations* (Armonk, N.Y.: M. E. Sharpe, 1999).

8. State of Indiana (website), "About ISCBA," accessed November 16, 2020, https://www.in.gov/iscba.

9. For an overview of authority fiscal power and governance, see Foster, *Political Economy*.

10. Robert A. Caro, *The Power Broker: Robert Moses and the Fall of New York* (New York: Alfred A. Knopf, 1974).

11. Alberta M. Sbragia, *Debt Wish: Entrepreneurial Cities, US Federalism, and Economic Development* (Pittsburgh, Pa.: University of Pittsburgh Press, 1996); Dennis R. Judd and James M. Smith, "The New Ecology of Urban Governance: Special-Purpose Authorities and Urban Development," in *Governing Cities in a Global Era: Urban Innovation, Competition, and Democratic Reform*, ed. Robin Hambleton and Jill Simone Gross (New York: Palgrave Macmillan, 2007), 151–60; James M. Smith, "'Re-Stating' Theories of Urban Development: The Politics of Authority Creation and Intergovernmental Triads in Postindustrial Chicago," *Journal of Urban Affairs* 32, no. 4 (2010): 425–48; Erik Swyngedouw, "The Post-Political City," in *Urban Politics Now: Re-imagining Democracy in the Neoliberal City*, ed. Gideon Boie and Matthias Pauwels (Rotterdam: NAi, 2007), 58–76.

12. Dennis R. Judd and Dick Simpson, "Reconstructing the Local State: The Role of External Constituencies in Building Urban Tourism," *American Behavioral Scientist* 46 (2003); Judd and Smith, "New Ecology."

13. Heywood Sanders, "Building the Convention City: Politics, Finance, and Public Investment in Urban America," *Journal of Urban Affairs* 14 (1992): 135–59.

14. David Greising, "McPier to Fund 2016 Bid," *Chicago Tribune*, March 14, 2007.

15. Joe Nocera, "The Real Port Authority Scandal," *New York Times*, April 21, 2014; Charles Bagli, "Developer's Skyscraper Is Focus of Latest Dispute at Rebuilt Trade Center," *New York Times*, March 16, 2014.

16. David M. Levitt, "Port Authority Reaches Deal on Silverstein, 3 World Trade," Bloomberg News (website), June 25, 2014, www.bloomberg.com/ news/articles/2014-06-25/port-authority-reaches-deal-on-silverstein -3-world-trade.

17. See Heywood Sanders, *Convention Center Follies: Politics, Power, and Public Investment in American Cities* (Philadelphia: University of Pennsylvania Press, 2014), 67.

18. Sanders, 67.

19. Fran Spielman, "City Council Launches Emanuel's Infrastructure Trust," *Chicago Sun-Times*, January 20, 2014. The CIT, created under Rahm Emanuel, was disbanded by his successor Mayor Lori Lightfoot.

20. Clarence N. Stone, *Regime Politics: Governing Atlanta, 1946–1988* (Lawrence: University Press of Kansas, 1989).

21. Clarence N. Stone, "The Empowerment Puzzle: In Pursuit of a New Dimension in Governing the City" (paper presented at the annual meeting of the American Political Science Association, Chicago, Illinois, August 29–September 1, 2013); Dennis R. Judd and David Laslo, "The Regime Moment: The Brief but Storied Career of Urban Regimes in American Cities," in *American Urban Politics in a Global Age*, ed. Paul Kantor and Dennis Judd (New York: Routledge, 2015), 35–46.

22. Robert Salisbury, "Urban Politics: The New Convergence of Power," *Journal of Politics* 26, no. 4 (1964): 775–97; Judd and Laslo, "Regime Moment"; Stone, "Reflections on Regime Politics," 6–9.

23. Peter Eisinger, "City Politics in an Era of Federal Devolution," *Urban Affairs Review* 33 (1998): 319.

24. Stone, "Empowerment Puzzle," 22.

25. Stone, 2.

26. Alan Altshuler and David Luberoff, *Mega-Projects: The Changing Politics of Urban Public Investment* (Washington, D.C.: Brookings Institution Press, 2003).

27. Caro, *Power Broker*; Smith, "Re-Stating."

28. Stone, *Regime Politics*.

29. Caro, *Power Broker*; Annemarie Hauck Walsh, *The Public's Business: The Politics of and Practices of Government Corporations* (Cambridge, Mass.: MIT Press, 1978).

30. Smith, "Re-Stating."

31. Even before the Richard M. Daley era (1989–2011), Mayor Harold Washington (mayor between 1983 and 1987) worked with the Illinois state legislature to secure funding for the construction of a new White Sox stadium on the city's South Side. This is well documented in Costas Spirou and Larry Bennett, *It's Hardly Sportin': Stadiums, Neighborhoods, and the New Chicago* (DeKalb: Northern Illinois University Press, 2003).

32. Smith, "Re-Stating."

33. For more on this argument, see Larry Bennett, *The Third City: Chicago and American Urbanism* (Chicago: University of Chicago Press, 2010), 103.

34. Smith, "Re-Stating."

35. See Bruce Katz and Jennifer Bradley, *The Metropolitan Revolution: How Cities and Metros Are Fixing Our Broken Politics and Fragile Economy* (Washington, D.C.: Brookings Institution Press, 2013); Benjamin Barber, *If Mayors Ruled the World: Dysfunctional Nations, Rising Cities* (New Haven, Conn.: Yale University Press, 2013).

36. Bennett, *Third City*; see, for example, Peter Burns, "The Intergovernmental Regime and Public Policy in Hartford, Connecticut," *Journal of Urban Affairs* 24, no. 1 (February 2002): 55–73.

37. Susan Clarke, "More Autonomous Policy Orientations: An Analytic Framework," in *The Politics of Urban Development*, ed. Clarence N. Stone and Heywood Sanders (Lawrence: University Press of Kansas, 1987), 116–17.

38. Ray Long and Kathy Bergen, "McCormick Place Overhaul Becomes Law," *Chicago Tribune*, May 27, 2010.

39. The Chicago Bears and MPEA officials had advocated building a domed stadium as part of a convention center's expansion—the Chicago media tagged this proposal "McDome." The dome was never built because cost projections led to media reports suggesting that new local taxes would be required to build the arena. The convention center's expansion went forward while the dome did not.

40. Kathy Bergen, "DePaul Arena Part of Broader Plan to Boost Chicago Tourism," *Chicago Tribune*, May 16, 2013.

41. Bergen, "DePaul Arena."

42. Bergen, "DePaul Arena."

43. Kathy Bergen, "McPier Chief Pushes Mega-Hotel Complex, Arena Vision," *Chicago Tribune*, October 30, 2012.

44. Josh Noel, "Chicago Welcomes Its Newest Mega Hotel, Marriott Marquis, Opening Sunday," *Chicago Tribune*, September 9, 2017.

45. Kathy Bergen, "McPier Begins Assembling Land for Future Developments," *Chicago Tribune*, December 18, 2012.

46. McCormick Square (website), http://mccormicksquarechicago.com.

47. Danny Ecker, "McPier Rolls Out Ad Campaign for New DePaul Arena, Hotel," *Crain's Chicago Business*, January 27, 2015.

48. https://thecollectionatmccormicksquare.com.

49. Bergen, "DePaul Arena."

50. *Chicago Tribune*, "The Missing Piece," May 17, 2013.

51. *Chicago Tribune*, "The Missing Piece."

52. Ben Jorvasky, "Rahm's Latest Plan: Close the Schools, Build an Arena," *Chicago Reader*, May 23, 2013.

53. Jorvasky, "Rahm's Latest Plan."

54. Bergen, "McPier Begins Assembling Land."

55. Bergen, "McPier Begins Assembling Land."

56. Swyngedouw, "Post-political City."

57. Swyngedouw, 608.

58. Swyngedouw, 609.

59. Gordon MacLeod, "Urban Politics Reconsidered: Growth Machine to Post-democratic City?" *Urban Studies* 48 (2011): 2630.

60. MacLeod, "Urban Politics Reconsidered," 2635.

61. For example, Lori Healey was named the CEO of MPEA in 2015; Healey served as Richard M. Daley's chief of staff late in his tenure as mayor (Danny Ecker, "McPier Taps Former Daley Aide as CEO," *Crain's Chicago Business*, April 15, 2015). Healey replaced Reilly, who was MPEA's first CEO between 1989 and 1999 and then again between 2010 and 2015; Reilly was a former chief of staff to Governor James Thompson, who was a key player in creating the MPEA and funding the first renovation of Navy Pier. Yet another former political executive's chief of staff, Scott Fawell, held the CEO position at MPEA between 1999 and 2003. Fawell served as Governor George Ryan's chief prior to his appointment (by Ryan) to MPEA's top spot. Fawell was convicted for campaign fraud during his time as Ryan's chief of staff and was later convicted for bid-rigging charges while at the helm of the MPEA (Matt O'Connor, "Feds Probe Corruption at McPier," *Chicago Tribune*, December 4, 2003). The appointment of the MPEA CEO is now made by the nine-member board of directors rather than by the Governor of Illinois.

62. MacLeod, "Urban Politics Reconsidered."

2

Phantom Governments

*Multiple-Function Special Districts
as Substitutes for Municipalities*

Evan McKenzie

Special districts were originally created to play an interstitial role in local government, usually performing only a single function— such as water provision, fire protection, or mosquito abatement— that was largely technocratic and instrumental. For scholars and the press, they have been relatively invisible, operating outside the po- litical arena, where large questions of "Who governs?" were decided. However, some states have endowed special districts with nearly all the powers of municipalities, without the limitations of general- purpose local government, and in some cases allow these districts to be run by real estate developers with little public accountability or outside scrutiny. Those who control these multiple-function special districts (MFSDs) issue municipal bonds to build infrastructure in support of extensive residential development; tax district residents to pay the bondholders; govern communities as they wish, largely free from electoral accountability; and sometimes engage in highly profitable self-dealing between the subdivision they own and the district they control.

MFSDs go by different names and have varying powers and limi- tations in different states, but there are consistencies. At its core, the rise of MFSDs in different places represents a new way to solve an old problem: Who is to bear the cost and the risk of building infrastructure in large-scale residential development? Infrastructure systems must be constructed before the houses are built, and whoever bears those construction costs faces huge losses if the units fail to sell as anticipated. In past decades, municipalities generally assumed that responsibility. MFSDs are a new approach to solving this problem, and it is a solution that developers find advantageous and governments interested in growth and new infrastructure are often willing to accept. However, the spread of MFSDs challenges accepted principles of local democracy, visibility, and accountability. If building infrastructure now requires that developers be given their own local governments, and if those governments can deny people the ability to choose their own community leadership, then we need to consider the implications of MFSDs for notions of local democracy and accountability, and consider what sort of policy framework is needed to address such concerns. This chapter explores these issues by examining how MFSDs operate in the state of Florida.

The 2012 Census of Governments found it "particularly noteworthy" that "special districts . . . have increased from 12,340 districts in 1952 to 38,266 districts in 2012."[1] Special districts, not counting school districts, now outnumber the nation's 19,519 municipalities by almost two to one. Much of the growth in special districts

Figure 2.1. Local Governments in the United States, 2012

Local governments	90,056
Special purpose governments	51,146
Special districts	38,266
Single function	33,031
Multifunction	5,235
School districts	12,880
General-purpose governments	38,910
Municipalities	19,519
Townships	16,360
Counties	3,031

Sources: Hogue 2013; Keating 2013.

involved the creation of multiple-function districts to finance infrastructure for residential development. There are at least 5,235 MFSDs in the nation, and they have a variety of names and specifications in different states.[2] Regardless of the nomenclature, the principle is the same: existing general-purpose local governments want new development, but they are unable or unwilling to fund the infrastructure needed to support it. Consequently, special districts are created that issue bonds to build infrastructure and tax or assess the residents of the district to pay the bondholders. It is estimated that 40 percent of new annual infrastructure investing is financed by bonds, and more than half of the value of those bonds is issued by special districts.[3]

MFSDs are an increasingly popular vehicle for assuming the risks of financial loss. They can issue tax-exempt municipal bonds, so that district property owners must pay what they owe the district as a line item on their property tax bill. However, these districts are often free from tax and expenditure limits that hamper local governments. They are separate entities that have their own bond rating.

Yet, along with these advantageous characteristics, there are undemocratic features. Because these districts are largely invisible and their charges are relatively unnoticed and mysterious, John C. Bollens calls them "phantom governments."[4] Consequently, local government officials are not held electorally accountable for the costs they impose on residents. In many cases, they are controlled by developers, rather than by officials or voters, during their critical early years. As discussed below, they can be set up so as to offer large financial windfalls to real estate developers. Significantly, although they are governments, special districts are not necessarily subject to popular control through the ballot box in the same way as municipalities normally are. District directors can make major decisions involving hundreds of millions of dollars free from electoral accountability. Even if residents penetrate the veil of invisibility that surrounds district affairs, they may find that they are unable to change anything because of the way voting is weighted by property ownership, instead of by the normal "one person, one vote" principal that binds city governments. If a special district performs only one or a few related functions, voting by property owners only, and on a one vote per acre basis, is sometimes allowed.[5]

Phantom Governments in Action: Florida

Multiple-function districts exist under different names in several states, including California, Colorado, Florida, Maryland, New Hampshire, Connecticut, Georgia, and Texas.[6] I will consider how MFSDs operate in Florida, which has 443 MFSDs, more than any other state except Colorado and Texas, and including some of the largest and fastest-growing districts in the nation.[7] The state legislature has passed laws that facilitate the rapid spread of these entities, and there is little or no oversight of their activities. Florida has a few huge districts that were specially created by the state legislature and hundreds of others that were brought into existence through procedures set out in a general statute. As will be explained below, the actions of the legislature and the courts seem to be aimed at creating a developers' paradise with maximum freedom and minimal oversight. The real estate developers who establish and control these districts have great discretion regarding their financial practices, and in some cases developers are able to maintain control indefinitely, effectively denying district residents the ability to choose their leadership. Florida law has also given developers the power to act through the special district government when it suits them, while on other occasions they can conduct their affairs directly through the private corporation when that is more advantageous. For example, the developer, acting through the district, can exercise the power of eminent domain or issue municipal bonds. At the same time, the developer is also a private business corporation that owns property in the district and has all the attendant rights of that status. This hat-swapping has led to developer behavior so questionable that it has attracted the attention of the federal government, as explained below.

Ave Maria and Celebration: Perpetual Corporate Control

In Collier County, Florida, is a community called Ave Maria. It is home to about twenty-eight thousand people on a tract of land totaling 10,805 acres. The community is located east of the Gulf Coast city of Naples and only a few miles from Immokalee, a poor Hispanic community in the heart of Florida's tomato industry, where the U.S. Department of Justice successfully prosecuted seven growers for holding more than one thousand workers in involuntary servitude.[8] Ave Maria has all the attributes of a thriving small city, and more. It is home to an eponymous university and law school; it has a burgeoning crop of businesses and a growing population of relatively affluent people. At its center is the only church allowed in town: an enormous and architecturally renowned Catholic church called the Ave Maria Oratory. Ave Maria's residents have many things to appreciate about their community, but participation in local self-governance is not one of them. This is because Ave Maria is not a municipality but a special district. The Ave Maria Stewardship Community District is authorized under Title 189 of the Florida Statutes. The residents of the district cannot vote to choose their local government, and because of the nature of this district, it is possible that they never will.

Specially authorized by the Florida legislature and signed into law by Governor Jeb Bush in 2004, Ave Maria is governed by a five-person board of directors who are chosen by the developers of the community. These developers are Barron Collier Companies, an organization so consequential that its founder, Barron Collier, gave his name to the county, and billionaire Tom Monaghan, the founder of Domino's Pizza and former owner of the Detroit Tigers. Monaghan is an ultraconservative Catholic who envisioned Ave Maria as a utopian "ticket to Heaven" for the Catholic faithful. The university and the law school are explicitly and assertively dedicated to restoring the values of a brand of Catholicism that predates Vatican II.

Women and reproduction are given special treatment under Monaghan's rule. At Ave Maria University, Monaghan mandated that all female employees wear skirts, with slacks and pantsuits forbidden. And despite the fact that the university is exempt from having to pay for contraception coverage for its employees under the Affordable Care Act, it sued the federal government nonetheless.[9] Moreover, while the university and law school are private corporations that are exercising their Hobby Lobby religious-freedom rights, the district itself is a public government. The infrastructure at Ave Maria was financed by the sale of tax-exempt municipal bonds.[10] Under the authority of its enabling legislation, the Ave Maria Stewardship Community District (AMSCD) can build and maintain infrastructure and provide services for:

- Water management and control
- Construction of roads and bridges
- Water supply, sewer, and wastewater
- Public transportation, including buses and parking
- Environmental cleanup
- Conservation and wildlife habitat
- Contracting and working with other governments and homeowner associations
- Parks and cultural and recreation facilities
- Health-care facilities
- Fire prevention and control
- School construction
- Security, including guardhouses, gates, fences, patrol cars, and other related activities, but without directly exercising law-enforcement powers, for which it is authorized to contract with other governments, presumably Collier County
- Mosquito control
- Garbage collection

Despite having all these governmental powers, Ave Maria's five-person board of supervisors is not elected by the residents of the district, and instead supervisors are chosen for four-year terms by the developers, because voting is done on a "one acre, one vote" basis, and the developers own most of the land in the district. These supervisors are picked by the developers, rather than by the residents, and it is entirely possible that this situation will never change. The residents of Ave Maria may be forever denied the right to vote for the leadership of their local government, so that the developers could be in control as long as Ave Maria exists.

It is understandable, and oftentimes necessary, that developers of new communities have total control when the project is created and for some time thereafter. They need to be able to subdivide the property, create the infrastructure and connect those systems to the residential lots, set up and run the sales and marketing operation, and in general launch the new community before there are enough residents to carry out any of these activities. This is because the developer is intensely and legitimately interested in controlling the new community in order to make sure the sales operation is successful. The developer's interest at this early stage is understood by the law to outweigh the owners' interests, which is why developers are always authorized to control the project for some term of years that varies from state to state.

However, it is assumed that developers will eventually relinquish their control over the development and that unit owners—residents and homeowners—will take over their own local government. In the case of homeowner association–run subdivisions, the law always clearly sets out when and how this transfer of control will take place. But with legislatively authorized special districts created under Chapter 189 of the Florida Statutes, such as Ave Maria and Celebration, the Walt Disney Company development in the Orlando area, the turnover arrangements are much murkier and appear in those cases to have been set up so that developers can maintain control in perpetuity.

The unusual provisions inserted into the governing documents of these special districts evidence the developers' concern about maintaining long-term control over all the property in the districts. Celebration is a planned community ultimately governed by the legislatively created Reedy Creek Improvement District. Disney set up an arrangement by which the corporation would have veto power over all homeowner-association decisions as long as Disney owned any property within the development. Because Disney owns all the commercial property, and has no intention of selling it, in effect Disney can maintain control of the homeowners' decisions forever.[11] This is an extraordinary situation.

At Ave Maria, the control issue is more complex and even disputed. But internal memos circulated among the parties involved in the development process make it clear that they intended to keep indefinite, possibly perpetual control of Ave Maria.[12]

Monaghan and Barron Collier formed an equal partnership called Ave Maria Development, and the partnership is run by an executive committee that has the power to make all important decisions, including selecting the members of the AMSCD Board of Supervisors. Two of the five seats on the board were scheduled eventually to be occupied by representatives elected by the residents of Ave Maria, but a controlling majority of three of the five seats would remain in the hands of the majority property owners, who are the developers, forever. Barron Collier executives and their attorney deny that they wish to maintain control forever and insist that they will voluntarily relinquish control to the residents eventually.[13]

Moreover, in the development stage, the issue of perpetual control was central to the planning process. In an internal memo, one Barron Collier executive wrote to the company's president: "I believe we are all in agreement that *the major decision factor on the size of the district is the control issue.* At what point do the residents (electors) have the power to control the decisions of the board and affect the value of the undeveloped land?"[14] Ultimately, the convoluted language of the enabling act that the developers' lawyer drafted leaves the control issue firmly in the developers' hands. As journalist Liam Dillon put it: "According to Ave Maria's law, the district's registered voters gain control over the district when more than half of it is developed. The town, at its completion, doesn't meet that mark." Only if the developers build residential lots outside the town will it be possible for the registered voters to control the district.[15]

Florida CDDs and Developer Enrichment: The Villages

Ave Maria and Celebration were created as "stewardship districts" by a specific legislative act under Chapter 189 of the Florida Statutes. It could be argued that these are unique situations, and that any lack of democratic accountability in those districts is the result of special lobbying efforts by the developers, which included drafting the enabling legislation, which used confusing language whose meaning was understood only by the developers.

In order to evaluate what is being done with MFSDs in Florida, it is necessary to step beyond these specially chartered Chapter 189 stewardship districts and consider the hundreds of MFSDs that were created under Chapter 190, the general law for the creation of Community Development Districts (CDDs). A massive project called The Villages was developed using Section 190 CDDs. Despite provisions in that law that mandate eventual turnover of CDDs from control by the developer to district directors elected by registered voters, no such transition has taken place. Moreover, the developer was able to use his control over the district and the subdivision to enrich himself to the tune of hundreds of millions of dollars. As David M. Hudson observes, "A central element in the approach taken initially in 1975 was to grant to private developers limited governmental status as a special improvement district in order to operate and finance the cost, delivery, and maintenance of certain predevelopment capital improvements such as water, sewer, road and drainage systems and other community facilities."[16]

Chapter 190 was enacted in 1980 in order to simplify the process by which MFSDs were created, eliminate the need for special legislative action, and standardize the structure and powers of these districts. Of the 1,635 special districts in the state of Florida, 575 are CDDs. The list of functions and powers of CDDs is spelled out at length in Section 190.012, and the language closely parallels Ave Maria's enabling legislation. The functions of these districts are in most respects those of municipalities. Districts of one thousand acres or more are created by the Florida Land and Water Adjudicatory Commission upon petition by the developer, and districts of under one thousand acres are created by the county commission of the county where the majority of the land is located. Under Chapter 190, a CDD is governed by a five-person board of directors. Within ninety days after creation of the district, the original landowners must choose the board of directors on a "one acre, one vote" basis. Because this first meeting takes place before lots are sold, the developer has all the votes and fills the board with developer representatives. The directors do not need to live in the district or be qualified electors. Two members serve for two years and three serve for four years. Elections take place thereafter every two years, at which point either two or three directors are up for election.

The transition to resident control, with elections by qualified electors in a public election, begins at six years after creation of the district, if it is smaller than five thousand acres, or at ten years after creation if the district is five thousand acres or larger. However, only two of the directors are replaced by vote of qualified electors at six or ten years. Moreover, this election is held only if there are enough qualified electors—that is, residents of the district eligible to vote. There must be at least 250 electors in districts of under five thousand acres, and at least 500 electors in districts of over five thousand acres. If there are not sufficient electors, then landowner control of the board continues.

The net effect is that developers control the majority of the five seats on the board of small districts for at least eight years, and with large districts for at least twelve years. This means that all the important financial decisions about bond issuance and other matters are made by a developer-controlled board.

The Florida law creating CDDs was challenged on the grounds that by prescribing "one acre, one vote" elections it violated the equal protection clause under the rule of *Reynolds v. Sims*. The Florida Supreme Court ruled on this challenge in the case of *Florida v. Frontier Acres Community Development District* and held that property-based voting was legal. Even though Section 190 gives CDDs a long list of specific powers, the court held that they were single-purpose districts, nonetheless, because the legislature had a "narrow objective" in creating this enabling act. That purpose was

> to address *this State's concern for community infrastructure and to serve projected population growth without financial or administrative burden to existing general purpose local governments* . . . Consistent with this objective, the powers exercised by these districts must comply with all applicable policies and regulations of statutes and ordinances enacted by popularly elected state and local governments. Moreover, the limited grant of these powers does not constitute sufficient general governmental power so as to invoke the demands of Reynolds. Rather, *these districts' powers implement the single, narrow legislative purpose of ensuring that future growth in this state will be complemented by an adequate community infrastructure* provided in a manner compatible with all state and local regulation. (emphasis added)[17]

A study of CDDs in Florida showed that as of July 2014, 221 of the 575 then in existence were in financial distress, in that they were in default on their bond obligations or otherwise not meeting their financial obligations.[18] The report found that notwithstanding expressed legal requirements in the state-created charter and other related general laws, there are structural inadequacies that have enhanced the impact of the financial decline of CDDs. Such structural inadequacies include: (1) uninformed and counterproductive sales and marketing of parcels; (2) ineffective ongoing financial disclosure; (3) "over-leveraged" non-ad valorem assessments imposed and levied on real property by district boards; (4) inadequate and ineffective validation proceedings; and (5) unclear disclosure of the demarcation between homeowner associations and CDDs.[19]

Perhaps the most troubling findings in the report concern the lack of reporting or accountability to, or oversight by, any other agency of state government. The report found that "for various reasons, there is little use, reliance and enforcement of reporting from CDDs to state and local governments. This has eroded the ability of state and local governments to exercise applicable oversight . . . Accountability of CDDs is, to the extent that state government has involvement with the operations of CDDs, poorly defined and fragmented."[20] The amounts of these defaulted or delinquent CDD bonds are staggering.[21] The evidence of costly dysfunction calls into question Florida's policy of engaging in minimal regulation or oversight of its many MFSDs.

The Villages: Special Districts and Developer Enrichment

In addition to the lack of external oversight, Florida's MFSDs are structured so that democratic processes are not necessarily able to function well. The fact that developers are allowed to control the boards of directors of CDDs and also entirely control the subdivision within it creates a conflict-of-interest situation. Paul D. Asfour observed that this gives rise to the potential for abuse, noting: "The Florida Legislature determined that since a developer was assuming most of the risks when developing property, it would allow obvious conflict of interest votes by developer-controlled boards. The Florida Supreme Court agreed. However, the Legislature failed to allow for the possible financial harm that a developer-elected board could cause a district and the residents within its boundaries, by permitting conflict of interest votes that resulted in financial harm to the district and the residents."[22]

This situation is illustrated by a development known as The Villages, located in central Florida in Sumter County, that was founded in 1992 by developer H. Gary Morse. It is an age-restricted community, where nobody under the age of nineteen is permitted to reside and where 80 percent of the homes must have at least one resident over the age of fifty-five. The U.S. Census Bureau emphasized the development's growth rate in a press release, noting that The Villages was the fastest-growing metro area in the nation.[23] It has sixty-three recreation centers, 540 holes of golf in numerous courses, 216 softball teams in seventeen leagues, a polo stadium, a 2,200-student charter school for employees' children, seven fire stations, and eight major grocery stores.[24]

Morse funded the infrastructure for The Villages by creating a dozen CDDs that issued about $900 million in CDD bonds. At the time, being the sole landowner, he was in complete control of the CDDs' boards of directors. He was also the developer and owner of the property in the subdivisions that would eventually be occupied by residents of The Villages. At the time when these financial decisions were made, the land was unoccupied, so Morse controlled both the CDDs and the subdivisions. He proceeded to engage in a series of complicated transactions in which he sold subdivision assets to the CDDs. These assets included the common areas of the subdivisions, such as golf courses, swimming pools, and many other facilities. He also sold to the district the association's most valuable asset, which is the assessment stream, meaning the power to collect payments from the owners for the right to use these recreational facilities. He priced these assets using his own appraiser.

Acting through the boards of directors of the CDDs, Morse issued municipal bonds to pay the subdivisions for these assets. The eventual residents of the subdivisions are obligated to pay the bondholders for thirty years. Through these sales of common elements to the districts, an enormous amount of money went into Morse's pockets. *Orlando Sentinel* reporter Lauren Ritchie has been following this situation for years. She summarized it as one in which the special districts in The Villages "owed a stunning $709 million on outstanding loans they took out partly to pay developer Gary Morse for everything from future fee collections to retention ponds, sewer plants, clubhouses, swimming pools and golf courses."[25]

There was a potential conflict of interest in the developer's pricing and selling the developer's subdivision assets to the developer-controlled district. There was also a question as to whether the residents of the district were paying for the same recreational and infrastructure assets twice: once as part of the purchase price of their homes and then again in the form of thirty years of bond payments to the district. The residents purchased their units for market prices that presumably reflected the existence of the amenities and infrastructure. But because Morse had already sold the amenities and assessment stream (in essence, the cash flow) to the CDD, he argued that the sales price didn't include the recreational assets. Is this actually true, Ritchie asks, or is it just a sleight of hand? As Ritchie phrases it, the ultimate question concerns whether the development was intended to function as a legitimate government or was more of a financial device to enhance the profitability of the project.[26]

The Internal Revenue Service (IRS) was concerned as well. It raised questions about these bond transactions as early as 2003, saying that their decision to close an earlier case "should not be construed as an approval of your method of operations. We have concerns regarding: the amount of control the developer has over the issuer; the questions of value of the assets sold by the developer to the issuer as these are not arm's length [transactions]; the treatment of income and expenses . . . ; [and] compliance with state law."[27]

The IRS eventually turned its attention to The Villages again. In the same way that the developers of Celebration and Ave Maria sought to create perpetual control of their special districts, Morse had done similar things with the CDDs in The Villages, seeking to contravene the intent of the law that CDDs should eventually transition to owner control. There would never be enough resident votes to move from landowner control to resident election by qualified electors of the district. In 2013 the IRS ruled that the Village Center CDD was not, in fact, a political subdivision but instead a private activity, stating, "We believe that an entity that is organized and operated in a manner intended to perpetuate private control, and to avoid indefinitely responsibility to a public electorate, cannot be a political subdivision of a state," under Section 103(c)(1) of the Internal Revenue Code.[28] The effect of this ruling was to render $426 million in Villages bonds taxable, as private activity bonds.

This bombshell ruling threatened not only the hundreds of millions of dollars in bonds issued by The Villages CDDs, but in fact worried developers of many other special districts in Florida where they had set up the acreage so as to remain in perpetual control. Those potentially concerned included Disney, developer of Celebration. Morse died in 2014, but his company appealed the IRS ruling. To deal with the uncertainty the ruling created in the bond market, the company switched to an issuance of $257 million in new taxable bonds instead, pending the outcome of the ruling.[29]

In 2016 the IRS closed its long-standing audits of The Villages CDD bonds, noting that the bonds had by then been redeemed.[30] However, the issues raised were of sufficient concern that the Department of the Treasury and the IRS proposed a set of new rules that would redefine the term "political subdivision" for the purposes of tax-exempt bonds. The new rules would have required that, in order for the bonds to qualify as those of a political subdivision, the district would have to exercise at least one sovereign power (eminent domain, police power, or taxation); serve a governmental purpose in a manner that provides "a significant public benefit with no more than incidental benefit to private persons"; and be "governmentally controlled," meaning that it must be controlled either by a state or local government or by an electorate that is not "unreasonably small." These regulations would have prevented developers from using quasi- governmental entities, such as CDDs, to issue tax-exempt bonds while retaining virtually all the control and creating financial windfalls for themselves.[31] However, on April 21, 2017, President Donald Trump issued an executive order that instructed the IRS to identify regulations that "impose an undue financial burden on United States taxpayers" or "add undue complexity to the Federal tax laws" or were beyond the authority of the IRS.[32] The Treasury targeted eight regulations to do away with pursuant to this order. One of them was the proposed new rule for political subdivisions, which they said appeared to constitute an undue burden and add undue complexity.[33] This struggle between the developer and the IRS over The Villages special districts may seem arcane, but it speaks to the potential for MFSDs to embody private values and serve private purposes.

Private Values in Public Institutions?

Florida's policies regarding MFSDs evidence a policy of attracting large-scale real estate development that offers little protection against the potential for undemocratic and self-serving actions by the developers who control these governments. Other states have expanded the powers of special districts, but under laws that are more protective of the rights of residents living in the districts and with more oversight of the actions of MFSDs. Under a different policy framework, MFSDs can be created with reduced risk of developer self-dealing and autocracy.

California is one example of such an approach, where the perceived advantages of MFSDs seem to be obtainable with greater governmental oversight. In 2017 there were 321 multiple-function Community Service Districts (CSDs) in the state.[34] They operate under a set of laws that the California legislature rewrote and consolidated in 2005.[35] This new law provided that a CSD could be created as "a permanent form of governance that can provide locally adequate levels of public facilities and services" and "a form of governance that can serve as an alternative to the incorporation of a new city." In order to do this, a CSD would need the powers of a municipality, and the revised law provides that potential. CSDs have a list of thirty-one powers that allow them to hire staff, issue bonds, provide a wide range of services and infrastructure, create a police force, enact criminal ordinances punishable by arrest, and exercise eminent domain.[36]

The basic term of the new law empowers CSDs to function in much the same ways as Florida's MFSDs do. However, unlike the directors of CDDs and stewardship districts in Florida, California CSD directors are chosen in public elections by registered voters of the district. The California Supreme Court addressed the issue of voter control of MFSDs in *Burrey v. Embarcadero Municipal Improvement District*, 5 Cal. 3d 671 (1971), and ruled that such districts are bound by the "one person, one vote" rule.[37]

Not only are California's judicial policies more protective of residents' political rights, but the districts are subject to substantial local administrative oversight of their creation and operation. Each of California's fifty-eight counties has a Local Agency Formation Commission (LAFCO) that regulates the creation of special districts, rules on annexation of land into existing cities, discourages sprawl, and facilitates orderly division of function among all forms of local government. The adequacy of LAFCO supervision of special districts is itself subject to oversight, most recently by the Little Hoover Commission in 2017. The commission made detailed recommendations to improve special district functioning under LAFCO scrutiny, including particular attention to the adequacy of reserve funds in the interest of securing long-term financial stability for the districts.[38] California's approach demonstrates that MFSDs need not necessarily operate as far outside the accepted norms of democratic governance and oversight as they do in Florida.

Yet, even under supervision, the decision to rely on special districts as substitutes for municipalities raises important questions. In her study of special district formation, Nancy Burns concluded that special districts represent "private values in public institutions." She found that they are "often created for reasons that impair their ability to be democratic training grounds," a function that local governments are assumed capable of performing. Instead, special districts "discourage participation" because of their invisibility. They are often created either by a single self-interested individual, usually a real estate developer, or by small, self-interested groups, such as a few manufacturers, and the individual's or group's private values are then institutionalized as the values of the government.[39]

Burns's concluding observations hold up well when applied to the rise of MFSDs:

Americans have also created a realm of particularly unaccountable and unrepresentative politics that has attendant benefits and problems. The benefits of special districts are that they can fund and provide services and infrastructure; they are able to get things done in a fragmented American polity. The difficulties are two: They do this while no one watches except interested devel-

opers, and they are gradually becoming the realm where much
of the substance of local politics happens. Thus local politics becomes quiet, not necessarily through the consensus that the earlier studies of suburbia noted, but rather through the invisibility
of special district politics.[40]

James Leigland contends that "particularly with regard to borrowing, many special purpose governments appear to operate
virtually without guidance, coordination, or oversight of parent
government officials." And he found that much of the money flowing through special districts may not be going to address the most
important needs, because these special purpose governments are
"isolated from broader policy planning frameworks."[41]

The problems with special district politics that Burns and Leigland recognize are even more pressing when the districts in question are not a multiplicity of single-purpose districts but large,
multiple-function districts entrusted with a whole range of government functions and the powers to carry them out. In this case, there
are at least three important ways in which the politics of government by MFSD differs from what we typically expect from municipal governance:

Invisibility: The literature on special districts is replete with
terms such as "invisible," "ghost," and "phantom." The public
knows little about the special districts in their area, what they do,
who runs them, or how much they cost. This lack of knowledge
suggests that people are ultimately unable to understand the real
costs of housing. And the media, with few exceptions, do not cover
special district politics. Those who do have a difficult task ahead of
them because they must penetrate the dense thicket of legislation,
financial data, and rationalizations thrown up by the developers
and their lawyers and managers. At the end of that inquiry is the
reality of confronting powerful and wealthy interests who fiercely
defend their position.

Lack of oversight and accountability: Although it is possible for
a state to create an oversight system for special districts, the complexity of the web of special districts, the variety of their activities,
and their independence all make this a challenging prospect. Most

special districts are, by definition, independent governmental entities. There are fewer dependent special districts that are governed by a county board of supervisors or a city council. These independent districts have their own directors, managers, staff, auditors, records, meetings, rules, and procedures. They hire lawyers and sue to defend their interests, and create lobbying organizations to protect themselves in state legislatures. Moreover, state legislatures are not enthusiastic about taking on this responsibility, nor do they find support for paying the cost of trying to supervise or oversee the activities of a host of special districts across a state.

Lack of electoral democracy: State legislatures often make it possible for special districts to operate free from meaningful electoral control. Some directors are appointed instead of elected. In other cases, there are elections, but the voting is based on owning acres in the district instead of being a resident of the district. The constitutional precedents that govern special district elections evidence a judicial policy of deference to state legislatures. And even where there are elections, as in California, the invisibility of special district affairs to the public and the media make these elections relatively meaningless in most cases.

These characteristics of MFSD governance and politics may trouble those who value cities, but the same characteristics are exactly why MFSDs are so popular with developers. It is easy to understand why developers would want to have their own governments, but it is harder to understand why state legislatures give developers such a gift. Further research may help us understand why state legislatures feel it necessary to do this. All these entities—cities, counties, and special districts—are creatures of the state legislature and state constitutions. We need to understand why some legislatures see so much value in government by special district instead of by municipality. We need to ask whether state and local government have arrived at a place where it is necessary to give developers their own local governments in order to build infrastructure. And if we are going to create what are, for all practical purposes, city governments in which people cannot vote to choose their own community leadership, then we need to ask whether it is possible to have cities without citizens.

Notes

1. Carma Hogue, *Government Organization Summary Report: 2012* (Washington, D.C.: U.S. Census Bureau, 2013), 4.

2. Stephen Owens, Chief of the Government Organization and Special Programs Branch of the Governments Division at the U.S. Census Bureau, said: "Community development districts that are put in place to finance the infrastructure for new development are growing in several states. These are known by a variety of names, but the underlying principle is the same." Michael Keating, "Census Bureau Reports Continued Growth in Special Districts," *Government Product News* (2013), https://www.americancityand county.com/2013/09/27/census-bureau-reports-continued-growth-in -special-districts-with-related-video. It is also important to note that MFSDs are unlike common-interest housing developments, or CIDs, in that MFSDs are governmental entities with taxing and other powers, while CIDs are private nonprofit corporations.

3. James Leigland, "Public Infrastructure and Special-Purpose Governments: Who Pays and How?," in *Building the Public City: The Politics, Governance, and Finance of Public Infrastructure*, ed. David Perry (Thousand Oaks, Calif.: Sage, 1994), 144.

4. John C. Bollens, *Special District Governments in the United States* (Berkeley: University of California Press, 1957), 30.

5. The United States Supreme Court established this principle in *Salyer Land Co. v. Tulare Lake Basin Water Storage District*, 410 U.S. 719 (1973), and then in *Ball v. James*, 451 U.S. 355 (1981), the court ruled that special districts were justified in limiting voting rights to property owners.

6. Nadav Shoked, "Quasi-Cities," *Boston University Law Review* 93, no. 6 (2013): 1971–2032, 2003–5. Shoked's article is a thorough legal analysis of multiple-function special districts that argues for a new theory to guide decisions about when these alternatives to municipalities should be created.

7. U.S. Census Bureau, *Special District Governments by Function and State: 2012*. 2012 Census of Governments. Table ORG-009. Data cited for Florida, California, and Texas are from this table.

8. Sean Sellers and Greg Asbed, "The History and Evolution of Forced Labor in Florida Agriculture," *Race/Ethnicity: Multidisciplinary Global Contexts* 5, no. 1 (Autumn 2011): 29–49.

9. *Ave Maria Foundation v. Sibelius*, filed December 20, 2013, 13-cv-15198 (E.D. Mich.), 14–1310 (6th Circuit.)

10. Liam Dillon, "Ave Maria: A Town Without a Vote," *Naples Daily News*, May 9, 2009, http://archive.naplesnews.com/news/local/ave-maria—-a -town-without-a-vote-now-and-forever-ep-398411826-343995352.html.

11. Douglas Frantz and Catherine Collins, *Celebration, U.S.A.: Living in Disney's Brave New Town* (New York: Henry Holt, 1999), 167; Richard E.

Foglesong, *Married to the Mouse: Walt Disney World and Orlando* (New Haven, Conn.: Yale University Press, 2001), 164.

12. This issue was thoroughly plumbed by Liam Dillon, an investigative reporter for the *Naples News*, in a three-part series of articles collectively titled "Ave Maria: A Town Without a Vote," May 9, 10, and 11, 2009.

13. Liam Dillon, "A Town Without a Vote: Residents' Control Hinges on Trust," *Naples News*, May 11, 2009.

14. Tom Sansbury, Memo to Paul Marinelli, "Ave Maria Stewardship Community District: Size Determination," September 5, 2003.

15. Dillon, "Ave Maria," May 11.

16. David M. Hudson, "Special Taxing Districts in Florida," *Florida State University Law Review* 10, no. 1 (1982): 64.

17. *State of Florida v. Frontier Acres Community Development District*, 472 So. 2d 455 (Florida 1985).

18. Sarah Ayers, "Community Development Districts: Financial and Accountability Issues" (Tallahassee: Leroy Collins Institute, Florida State University, July 2014), http://collinsinstitute.fsu.edu/sites/default/files/ CDD%20report%20FINAL%20Revised-Reformatted%207%2003%2014 .pdf.

19. Ayers, "Community Development Districts."

20. Ayers, "Community Development Districts."

21. Matthew Schifrin, "Potemkin Villages," *Forbes*, September 17, 2009.

22. Paul D. Asfour, "The Potential for Abuse in Developer-Controlled Community Development Districts," *Barry Law Review* 19, no. 1 (2013): 14.

23. U.S. Census Bureau, "Sumter County, Fla., Is Nation's Oldest, Census Bureau Reports," June 23, 2016, release number: CB16–107.

24. Ryan Erisman, "82 Cool Facts about The Villages," updated November 10, 2020, www.thevillagesfloridabook.com/82-cool-facts-the-villages.

25. Lauren Ritchie, "IRS Trying to Get to Bottom of Villages Bond-Financing History," *Orlando Sentinel*, September 7, 2008.

26. Lauren Ritchie, "Don't Stress over IRS Ruling on Villages Bonds," *Orlando Sentinel*, June 12, 2013.

27. Lauren Ritchie, "IRS Trying to Get to Bottom."

28. Internal Revenue Service, National Office Technical Advice Memorandum, May 09, 2013, number 201334038, release date August 23, 2013.

29. Toluse Olorunnipa, "Florida's Villages Shifts to Taxable Debt Amid IRS Probe," Bloomberg News (website), September 21, 2014, www.bloomberg .com/news/articles/2014-09-22/florida-s-villages-shifts-to-taxable-debt -amid-irs-probe.

30. Lynn Hume, "Why IRS Dropped Its Challenge to Florida CDD Bonds," *The Bond Buyer*, July 19, 2016.

31. Internal Revenue Service Bulletin 2016:10, REG-129067-15, "Definition of Political Subdivision," March 7, 2016.

32. Presidential Executive Order 13,789, "Presidential Executive Order on Identifying and Reducing Tax Regulatory Burdens" (April 21, 2017).

33. Internal Revenue Bulletin 2017:30, Notice 2017–38, "Implementation of Executive Order 13789 (Identifying and Reducing Tax Regulatory Burdens)," July 24, 2017.

34. Little Hoover Commission, *Special Districts: Improving Oversight and Transparency*, report no. 239, August 2017, 17.

35. California Association of Local Agency Formation Commissions (CALAFCo), "Community Needs, Community Services: A Legislative History of SB 135 (Kehoe) and the 'Community Services District Law'" (2006), http://calafco.org/docs/CNCSReport.pdf.

36. CALAFCo, "Community Needs, Community Services."

37. *Burrey v. Embarcadero Municipal Improvement District*, 5 Cal. 3d 671 (1971), 676–77.

38. Little Hoover Commission, *Special Districts*, 2.

39. Nancy Burns, *The Formation of American Local Governments: Private Values in Public Institutions* (Oxford: Oxford University Press, 1994), 116.

40. Burns, 117.

41. Leigland, "Public Infrastructure," 165.

3

Governing Detroit
The Withering of the Municipal State

Peter Eisinger

As Detroit's fiscal fortunes collapsed in the decade or so before the declaration of municipal bankruptcy in 2013 and then in the period during which the bankruptcy itself played out, three developments occurred that greatly diminished the scope and authority of the city's government. At the start of the crisis, Detroit, which shrank precipitously in population in preceding decades and became a majority-black city, could not pay debts of $18 billion, the subject of the 2014 bankruptcy proceedings and the reason for the state appointment of an emergency manager. Although the mayor, Mike Duggan, handily reelected in 2017, eventually managed to assert a certain degree of *political* power in city hall, despite the diminished local institutional structure, the evisceration of city government itself remains a notable development. The latter occurred in several ways. First, many of the city's responsibilities and assets were divested by reallocating them to regional authorities, the county, the state, nonprofit agencies, and even for-profit creditors. Most of this divestment occurred on the initiative of the state of Michigan under business-oriented Republican Governor Rick Snyder with a likewise Republican State House and Senate. Second, private foundations, as well as individual philanthropists and developers, increasingly provided funding for major capital projects and, more unusually, for both debt relief and many ordinary, ongoing operational public functions. Third, the economic revival of the city—or more precisely the revival of its public and private downtown real estate rather than its industrial or commercial base—became increasingly influenced or controlled by a few private individual developers.

The result of these three developments has been a much smaller government with fewer responsibilities, less capacity, and less authority. Not only does the city control fewer public functions and public agencies, but its ability to engage in responsible fiscal planning is often limited by its dependence on the priorities and reliability of private funders. Furthermore, the city government must share a role with private real estate developers who have an outsized influence on the projects that are shaping the city's future. To some degree all these developments have brought relief to the city. Yet in the long run, they also marginalize and diminish municipal government, raising issues of authority, sustainability, and accountability for the city.[1] Part of the problem, as B. D. Ryan points out, is that the city has never had either the inclination or the capacity to develop a centralized housing, planning, or urban-design policy.[2] Without such a tradition, and in its current helpless state, the city represents a blank slate for grand schemes. As Ryan puts it, "When left to their own devices, cities such as Detroit simply answered the wishes of the loudest and most powerful voices."[3]

Divesting Public Responsibilities

For the year and a half when Detroit was in formal bankruptcy, *all* municipal functions were controlled by Kevin Orr, the state-appointed emergency manager.[4] Specifically, Orr had the sole power to manage the budget, dispose of city assets to settle its debts, and administer and even abrogate its labor contracts. The city council was superfluous, and the mayor had only those oversight powers granted by the emergency manager. When the term of the emergency manager ended in 2014, the city still did not recover the full scope of its authority. The Financial Review Commission, established by the state and lodged in the Michigan Department of Treasury, will exercise fiscal oversight at least until 2027. The Commission must review the city's financial plans, approve any borrowing, and approve or reject any contract for goods or services costing more than $750,000. Five of the nine board members were appointed by the governor, the effect of which was to reassign the city's fiscal powers to the state. At the end of the 2018 fiscal year, however, the city had a $38 million surplus, and the commission voted to end its oversight. Nevertheless, at any time during the next decade, the commission and its fiscal powers can be reinstated.

If these constraints over the city's budget have been removed, other changes in the scope of direct municipal authority are meant to be more permanent. As the city headed toward fiscal crisis in 2012, the state transferred responsibility for street lighting from the city to a special Public Lighting Authority. Although the mayor and city council appoint the five-member board, the Authority has independent bonding powers and is not subject to direct municipal control. Furthermore, the Authority is funded by the dedicated revenue from the Detroit Utility Users Tax that the city had previously collected for general operating expenses. The city has also been relieved by the state of what appear to be fairly ordinary administrative tasks: for example, the state now collects the city's income tax.

One of the most recent changes, mediated by the bankruptcy court, represents perhaps the most significant new regional arrangement: the Great Lakes Water Authority. Whereas Detroit once owned the regional water-distribution system and set the rates for the sale of water from its water-treatment facility to 127 suburban communities, the new regional authority, created by the state, is governed by a board with a majority of suburban representatives. The city now leases its water infrastructure to the suburbs and the new board now sets the water rates. The new water and sewer authority is part of a more general push for regionalization that does not always involve reallocating the city's municipal functions but simply establishes another higher layer of authority. For example, in 2012 the state created a four-county Regional Transit Authority to plan for and coordinate mass transit in the metropolitan area, including within the city itself. By most accounts the Regional Transit Authority has been a failure. A regional transportation millage vote failed in 2016, largely because of resistance by voters in the suburban counties and opposition by their county executives. The city has been a marginal player in transportation projects, even within its own borders. For example, the new three-mile light-rail down the city's main street was planned and funded by private investors, non-profit organizations, and the state and federal governments. The light-rail's original name, the M-1 Rail, was changed to the QLine in recognition of the key financing role of Quicken Loans' CEO Dan Gilbert. Detroit's involvement was limited mainly to coordinating the city's bus service to serve the light-rail stops.

Other municipal functions have been reallocated by the city itself to other providers. The city's 2013 budget eliminated own-source funding entirely for the Department of Health and Wellness Promotion, transferring most of its functions, including the administration of the Women, Infants, and Children food program and Medicaid enrollment, to a nonprofit contractor called the Institute for Population Health. Then the functions of the city's Department of Human Services, including food assistance, shelters, Head Start, and weatherization, were contracted out to the Wayne County Metropolitan Community Action Agency and the Community Development Institute. In 2014 the city leased the crown jewel of its public park system, Belle Isle, designed in the nineteenth century by Frederick Law Olmsted, to the state of Michigan for the following thirty years. There is now a fee for out-of-state visitors. In the same year, after nearly a century of municipal ownership, the city transferred the Detroit Institute of Art to a nonprofit organization funded by a three-county regional tax base. Next, the city council privatized trash collection in 2014, signing a five-year contract with a private disposal company.

Finally, the city has had to relinquish various valuable assets to certain creditors as part of the bankruptcy settlement. Notably, two bond insurance companies that had significant claims against the city, Syncora and Financial Guaranty Insurance, were granted revenues from two major municipal parking garages, and both companies secured options and financial assistance from the city to develop large tracts of prime land owned by Detroit.

This steady divestment and reassignment of municipal government responsibilities and assets suggest contradictory implications. On the one hand, an overburdened, underresourced city government has been steadily relieved of functions it could not perform effectively. When the city leased Belle Isle to the state, much of this historic park was decrepit, and the city's Parks and Recreation Department was on the verge of closing half the roughly three hundred parks in the system for lack of funding for maintenance. Similarly, the creation of the Public Lighting Authority took the burden of street lighting out of the city's hands and lodged it with a new agency, endowed with its own borrowing powers and unencumbered by a history of ineffectiveness.

An additional consequence of some of these changes has been the regionalization of certain responsibilities, particularly of the responsibility for water. The once municipal Detroit zoo (2006) and art museum (2014) are also both funded on a three-county basis and managed by nonprofit entities. This sort of reorganization has been a standard plank of metropolitan reformers for decades, propelled by the argument that regionalization broadens the tax base, generates economies of scale, and reconciles the geographical scope of formal responsibility with that of the problems or functions to be addressed.

If there are positive consequences of municipal divestment, however, there are also costs. The fragmentation of authority for local functions recalls the sort of administrative and political decentralization first established during the nineteenth century with weak-mayor systems. These arrangements were designed originally to check the power of the city executive, but reformers quickly realized that such arrangements often led to policy and planning paralysis. Independent authorities with their own power bases and distinctive constituencies often had no compelling reason to cooperate or coordinate with one another. Weak mayors had little leverage to create effective coalitions or regimes to move on big projects or to integrate policy approaches or planning. While divesting Detroit government of various functions may increase governmental effectiveness within each of those separate policy domains, city government itself in such a highly decentralized system becomes a less and less consequential player on a crowded stage. The mayor has steadily lost formal influence over functions that office once controlled. City hall in such a system no longer serves as a focal point for coordinated action, sitting at the heart of the old executive-centered coalition of New Haven fame.[5] Both its capacity and its authority are significantly diminished.

There is yet another cost to a highly decentralized system: democratic accountability is reduced, particularly for central-city, overwhelmingly black voters. Regional bodies and nonprofit entities have different constituencies than those to which city hall must respond, and some of the new service providers are beyond the reach of city voters altogether when the governing authority is transferred from a municipal agency to a body appointed by actors from outside the city, as with the new water and street-lighting authorities.

The Increased Role of Private Financing of Public Functions

The severe, long-term decline in the city's population, the relocation of the automobile industry, and the collapse of the local housing market greatly reduced the city's income- and property-tax revenues.[6] With its vastly diminished coffers, the city could not maintain basic services, much less embark on large development undertakings, social- and economic-justice initiatives, or maintenance projects. A third of the bus fleet was out of commission and could not be repaired; aging police and fire vehicles and equipment could not be replaced; the grass in the parks could not be mowed. The sight of a city street sweeper, even in 2018, was so unusual as to elicit surprise.[7] Thousands of abandoned structures—including houses, factories, office towers, and strip malls—could not be rehabilitated, repurposed, or torn down. As public services languished, philanthropic foundations increasingly stepped in on an ad hoc basis to finance these various functions.

Between 2007 and 2011, private foundations, such as Kresge, Skillman, Ford, and Kellogg, allocated $628 million to public projects and functions in Detroit, vastly increasing their historic involvement with the city. A combination of onetime foundation and corporate grants saved the city from closing half its parks in the summer of 2013, and other private grants provided funds to purchase new police cars, ambulances, and fire-fighting equipment. After 2011 a consortium of foundations pledged an additional $330 million—a centerpiece of the so-called Grand Bargain—to cover a portion of the public pension fund's shortfall, in return for which the bankruptcy court shielded the publicly owned Old Master and Impressionist paintings in the Detroit Institute of Art from sale to satisfy creditors' claims against the city.[8] Other large grants include $150 million from the Kresge Foundation for implementation of the city's current planning framework, Detroit Future City, developed by a nonprofit consortium.[9] Kresge is also a major underwriter of the new QLine light-rail system along the Woodward corridor, a project in which there is no local public funding. Indeed, so pervasive is Kresge's financial involvement in Detroit that some observers suggest that the president of the foundation treats his organization as the city's "shadow government."[10] For-profit corporate entities have also provided significant funds for public functions, most notably a combination of grants and loans by JPMorgan Chase bank in 2014 totaling $100 million over five years for blight removal, workforce training, and small business loans. Private investors are central to the QLine light-rail project as well.

Private funding for public purposes, it could be argued, provided an emergency backstop that quite possibly stemmed the city's slide into irredeemable destitution. Such foundation commitment to a distressed city is highly unusual. No other city in the United States has been the recipient of so much foundation money, nor have other cities typically received foundation support for ordinary operations and maintenance of standard public services. But as important as such money has been for Detroit, it raises significant issues of concern: it is not sustainable, it makes fiscal planning difficult, and it raises accountability problems.

Unlike a tax system, which can be designed and adjusted to guarantee a steady revenue stream, foundation funding is in no way sustainable. Foundation priorities may change; foundation endowments may dry up in hard financial times.[11] For foundations, particularly for national rather than regional or local foundations, focusing on one city can be a slippery slope: other cities will begin to seek foundation financial assistance, generating competition for Detroit. In any event, foundations are under no obligation to supply financial assistance year after year, a particularly grave challenge for a city function that relies on such funding for current operations and maintenance.

Because foundations give money according to their own priorities and the state of their own resources, a city that relies on such assistance will find it difficult to perform any long-range budget planning. Foundation monies can dry up at any time. Furthermore, the presence of private funding acts as a disincentive to make hard fiscal decisions regarding both the local tax regime and local expenditures.

One additional problem with high foundation funding is that the voters and their elected leaders have no authoritative voice in establishing spending priorities. The decision, for example, to pay for blight removal may be important to the city's long-term recovery prospects, but that is a decision made in boardrooms, not city hall. Foundations may, perhaps, feel they are morally accountable, but they are not formally accountable.

The Dominant Role of Private Developers

Developers have always had a central role in building the American city. Even the great federal public programs—including urban renewal, the Carter-era Urban Development Action Grants, and urban enterprise zones—all relied heavily upon private initiative and active private partners. And much urban development, historically, has taken place without significant government involvement, with the formal local-government role limited to no more than the passage of accommodating zoning laws and perhaps the provision of tax incentives.

But typically, in the development realm, local officials and public bodies—mayors, planning departments, economic-development commissioners, strategic-planning and visioning bodies, community-planning boards, and the like—provide frameworks, ideas, resources, constraints, and checks on private ambition. Visionary mayors, entrepreneurial economic-development directors, and active citizen planning boards are fixtures in many cities, and private developers must cooperate and contend with them. But development in Detroit—primarily investment in downtown properties and sports and entertainment facilities—was pursued during the city's descent into bankruptcy and fiscal takeover by the state almost entirely according to the visions of a very small number of private developers. As Mayor Dave Bing famously said, "My job is to knock down as many barriers as possible and get out of the way."[12] Most investment in the last decade has occurred in the roughly

7-square-mile downtown, a small area within the 139-square-mile city footprint, and much of it has been geared to the small middle-class population of downtown workers and residents.

Detroit boosters point to the recent planning exercise that produced a framework for the city's development and transformation, Detroit Future City, which involved hundreds of public meetings and hearings by the nonprofit organizers of this effort. But Detroit Future City, by its own account, is an aspirational document, without teeth or the means to raise its own resources beyond the beneficence of its foundation funders. No private developer need be constrained by the proposals in the plan. It does not establish a set of priorities or communal values that must guide the city's transformation. It does not establish authoritative guidelines or goals for the city's public authorities. And by all accounts, it is moribund, ignored by developers and the current mayor alike.[13]

By far the dominant figure in the city's development in the last decade has been Dan Gilbert, a Detroit native who made his fortune as the founder of Quicken Loans, which services the online mortgage market and has been the target of successful federal action and other lawsuits for its dubious lending practices.[14] By 2018 Gilbert had purchased more than ninety Detroit properties, all clustered in the downtown, investing more than $1.5 billion in abandoned or half-empty office towers, a casino, parking structures, the old police headquarters, a hotel, and large vacant lots. Gilbert employs an estimated 12,500 workers downtown in his various companies. Besides owning a major proportion of the productive downtown property, Gilbert has sought to create a festive ambience, in part by co-opting public spaces, to attract and preoccupy his young workforce: he designed and funded street furniture, food trucks, a dog run, and even a summer "beach" with trucked-in sand in a downtown square. He has installed his own surveillance cameras to enhance public safety, created a bike-rental service, and financed a freeway off-ramp to funnel traffic more efficiently to his casino. To serve his largely young workforce, some of whom now rent in downtown housing developments, Gilbert has recruited retail and restaurant businesses to fill the ground-floor levels of his office properties, developed a residential complex in a neighborhood adjacent to the city core, and created a high-speed internet service for the area. Indeed, so numerous are his projects and so all-encompassing is his vision of the future city that the *National Journal* has called him Detroit's "*de facto* CEO."[15]

Gilbert is not the only entrepreneur developing downtown Detroit. Mike and Marian Ilitch, whose wealth derived initially from Little Caesars Pizza, have been the central force in developing the city's considerable array of entertainment amenities. The Ilitch family (Mike died in 2017) laid the foundation for a downtown entertainment district by renovating the old Fox Theater, a rococo 1920s movie palace, in 1988. It now hosts major live music acts. Then a little over a decade later, they built a new stadium, across the street from the theater, for their Detroit Tigers baseball team. The Ilitch family also owns the MotorCity Casino Hotel on the district's western edge. Recently, they also built a new hockey arena for the Red Wings, just north of the downtown. The city played no role in planning any of these facilities, although it did transfer thirty-nine parcels of city-owned land to the Downtown Development Authority, the action arm of the city's nonprofit economic-development agency, for one dollar. The Authority then leased the land to the family rent-free for ninety-five years.

Gilbert, the Ilitch family, and a handful of others have indubitably made Detroit a more pleasant and interesting place to live for the small upper-middle class that works in or visits the downtown (approximately three-quarters of the downtown workforce still lives in the suburbs). But the food trucks and the baseball stadium and the sand beach and the freeway off-ramp to the Gilbert casino do not seem to serve the central interests or tastes or needs of the vast majority of the city's population. Given that a third or more of Detroit's residents live below the poverty line and the proportion of the city's college graduates is the smallest of any large city in the United States, such amenities would seem to represent a badly calibrated sense of priorities.

To some extent, the problem can be traced to the absence of government participation in the development process. Although Mayor Duggan has lately managed to amass the political clout to appear on the podium with private actors for the announcement of each new development project, there is little indication that such activity has been initiated or shaped or constrained by municipal development institutions. The Detroit Economic Growth Corporation, a Coleman Young–era creation, has been marginalized.[16] There is no institutional forum for debate about the direction the city is taking. And there is no accountability, because local government is diminished: its authority is attenuated, its resources are scarce, and its functional scope is reduced.

Even after being absolved of full liability for its debts, Detroit's financial prospects are not good. Bankruptcy proceedings were not a cure. The end result is a weaker city, stripped of any vestiges of freedom of action, less able to confront its maladies and less attractive to immigrants and business firms seeking economic opportunity. Both own-source and state-shared revenues are projected to decline or stay flat into the mid-2020s. Population flight has left the poorest behind: 59 percent of Detroit children lived in poverty in 2013. A United Way study calculates that fully two-thirds of the city's population (including the 38 percent who live under the poverty line) cannot afford basic housing and health-care needs, even when they are working. In essence, and in line with this volume's themes, one could say that the largely imposed solution of "shadow government"—ceding city powers to private or other external entities—for the city's woes is no solution at all for most of Detroit's residents.

A city without a consequential government becomes a blank slate for the ambitions, plans, and schemes of actors for whom common purpose and communal norms are not, perhaps, the top priority. As Detroit's functions have been reallocated to other public and private entities, its scope of authority has diminished. As responsibility for financing public functions has increasingly been assumed by private funders, the city's path to fiscal security and stability has been jeopardized. As the development initiative has been consolidated in the hands of a few private entrepreneurs, the city's future shape is no longer an issue of debate in the public arena.

This is not to say, of course, that a strong government is necessarily a virtuous government, responsive to the people and reliable in its exercise of authority for some idea of the public good.

Governments can be (and in the case of Detroit often were) corrupt and ineffective. Nor is this to say that good cities cannot ever be built by benevolent private actors. But the dismantling of municipal government in Detroit somehow offends the ideal of local democracy, which, for all its flaws, nevertheless remains the most effective way to represent communal interests. None of the current visions, accordingly, identifies a path that will employ large numbers of Detroit residents with little formal education beyond high school.

What is a reasonable middle ground between the inadequate visions mentioned here? There can be a practical if modest future for Detroit as a functioning working-class city, even in the absence of a robust municipal government infrastructure, if the political will is there. The city could use inclusionary zoning to expand and concentrate affordable-housing options. It could recruit immigrants, as some other cities are doing (Pittsburgh, St. Louis, and Nashville, among others), say, by offering cheap housing from its huge stock of city-owned tax-delinquent properties; creating an office of immigrant affairs; and tailoring bilingual schools to target populations from Africa, the Middle East, and Central America. Immigrants tend to create their own small business economies wherever they settle in dense enough numbers. And the city could also declare a moratorium on using any sort of public subsidies to support downtown-development projects.[17]

In the nineteenth century, many of the great industrial barons spent some of their great fortunes on public institutions or on private institutions for the public good—libraries, museums, mass-transit systems and stations, concert halls, schools and universities, and hospitals. Absent similar voluntary impulses among Detroit's new economic barons, imagine the impact if the city could levy exactions from its developers to finance projects for the public good in return for the necessary building permits and other public cooperation. Perhaps some would take their capital elsewhere, but some of them profess to be committed Detroit partisans. Some might surely be willing to exchange permits for financial support for schools or parks or libraries or youth centers or neighborhood clinics or fire stations or low-income housing or new computers. This is a vision of Detroit as a city that functions for its working class and poor and promises a more achievable and equitable future.

Notes

I am indebted to Robin Boyle for his careful reading and helpful comments on an earlier version of this chapter.

1. Some scholars speak of the "local state," but the focus of this chapter is *municipal* government and its diminishment in relation to other administrative entities, both public and private, some of which are themselves local government bodies, such as county government and special regional authorities. See, for example, Helga Leitner, "Cities in Pursuit of Economic Growth: The Local State as Entrepreneur," *Political Geography Quarterly* 9, no. 2 (1990): 146–70.

2. B. D. Ryan, *Design after Decline: How America Rebuilds Shrinking Cities* (Philadelphia: University of Pennsylvania Press, 2012), xiii.

3. Ryan, 184.

4. The best account of the causes and dimensions of the bankruptcy and the subsequent settlement is Reynolds Farley, "Detroit in Bankruptcy," in *Reinventing Detroit: The Politics of Possibility*, ed. Michael Peter Smith and L. Owen Kirkpatrick (New Brunswick, N.J.: Transaction, 2015), 93–112.

5. This was the characterization of the local political structure of New Haven in Robert Dahl's classic, *Who Governs?* (New Haven, Conn.: Yale University Press, 1961).

6. For a full discussion of Detroit finances, see City of Detroit, *Disclosure Statement with Respect to the Plan for the Adjustment of Debts of the City of Detroit* (Detroit, Mich., February 14, 2014), https://detroitmi.gov/Portals/0/docs/EM/Bankruptcy%20Information/Disclosure%20Statement%20_Plan%20for%20the%20Adjustment%20of%20Debts%20of%20the%20City%20of%20Detroit.pdf.

7. Chad Livengood, "State Ends Direct Oversight of Detroit Finances," *Crain's* (website), April 30, 2018, www.crainsdetroit.com/article/20180430/news/659466/state-ends-direct-oversight-of-detroit-finances.

8. Susan Drake Swift, "Detroit's 'Grand Bargain' and the Partnership that Propelled It," *Independent Sector* (blog), January 12, 2016, http://bit.ly/2NP1yLr.

9. Detroit Future City, *Detroit Strategic Framework Plan* (Detroit, Mich., December 2012), https://bit.ly/2NRytPp.

10. Suzanne Perry, "Detroit Tests What Foundations Can Do to Rescue Troubled Cities," *Chronicle of Philanthropy*, October 20, 2013.

11. Kresge, for example, shifted its focus in 2014 from Detroit to more general problems of inequality, leaving Detroit recipients without a relatively assured source of support.

12. Quoted in David Segal, "A Missionary's Quest to Remake Motor City," *New York Times*, April 14, 2013.

13. Robin Boyle, email message to author, June 29, 2018.

14. Tom Perkins, "On Bill Gilbert's Ever-growing Rap Sheet, and Corporate Welfare," *Detroit Metro Times*, August 30, 2017, www.metrotimes.com/news-hits/archives/2017/08/30/on-dan-gilberts-ever-growing-rap -sheet-and-corporate-welfare.

15. Tim Alberta, "Is Dan Gilbert Detroit's New Superhero?," *Atlantic*, February 27, 2014.

16. Boyle, email.

17. Peter Eisinger, "Reimagining Detroit," *City & Community* 2, no. 2 (June 2003): 115.

Part II

The Evolving Role of Public-Private Authorities

4

Transportation Empires in the New York and Los Angeles Regions

From the Old to the New Politics of Governance and Development

Steven P. Erie, Scott A. MacKenzie, and Jameson W. Doig

> While political scientists concerned with urban politics
> have recently been preoccupied with business influence
> and economic development policy, they have devoted
> remarkably little attention to the *politics* of direct public
> investment.
>
> —Alan Altshuler and David Luberoff, *Mega-Projects*

Urban scholars have long recognized the crucial role of infrastructure investment in the development of cities and regions.[1] Physical infrastructure—including roads, rail, water, sewer, power, and other material systems—constitutes the "technological sinews" of urban places.[2] To grow and thrive, all cities must devise means to move goods and people efficiently within and beyond their borders. Gathering the resources to plan, finance, and manage transportation systems is a major collective undertaking for urban practitioners and a critical issue in the study of urban development and governance.

Since the early twentieth century, most investments in transportation infrastructure—highways, airports, seaports, rail systems, and the like—have been planned, financed, and constructed either by governments or by private firms under close government supervision.[3] With the exception of interstate highways, where the federal government assumed the lead role, primary responsibility for transportation infrastructure devolved to state and local governments.[4] Local governments own and operate nearly all the nation's airports and seaports, as well as a large share of its commuter-rail systems. And while private firms own and operate much of the nation's freight-rail system, decisions by local public officials determine whether and how freight-rail facilities connect to seaports and other transportation nodes.

Despite the obvious importance of transportation in urban development, and recognition of the dominant role of state and local governments, relatively little work focuses on how the governance of local and regional transportation systems is organized. In many cities and regions, special-district governments or public authorities have been created to plan, finance, build, and manage airports, seaports, and freight-rail systems.[5] In other places, these functions are carried out by city or county government departments. Even among cities and regions that employ public authorities, there is substantial variation in the geographic and functional scope of transportation agencies, the resources available to them, and the rules mediating their relationships with local elected officials and private-sector actors. Such diversity in the governance of transportation infrastructure challenges existing scholarship, which asserts that all cities must foster economic development and that internal political factors are irrelevant to the pursuit of this objective.[6] Do differences in how infrastructure investments are financed, and transportation systems are governed, really matter? Does the decision to lodge responsibility in single-purpose municipal agencies, as opposed to a multipurpose regional authority, influence how the interests of local residents, elected officials, businesses, and others are represented? Why have cities and regions developed such different approaches to the governance of transportation infrastructure? Do these differences contribute to differences in performance and policy-making capacity?

We address these questions in examining the evolution and performance of governance arrangements for transportation systems in the New York and Los Angeles regions. We focus on seaport, freight-rail, and airport networks that connect these regions to the rest of the nation and the world.[7] Our survey of more than one hundred years of transportation development and policy-making reveals the importance of both formal and informal collaboration between public officials and private-sector actors. While our account emphasizes the activities of professional bureaucrats who oversee the major seaport, airport, and freight-rail facilities, it also highlights contributions by private-sector policy entrepreneurs, including local business groups, the maritime and airline industries, railroads, organized labor, environmental groups, and other stakeholders. Leadership by private actors helped establish the first large-scale facilities in both regions. Their collaboration in policy innovation and institutional changes later enhanced the capacities of transportation agencies. More recently, their political activity (especially in Los Angeles) has shaped how transportation officials respond to the challenges they face. We believe that examining earlier periods of transportation development—that is, the "old" politics—provides useful context for understanding the "new" politics of public–private partnerships and quasi-public development corporations.

Our choice of cases is motivated by the preeminent role of these regions in the nation's international trade traffic. Table 4.1 lists the nation's top-ten trading centers for 2016. New York and Los Angeles are the nation's top-two centers of foreign commerce, far exceeding other metropolitan areas. Los Angeles ranked first in the value of vessel-cargo shipments and third in the value of air-cargo shipments. New York ranked first in air cargo and second in vessel cargo.[8] Table 4.2 lists the nation's top-ten global gateways. New York and Los Angeles house the top-two gateways, four of the top five, and five of the top ten. These include three of the nation's premier seaports in terms of the value of merchandise trade and two of the busiest airports for passenger and cargo traffic.

In addition to their unique status as leading international trade hubs, these cases differ markedly in how their transportation systems are governed. In New York a single bistate agency, the Port

Table 4.1. U.S. Merchandise Trade by Shipping Mode, 2016
(in billions of dollars by customs district)

Rank	District	Vessel	Air	Land	Total
1	Los Angeles	373.2	102.7	2.1	477.9
2	New York	187.8	203.1	3.3	394.2
3	Laredo	1.1	0.5	279.9	281.5
4	Detroit	2.7	5.4	233.7	241.9
5	Chicago	1.4	143.7	32.1	177.1
6	Seattle	81.9	19.5	71.6	173.1
7	New Orleans	83.5	73.9	8.6	166.0
8	Houston	147.8	14.2	0.4	162.5
9	Savannah	100.6	39.5	2.0	142.1
10	San Francisco	63.3	57.7	0.3	121.2

Source: U.S. Department of Commerce, Bureau of the Census, *FT 920 U.S. Merchandise Trade: Selected Highlights* (Washington, D.C., December 2016).

Table 4.2. Top U.S. Global Gateways, 2015
(merchandise trade in billions of dollars)

Rank	Gateway	Type	Exports	Imports	Total
1	Port Newark/Elizabeth	Water	46.9	155.8	202.6
2	Port of Los Angeles	Water	31.4	166.9	198.4
3	Laredo bridges	Land	91.6	106.3	198.0
4	JFK Int'l. Airport	Air	90.4	95.1	185.5
5	Port of Long Beach	Water	31.0	123.3	154.2
6	Chicago airports	Air	45.7	96.0	141.8
7	Port of Houston	Water	75.9	58.7	134.6
8	Detroit bridges	Land	70.0	59.2	129.2
9	L.A. Int'l. Airport	Air	49.0	50.9	99.9
10	Port of Savannah	Water	25.8	61.5	87.3

Source: U.S. Department of Transportation, Bureau of Transportation Statistics, National Transportation Statistics (February 2017), Table 1-51.

Authority of New York and New Jersey (PA) owns and operates all essential airport and seaport facilities. In Los Angeles these responsibilities have been lodged in multiple single-purpose municipal airport, seaport, and freight-rail agencies. We argue that differences in how these transportation systems are governed have shaped the performance of transportation agencies and their proclivity for developing innovative programs and policies. The PA used superior financial resources, greater insulation from local elected officials and voters, and an "open-ended" legislative mandate to expand its activities beyond its original mission. Financial flexibility has also enabled the PA to take on revenue-losing projects and weather economic downturns, such as the 2008 global recession. L.A.'s major transportation agencies—including the Port of Los Angeles (POLA), the Port of Long Beach (POLB), and Los Angeles World Airports (LAWA)—while not endowed with the flexible revenues of the PA, have thrived by appealing to local elected officials and voters for greater authority and resources. However, the decisions of these three L.A. agencies reflect far greater deference to local concerns, including wider social objectives.

Our analysis, based on primary-source materials, interviews, and secondary literature, indicates that differences in how transportation systems are governed in these two regions reflect the consequences of decisions taken in the early twentieth century. Political leaders were influenced by Progressive Era arguments—such as that insulating administrative decisions from political pressures would lead to more innovative and effective policies. The configuration of local and state politics in the two regions dictated different governance arrangements to accomplish their goals. In delegating to public authorities, state officials in New York and local officials in Los Angeles created and empowered a new class of actors—professional transportation bureaucrats. Our case studies draw upon *agency theory* and *historical institutionalism*, which emphasize how institutional choices at one moment can over time push regional development onto distinct tracks.[9] We explain how agency design has encouraged entrepreneurial behavior at these agencies.

Governance Quandaries

Research on urban economic development has focused on the ability of cities to overcome structural conditions that limit their autonomy and support for redistributive policies. Since Paul E. Peterson's influential study *City Limits*, scholars have been attuned to conditions, such as subordinate legal status and interurban competition, which privilege economic-development objectives and limit cities' support for redistributive policies.[10] Peterson argued that development programs attract little controversy, a much-disputed claim.[11] Subsequent scholarship has focused on the entrepreneurial strategies cities use to overcome their limited legal authority and reductions in federal assistance.[12]

One tool in the arsenal of cities is public authorities. The proliferation of these special-purpose governments introduced competition-based efficiencies but has been criticized for duplicating services and reducing public participation.[13] Nonetheless, by allowing local governments to assume large debts while adhering to state and local fiscal requirements, public authorities provide a flexible mechanism for engaging financial markets.[14] Today, public authorities are responsible for most bonds used to finance infrastructure.[15] The frequent use of special-purpose governments to plan, finance, and manage transportation investments can obscure important differences in their institutional arrangements, including geographic scope. Regional authorities manage 55 percent of U.S. seaports, while state and bistate authorities govern 19 percent, and city and county departments or agencies oversee 26 percent, respectively. In contrast, city and county agencies manage most airports, though regional and bistate authorities are prevalent in large metropolitan regions.[16] The functional and financial characteristics of these agencies also vary significantly.[17]

The practice of delegating responsibility for planning, financing, and managing transportation systems springs from the reality that elected officials are ill equipped to handle these functions. Local and state governments require the expertise of professional planners, engineers, and managers; financial-sector resources; and stakeholder input. The task of institutional design is less about setting up a "stand-alone" agency to impose solutions and more about arranging agency hierarchies, incentives, and sanctions to facilitate cooperation among public and private actors—that is, modifying *governance* as opposed to government.[18] The transportation agencies created by acts of delegation appear to be semi-independent command-and-control structures, but they serve also as institutional anchors of larger networks organized to carry out policies and programs. The rules that structure an agency's decision-making in its early years can foreclose or privilege particular courses of action, shape the rights and influence of actors, and influence the incentives and capacity for policy innovation.

Principal-Agent Models and Transportation Governance: Theory and Methods

One useful analytical tool for understanding the governance of transportation systems is agency theory. The creation of a public authority sets up a classic principal–agent relationship, whereby one or more elected bodies (the principal) delegate resources and authority to a transportation agency (the agent). However, because elected officials often cannot easily observe agency actions and because the preferences of elected and appointed officials are seldom identical, "agency loss" occurs—that is, agency activity strays from the objectives of those responsible for delegation.[19] Principal–agent models can describe relationships between Congress and federal agencies. Some scholars argue that bureaucrats and special interests use their information advantages to achieve nonmajoritarian policy outcomes.[20] Others believe that Congress retains the upper hand, using implicit threats, committee oversight, and administrative procedures to control bureaucrats.[21] Still others find that presidents, using appointments, unilateral actions, and other tools strongly influence bureaucratic activities.[22] Alternatively, Daniel Carpenter explains how federal agencies, such as the Food and Drug Administration, can develop an independent capacity to design and implement innovative policies. Through careful preservation of their reputation and cultivation of coalition partners, federal agencies can prevail against significant congressional opposition.[23]

While local governments frequently delegate to public authorities and, increasingly, to private-sector organizations, urban scholars have made little use of agency theory. Nonetheless, state legislation and local charter provisions can enable public authorities (the agents) to influence elected officials (the principals). Similarly, the limited capacity of state and local legislatures offers reason to question the effectiveness of many tools of legislative control. Thus, the opportunities for bureaucratic autonomy at the subnational level are likely to be at least as great as they are at the federal level.

Empirical studies provide ample evidence of the risks of delegation. Robert A. Caro's study of Robert Moses, for example, details how bureaucrats might use superior information and resources to initiate large-scale infrastructure projects with little input or oversight from local elected officials and voters.[24] Some scholars find that many public authorities are designed expressly to limit participation from local communities.[25] Others explain how overestimating benefits and underestimating costs (optimism bias) and deliberate misleading of elected officials shape infrastructure megaprojects.[26] Indeed, a recent cross-national survey concluded that cost overruns, delays, and overstatement of project benefits are the norm.[27] These and other studies emphasize the powerful influence of the business community, developers, and other special interests, and suggest that delegation by local governments will often result in abdication.[28]

What might prevent this pattern or other kinds of shirking by the agencies tasked with planning, implementing, and managing transportation infrastructure? While no configuration of institutions and actors will eliminate agency loss entirely, we emphasize two factors that can preserve agency integrity and enhance performance. The first, institutional design, refers to contract language, institutional checks, and other mechanisms that strengthen the alignment of interests between principal and agent and, thereby, steer the activities of officials toward the public interest.[29] The second, organizational reputation, focuses on professional norms and career objectives. While bureaucrats acquire the means to mislead the public, they also thrive by using these means to create positive impressions based on actual performance. By maintaining a reputation for honesty and competence, bureaucrats might enhance their institutional authority and resources. Indeed, doing so is instrumentally rational in relationships characterized by repeated interactions.[30] If a transportation agency consistently misleads elected officials, elected officials and voters will not grant the agency more resources in the future, and might curtail the authority of that agency.

A Historical-Institutionalist Approach

To assess how public authorities achieve and maintain independent decision-making power, we examine the evolution of the transportation agencies responsible for airport, seaport, and freight-rail networks in the New York and Los Angeles regions. Our comparison is set up as a "most similar cases" design. Both regions are large markets geographically positioned to support airport, seaport, and freight-rail infrastructure. The exposure of these regions to factors frequently cited to explain infrastructure investments—technology, economic shocks, and political forces—is similar across our cases. Governance, however, differs markedly between the two regions. So, too, we argue, does agency responsiveness to local concerns, and policy-making capacity.

These cases can shed light on the factors that powerfully shape differences in governance, but demonstrating this requires more than a static comparison of cross-sectional differences. Our historical case studies trace the emergence of different governance arrangements that shaped the transportation systems in New York and Los Angeles. In both regions, new institutions were created during the Progressive Era to address local transportation deficiencies. Those who designed these systems were concerned about political pressures, and they organized transportation agencies to be partially insulated. Our account exhibits several hallmarks of the historical-institutionalist approach.[31] We emphasize the Progressive Era as a "critical juncture" where new governance arrangements sent these regions along different development paths. These arrangements empowered a new class of decision makers: professional bureaucrats intent on developing transportation systems to improve efficiency of travel and to capture large shares of regional, national, and global trade flows.

While both regions empowered appointed transportation officials, the core institutional features under which they labored were quite different. In New York, with a harbor that touched both New

York City and New Jersey shores, and state officials' desire to insulate transportation systems from local political pressures, a bistate authority was created and, some years later, invested with enormous financial resources through bridge and tunnel revenues. Regional control of seaport and airport facilities ensued as an outgrowth of the PA's financial surplus and ambitions of its top managers. In Los Angeles, the creation of single-purpose semiautonomous municipal proprietary departments provided a measure of local control, while preventing elected officials from siphoning port and airport revenues. Regionalization of seaport and airport facilities was blocked by long-standing rivalries between the City of Los Angeles and its neighbors, later reinforced by the self-interest of appointed transportation commissioners and managers. Thus, bureaucratic autonomy favored regionalization in New York and impeded regionalization in Los Angeles.

We focus next on the activities of the transportation agencies empowered by governance reforms. We explain how and why different arrangements were negotiated in the 1920s. We describe how bureaucratic entrepreneurs in both regions secured and maintained some freedom from elected officials as these agencies undertook large public-works projects. The success of these efforts helps explain the relative stability of these arrangements, even in the face of changes in technology, unprecedented regional growth, and globalization. The agencies created nearly a century ago in these regions have continued to play a dominant role, though differences in governance have mediated each region's response to these forces.

Creating New Agencies

In the early twentieth century, public officials and business leaders in New York and Los Angeles faced transportation deficiencies generated by population growth, industrial development, and maritime demands. With federal policy makers paying little attention to cities, it was up to local leaders to devise solutions. It was apparent that exclusively relying on private-sector resources would be insufficient. Similarly, business leaders and reformers understood the dangers of overreliance on elected state and local governments. Few elected officials possessed more than a passing interest in transportation problems, and experience suggested that those officials might be more interested in job creation (patronage) than improved efficiency. Business leaders and reformers in New York pushed reluctant state legislatures to create an institution to overcome perceived weaknesses in the system of railroads and marine terminals. In Los Angeles, the business community, aided by fledgling harbor commissions, lobbied elected officials and voters for resources to spur port development. Delegation to such entities, however, posed significant risks. Elected officials were concerned that they were giving away power and that these semiautonomous agencies would require higher taxes or otherwise become unpopular. For private-sector reformers, the task was to shield transportation agencies from the vicissitudes of electoral politics and patronage claims of party-machine organizations.

Challenges in the New York–New Jersey Region

Governors of New York and New Jersey in the years before World War I understood the need to remedy port inefficiency. Half the nation's international trade passed through the port; but the Hudson River separated the major shipping piers in Manhattan and Brooklyn from the freight railroads, which terminated at the New Jersey shore.[32] Moreover, New York City's marine-terminal department was a weak, patronage-laden agency. On the New Jersey side, small municipal agencies had little capacity to pursue modernization. Leadership to overcome these problems initially came from Julius Henry Cohen, of the New York State Chamber of Commerce, who proposed creating a bistate agency with extensive power to develop modernization plans, including tunnels under the Hudson to carry rail-freight trains directly to New York's piers. This new agency would also control private development that might affect transport efficiency.[33]

State officials rejected some of Cohen's plans, but they did agree to create, via an interstate compact, a Port of New York Authority— renamed the Port Authority of New York and New Jersey (PA) in 1972—and to give it an unusual degree of political insulation. The PA would be controlled by six commissioners (three appointed by each governor for fixed six-year terms), have the power to issue bonds, and could retain the income from its projects.[34] Moreover, the PA was given an open-ended mandate: it was authorized to examine and *perhaps* carry out transportation projects in a Port District extending across twenty-one counties in two states. ("Perhaps," because the agency was given little beyond a Manhattan office and funds to employ a few railroad and port planners.) The agreement was reached despite protests from New York, Newark, Jersey City, and other municipalities on the western side of the Hudson River.[35] The interstate compact legislation was signed in 1921, and the two states also directed the PA to "solve" the rail-freight problem.

PA staff prepared a detailed plan to connect the railroads via tunnels under the Hudson River to New York's marine terminals, and they focused their energies throughout the 1920s on negotiations with the rail corporations. Meanwhile, private engineer Othmar H. Ammann began a public campaign in 1923 for a large vehicular bridge. He convinced New Jersey governor George Silzer to push the PA to build Hudson River crossings for motor vehicles too. Under pressure to show progress in meeting the region's transportation problems, the PA hired Ammann in 1925. Ammann's George Washington Bridge, completed in 1931, proved to be an engineering and toll-revenue success. Then in 1930–31, the PA acquired the money-making Holland Tunnel. Meanwhile, efforts to enlist railroad support for the underwater tunnel collapsed. Its rail efforts abandoned, the PA was seen thereafter as a vehicular "bridge-and-tunnel outfit." Governors and state legislatures agreed to this change in direction, and Governor Silzer played a role in advancing Ammann's preferences. But the main impetus was neither elected officials nor PA commissioners, but rather the skills and energies of Ammann and Cohen.[36]

Creating New Agencies in Los Angeles and Long Beach

The story of L.A.'s early harbor development is a riveting tale of urban rivalries, railroad hegemony, and political revolt.[37] In the 1870s, after the transcontinental railroad was completed, Los Angeles and San Diego battled to secure a rail connection to San Francisco that civic leaders believed would ensure regional growth and supremacy. To place a trunk line through Los Angeles, the Southern Pacific Railroad, the first long-distance rail line in the West, demanded a king's ransom in subsidies. In 1872 local voters approved a deal that granted Southern Pacific a $602,000 subsidy (equaling 5 percent of L.A. County's assessed valuation) and ownership of the rail link between downtown and the harbor. In doing so, Los Angeles secured the vital rail connection to San Francisco and the East, and marginalized San Diego, its main rival in Southern California.

The railroad proved to be a Faustian bargain, as Southern Pacific saddled the region with high shipping rates and poor service. This— and the railroad's meddling in local affairs—galvanized opposition. In the 1890s the Southern Pacific squared off against local business leaders and reformers to determine the location of the harbor. The Southern Pacific proposed a railroad-controlled harbor at Santa Monica; L.A.'s business community, including *Los Angeles Times* owner Harrison Gray Otis, countered with a proposal for a municipally owned harbor at San Pedro. Local initiative combined with federal support proved to be decisive for San Pedro.[38] Municipal ownership was facilitated by a state constitution that granted cities extensive home-rule powers, including expansive fiscal and land-use authority. It also ensured that local officials, not state officials hand-picked by Southern Pacific's statewide organization, would control the harbor.

In 1907 Los Angeles created a Harbor Department led by a three-person commission. Orchestrated at the local level, harbor development still required outside assistance. Federal money was needed to dredge the harbor in San Pedro and establish a breakwater. State approval also was needed to merge San Pedro and Wilmington into the City of Los Angeles in 1909. In 1911 the state legislature passed the Tidelands Trust Act, making port cities trustees of state tidelands along their waterfronts. By 1912 a portion of the breakwater was completed, and the first large wharf had been opened.[39]

Harbor development in Long Beach also had to overcome private profit-seeking and the city's remoteness from the waterfront. The rail link with Los Angeles was controlled by the Southern Pacific. As Los Angeles extended municipal boundaries to San Pedro and Wilmington, Long Beach officials consolidated control over nearby Terminal Island. In 1910 Long Beach ended its neighbor's waterfront conquest by annexing a one-hundred-foot-wide strip of land extending from its southeastern border to the Orange County line. In 1911 the city dedicated the Port of Long Beach, but harbor development was controlled by the private Los Angeles Dock and Terminal Company. City officials gradually increased their role. A commission overseeing harbor development was established in 1917, although attempts to raise money to place all port property under municipal control would languish until 1924.

While the pattern of single-purpose municipal agencies had been established, harbor commissions in Los Angeles and Long Beach were little more than appendages of local government. They had to rely on elected officials and voters for funds. In 1925 Los Angeles voters approved a new charter that increased the authority of the Harbor Department. The charter created the position of general manager, expanded the harbor commission, and gave it near total control over port development, financing, and personnel. In Long Beach a charter amendment gave the harbor commission control over a separate revenue fund.[40] Charter amendments in 1929 and 1931 gave the Harbor Department powers comparable to those enjoyed by counterparts in Los Angeles. With these changes both port agencies achieved "proprietary," or semiautonomous, status.

Exceeding Limited Delegation in New York and Los Angeles

The agencies that would dominate massive transportation systems in both regions were created through successive acts of delegation. By 1940 the PA had escaped the constraints of its railroad-focused plans and acquired resources to maintain a large portfolio of bridges and tunnels. Such developments were not anticipated by the original coalition of officials, businessmen, and reformers who had backed the 1921 compact. The PA's success in expanding its mission is partly explained by the compact's open-ended phrasing: the power to "purchase, construct, lease," and operate *any* transportation facility and to "make charges for the use thereof." However, in order to expand beyond freight rail, the PA needed approval by the governors and state legislatures. In 1927 the governors were given powers to ensure the PA would not stray from its principals' preferred policies; new state laws granted each governor a veto over PA projects and other activities.

Nonetheless, governors and state legislatures throughout the 1920s and beyond agreed to legislation allowing the PA to expand into vehicular bridge and tunnel construction, bus and airport operations, and, later, commuter-rail services and real-estate development. Attempts to abolish the agency, curtail its authority, or undermine its operations by layering it with patronage were defeated. Cohen, and his successors after 1942, assisted by allies in the business community and the press, maintained control. Local officials at times vigorously opposed them, but the success of the PA in carrying out projects on time and without scandal marginalized opposition. Crucial to its success was the work of Cohen, Amman, and other skilled entrepreneurs who controlled substantial funds (mainly toll revenue), embraced a risk-taking approach, and nurtured alliances with key members of the press and the business community.[41]

In the L.A. region, weak municipal harbor departments were dramatically strengthened by charter reforms. The ability of proponents of enlarged harbor authority to use the initiative process to appeal above the heads of mayors and city councils proved to be decisive. The Los Angeles Harbor Department was instrumental in organizing campaign committees—drawn from businesses, oil companies, shippers, railroads, and banks—to secure voter approval for increased authority and resources via bond measures. Six bonds totaling more than $30 million and twenty-three initiatives expanding its authority were approved between 1906 and 1928. By the 1930s the Harbor Department was self-supporting and handling more tonnage than any other port on the West Coast.[42] In Long Beach public–private collaboration was instrumental in acquiring greater authority and resources for the harbor commission. As in Los Angeles, bureaucratic empowerment was achieved primarily via the initiative process. Between 1906 and 1928, Long Beach voters passed ten bond proposals, totaling more than $16 million. Long Beach voters approved twenty-two charter amendments between 1905 and 1931 to strengthen the authority of harbor officials, usually with large majorities.[43] By 1931, when charter changes created a harbor district and a Board of Harbor Commissioners, Long Beach's seaport was handling more than a million tons of cargo annually.[44]

Thomas Romer and Howard Rosenthal explain how public agencies can use the initiative process to confront voters with a "take it or leave it" offer.[45] Voters cannot amend bond proposals. They must choose between the status quo (i.e., overcrowded harbor facilities) and more spending (on needed improvements). Thus, transportation officials in Los Angeles circumvented the tight control that theoretically should exist between elected officials and the agencies they create. Because voters ultimately control the degree of authority awarded to the POLA, the POLB, and the L.A. airport agency, transportation officials have ample incentives to cultivate a positive public image.

Mayors and city councils could be powerfully affected by the activities of these semiautonomous departments. Altering the departments' prerogatives, however, required elected officials to battle the coalitions supporting these agencies. In such battles L.A.'s transportation bureaucrats enjoyed superior organization and resources. Since the advent of district elections in Los Angeles in 1925, only council members representing districts that contain the port or airport have taken serious interest in department activities. Mayors have retained influence through appointments and, on occasion, succeeded in bending departments to their will. On balance, however, the departments have enjoyed substantial discretion in their pursuit of transportation investments and policy objectives.

Building Transportation Empires

The result of creative maneuverings by elected officials, business leaders, and the transportation entrepreneurs they empowered were two strikingly different governance arrangements. Of the two, the PA was by far the more innovative as the first multipurpose public authority in the United States and the first created via interstate compact. In contrast, Los Angeles created a municipal proprietary department with semiautonomous status, but one limited to planning, constructing, and operating a single public improvement or facility. The potent flexibility of the PA's structure was demonstrated in the mid-1920s, when it expanded to bridges and tunnels.[46] In 1935 the PA devised a new bond instrument, which ensured that new programs would be supported by revenues from all PA enterprises. Surplus revenues from moneymaking projects could underwrite initiatives of uncertain profitability. This step established the financial weaponry to expand PA activities into airports, seaports, rail transit, and ultimately the World Trade Center. Led by a governing board composed of gubernatorial appointees who served without pay, the PA was also unique in the degree of insulation it enjoyed from local elected officials.

In Los Angeles, reformers stuck to single-purpose municipal agencies to avoid empowering a regional entity that could be controlled by state officials in thrall to Southern Pacific kickbacks. This precluded the innovative project financing used by the PA. Nonetheless, harbor officials in Los Angeles and Long Beach achieved financial independence with the creation of proprietary harbor funds. Where these revenue funds proved insufficient, harbor officials resorted to the municipal credit card: general obligation bonds backed by host cities and, later, revenue bonds backed by agency revenues. Such enhanced financial flexibility reduced the ability of local officials to control their agents in the two ports.

A hallmark of transportation governance in Los Angeles was the citizen-commission system. Major departments were governed by five-member citizen boards appointed by the mayor with city-council approval. Commissioners were appointed for staggered five-year terms, giving them some independence. In Los Angeles, under the voter-approved 2000 charter, two members of the airport commission must live near the airports and one member of the harbor commission must live in the harbor district. Thus, affected local communities enjoy some representation.[47] The new charter also strengthened mayoral authority over executive directors.[48] Since 2000 mayors alone may remove commissioners. L.A.'s airport and port executive directors can be fired by the commissions with the mayor's assent, unless two-thirds of the council votes to reinstate. In contrast, POLB commissioners enjoy greater independence. They serve six-year terms, and the executive director serves at the pleasure of the commission.[49]

The defining features of these governance arrangements have proved difficult to modify. No local government, including New York City, possesses the power to seriously threaten the PA. In Los Angeles, efforts to regionalize transportation governance would need to overcome the area's fragmentation. Having witnessed L.A.'s attempt to annex the San Pedro waterfront and use its water monopoly to gobble up nearby cities and the San Fernando Valley, local governments have been very wary of their regional hegemon. We emphasize three consequences of these differences that recurred as these agencies expanded facilities to capture large shares of regional transportation activities. The first difference lies in the extent to which local groups influence these agencies' internal deliberations. In New York, the regional scope of the PA marginalizes local concerns; in Los Angeles, local concerns increasingly predominate. A second difference flows from the PA's financial flexibility. In New York, projects get bundled in ways that are not possible in Los Angeles. A third difference concerns the coalitions needed to approve large projects. More inclusive coalitions are needed to get things done in Los Angeles.

Adding Airports and Containerization to the PA Portfolio

The PA had by 1931 established an impressive reputation that it could use to fend off interference and that would aid its forays into new fields. By the early 1940s, the PA, led by Executive Director Austin Tobin, was ready to expand beyond bridges and tunnels. With the 1921 compact allowing the PA to carry out any "transportation and terminal" project—as long as the two states approved and the agency could pay for it—the PA's senior staff decided to survey regional transportation needs for promising opportunities. They would then obtain approval from commissioners and devise strategies to gain support from relevant interest groups, local officials, and the two states. Transportation bureaucrats, supported by the twelve commissioners, defined the direction the PA took. In time the agency's principals would be enlisted to endorse its plans.

Prime PA targets in the mid-1940s were the airports and seaports of New York City and Newark.[50] New York City had one functioning airfield, LaGuardia, and one under construction (Idlewild, now John F. Kennedy International Airport [JFK]), while Newark had its own airfield. Officials in both cities preferred to control their airports. Indeed, Robert Moses rushed through state approval for a New York City Airport Authority to operate and modernize LaGuardia and Idlewild, protecting them from the PA's wiles. Both cities also had seaports, and neither wished to yield their port facilities to a bistate agency. The PA would need allies to overcome this local opposition. In 1946–47 the PA gathered support from the region's newspapers and the Regional Plan Association, arguing that one agency could run the region's major airports more efficiently. The PA also convinced the major airlines that the agency could allocate substantial sums from bridge and tunnel tolls to modernize airfields, while municipal funds were likely to be limited.

When New York mayor William O'Dwyer and Robert Moses resisted, Tobin persuaded the bond houses to advise the mayor that they would not purchase city bonds for airport modernization because it was unclear that the airports would generate enough revenue to repay them. When Newark's elected officials objected, Tobin enlisted the state's governor to inform city leaders that they had better yield the airport—and the seaport—if they wished to obtain state funds to meet other city needs. City officials in both states reluctantly accepted the PA's offer, and the agency then won the approval of both governors and state legislatures. By the fall of 1947, all three airports and Newark's marine terminal were under PA control.[51] These efforts to secure the airports and seaports were led by PA career officials with elected officials and private-sector allies assisting when needed.

A somewhat different pattern of policy innovation occurred in the development of containerization in the early 1950s. A trucking executive, Malcom McLean, wanted to transport truck containers via ship, which matched up with the PA's willingness to experiment with ways to improve shipping efficiency. Discussions led to an agreement that the PA would begin hoisting truck containers onto ships at Port Newark. The first truck-to-ship containers moved between Newark and Puerto Rico, and soon after through the Panama Canal to the Port of Oakland, whose executives joined the experiment. Initial efforts were so successful that the PA, which had plans to expand its traditional break-bulk terminal at Port Newark southward into the city of Elizabeth, decided instead to develop the extensive new space as container terminals. These opening steps in the "containership revolution" were a collaboration between an external actor and senior PA staff. The two states readily agreed to facilitate matters. A plan to develop the new port at Elizabeth, New Jersey, was announced by Governor Robert Meyner, who thereby received credit for the innovative approach worked out entirely between PA staff and McLean and his aides.[52]

From Mines Field to LAX

Los Angeles International Airport (LAX) followed a familiar trajectory from fledgling department to global gateway. In 1926 the L.A. Chamber of Commerce began lobbying the city council to develop a municipal airport. One favored location was a three-thousand-acre bean field near the coast and sixteen miles from downtown. The city council agreed to lease the site, but with finances plummeting during the Great Depression, local officials had few available resources. As with the ports, early airport development required federal assistance. Urged on by Harry Hopkins, head of the Works Progress Administration (WPA), the city in 1937 purchased the future site of LAX for $2.7 million, thereby qualifying for WPA grants too. During World War II the federal government assumed control of the airport and improved the landing field. After the war, L.A.'s Department of Airports (LADOA) regained control. Its first postwar master plan targeted airlines serving nearby Burbank Airport. A second master plan in the 1950s was more ambitious, featuring a decentralized terminal design to accommodate jet airplanes that would revolutionize air travel. Having lagged behind other cities in airport development, Los Angeles emerged with the most modern facility in the United States. In 1959 LAX inaugurated the jet age with the nation's first transcontinental jet passenger flight.

In the early postwar era, the business, civic, and labor groups advocating LAX expansion also wanted to professionalize its governance. In 1947 Mayor Fletcher Bowron acceded to the wishes of LADOA and recommended that the department be given semiautonomous status similar to the Harbor and Water and Power Departments. The move was supported by the business community as an efficiency measure and by airlines as a way of protecting airport revenues. Voters approved a charter amendment to this effect later that year. By 1952 LAX was earning a profit. The coalition next turned to the challenge of financing the airport's second master plan. In 1956 a well-financed campaign directed by airport commissioner Don Belding and former L.A. Chamber of Commerce president Charles Detoy helped pass a $59.7 million bond for improvements.

Airport operations were overseen by skilled managers during this period. Under Francis Fox (1959–68), LADOA gained financial flexibility in the form of a 1963 charter amendment granting the ability to issue revenue bonds. No longer would large investments in airport infrastructure require voter approval. In 1967 Fox forged an agreement with the airlines to raise landing fees to repay revenue bonds. That same year an ambitious plan to develop new runways, terminals, and a buffer zone was approved by the airport commission. As in New York, LADOA officials cultivated support, among public- and private-sector actors and, ultimately, voters, for airport improvements.

The 1967 master plan was the high point of department autonomy. Starting in the 1960s, multiple stakeholders emerged to oppose and frustrate airport expansion, including the communities near the airport. To expand the airport, LADOA used both purchases and condemnations to acquire 579 acres, displacing thousands of residents. In 1971 the 1967 master plan was overturned after an expensive legal fight. LADOA officials were put on notice that the adverse impacts of airport operations could no longer be ignored. As a result, the new master plan for LAX in 1972 recommended a cap of forty million air passengers by 1990. Periodic disputes with nearby communities did not prevent airport officials from transforming LAX into an international hub. LADOA carried out a $500 million plan to modernize LAX for the 1984 Olympics. In June 1984 airport officials christened what would later be called Tom Bradley International Terminal, named for L.A.'s longest serving mayor. Between 1980 and 1992, air passenger traffic grew 40 percent and air cargo 55 percent. By the 1990s LAX was the world's fourth busiest airport and a regional economic engine. Though a key advocate for the aspirations of the city's transportation agencies, it was Bradley who resurrected the principal–agent relationship between elected officials and the city's commissions—converting term appointments into service at the pleasure of the mayor by having commissioners sign undated letters of resignation.

Containerization, Competition, and Cooperation in Los Angeles and Long Beach

The Great Depression hit the ports in Los Angeles hard. Several harbor bonds were defeated, a reversal of port officials' early success. Federal largesse, especially during World War II, when the U.S. Navy controlled the ports, compensated for voters' stinginess. The POLA positioned itself to take advantage of the postwar uptick in trade. Harbor officials campaigned for additional autonomy and financial resources, winning a charter amendment granting greater leasing and contracting authority and, in 1959, the ability to issue revenue bonds. The POLA used this authority to raise $50 million to build container facilities. In Long Beach, harbor officials fought equally hard to gain control over the oil money generated in the harbor. Voters passed charter amendments giving the Harbor Department control over oil revenues and tideland oil funds, though it did not receive revenue-bond authority until 1968. Moreover, in 1954 the city council was given greater control over the department's budget and salaries. Later, in 1980, voters signed off on a scheme to capture 10 percent of POLB's revenues for the city's tidelands operating fund.[53]

The two ports competed fiercely for container traffic. By the early 1970s, the ports were at rough parity with respect to the tonnage handled annually (26.1 million tons at Long Beach, 27.2 million at Los Angeles). Rivalry continued to undermine efforts to regionalize seaport operations. When L.A. mayor Sam Yorty, supported by his counterpart in Long Beach, revived a 1920s proposal to consolidate the facilities, commissioners overseeing the POLA and the POLB squashed the effort.[54] The regional control over port facilities achieved in New York proved unattainable in Los Angeles. To gain a greater share of Pacific Rim trade, port officials had to do more than deepen the harbor and modernize shore-side facilities. By the early 1980s, both ports were out of land, and freight-rail bottlenecks and truck congestion became intolerable. Solving these problems required the ports to overcome long-standing rivalries. During the 1980s the ports cooperated on several ground-access and freight-rail schemes. In 1987 they opened a $70 million facility to transfer cargo from trucks to trains. On-dock rail facilities were constructed to ease traffic. The capstone was the $2.4 billion Alameda Corridor project, which consolidated over ninety miles of railroad lines into a single grade-separated system connecting the ports and downtown railyards. In 1989 the ports created the Alameda Corridor Transportation Authority (ACTA) to oversee the project. To finance the project, port officials worked with the city and state governments to pressure the railroads with the threat of eminent domain. Ultimately, 80 percent of project costs were met by federal loans and revenue bonds backed by container fees and wharfage charges.

One final challenge lay in resolving conflicts between the ports and the small cities along the twenty-mile corridor. Groups in the corridor cities believed their communities were, through disruption and pollution, bearing the costs of improved freight-rail efficiency and wanted port officials to channel some revenues into a trust fund for economic revitalization projects. When ACTA failed to meet these demands, the cities sued. Though these suits were unsuccessful, ACTA created programs for minority contracting, local job training, and construction mitigation. As at LAX, port officials were put on notice that they could not ignore the voices of surrounding communities.[55]

Contemporary Challenges

By 1990 New York and Los Angeles had lapped the field in their transportation infrastructure investments. In 1990 the POLA was first, New York and New Jersey second, and the POLB third in container traffic. By 2000 the gap between the big three and the rest of the nation's seaports had widened considerably. The PA, ranked third behind the Ports of San Pedro Bay in 2000, was handling more than twice as many containers as fourth-ranked Seattle. In 2001 LAX was the world's third busiest airport for passengers and fourth busiest for cargo. New York was also handling a large share of the nation's air traffic. In both regions, bureaucrats designed solutions to transportation challenges and deployed their skills and resources to build broad political coalitions to implement them. Their successes over several decades enabled the PA and L.A.'s port and airport agencies to develop unique capacities for running large-scale public-works projects. Through careful stewardship of their reputations and active cultivation of supporters, the PA and L.A.'s transportation agencies achieved political legitimacy. Elected officials, private actors, and citizens believe that *these* agencies can solve regional transportation challenges. Those conditions—capacity and legitimacy—are crucial factors supporting the bureaucratic autonomy that can enable sophisticated policy innovation.[56]

Undermining Bureaucratic Independence in Both Regions

Such bureaucratic autonomy can be fleeting. In Los Angeles, charter-amendment campaigns succeeded in making seaport and airport administration largely independent of mayors and city councils. Between 1970 and 1990, however, elected officials pursued greater control. During the 1970s Los Angeles voters passed charter amendments granting the city council greater oversight over salaries at LAWA and the POLA, as well as veto authority over large leases. In 1991 Proposition 5 was passed, enabling the city council to veto decisions made by the city's citizen commissions. The POLB was not subjected to the same scrutiny, although a 1980 proposition that sanctioned revenue diversion from the port imposed term limits on harbor commissioners.

Elected officials were not the only actors interested in the policy deliberations of transportation agencies. Environmental activists and nearby communities raising quality-of-life issues sought greater influence. Their ability to do so was enhanced in 1970 with passage of the National Environmental Protection Act and Clean Air Act, and the California Environmental Quality Act (CEQA). CEQA requires public agencies to assess the environmental impacts of proposed projects and to mitigate negative impacts. Under the California Coastal Act of 1976, the California Coastal Commission has authority to review port master plans, giving it a veto over port expansion.

The 1970s also birthed a new fiscal regime. In 1978 California passed Proposition 13, which immediately cut property tax revenue by $7 billion.[57] Proposition 13 set a high bar for raising taxes: a two-thirds vote of the state legislature was needed to raise taxes and two-thirds voter approval was needed for special levies. State lawmakers were empowered to allocate property taxes among various local governments. In the early 1990s, state lawmakers used this authority to shift $3.6 billion from city and county governments to schools. By the early 1990s, L.A.'s transportation agencies were fending off local attempts to divert portions of their revenues.

The PA must also deal with environmental concerns and remains a target for local officials pushing their own development goals. Local elected officials and citizens, however, lack the tools of direct democracy that make them influential players in Los Angeles. State regulatory regimes in New York and New Jersey provide environmental groups with modest influence over PA projects. Governors are the only actors able to exercise leverage over PA deliberations, and they have not hesitated to use veto authority to force the PA to devote more resources to projects on a favored side of the Hudson. In Los Angeles, state regulatory authorities emerged as powerful new principals. Environmental rules enable environmental groups to challenge POLA's, POLB's, LAWA's, and other agencies' decisions. With city-council oversight and reversal now a real possibility, L.A.'s transportation officials must satisfy restive communities near their facilities. Recent mayoral appointment patterns, rules establishing local preferences in contract bidding, and greater community representation on the airport and harbor commissions have strengthened the forces of localism. In comparison, the PA stands as a recognizable offspring of Progressive Era reforms, a large agency whose projects continue to reflect a businesslike concern for efficiency.

The PA and Gubernatorial Intervention

Governors generally let the PA take the lead in defining issues and pursuing solutions as long as state funds are not implicated. There are exceptions, particularly when criticizing the PA allows governors to score points. One illustration concerned the agency's plan in the 1990s to dredge Newark Bay to permit large ships to dock at the Port Newark-Elizabeth marine terminals. New York governor George Pataki blocked the plan for several years, demanding that the agency first modernize terminals on the New York side of the Harbor. Pataki was joined by Mayor Rudolph Giuliani, who argued that the PA should return JFK and LaGuardia airports to local control. Here the PA's principal held a strong hand; without governor approval, the PA could not proceed with an essential project.[58] Another example is the rebuilding of the World Trade Center (WTC). Governors of New York pressed the PA to allocate money and staff to the project. The PA devoted nearly $2 billion a year to the WTC—a sum dwarfing funds for all other activities—and delayed modernization at the airports, bridges and tunnels. Here, too, the governors hold a strong hand, rearranging the priorities that PA commissioners and staff would otherwise pursue.

The WTC rebuilding illustrates the potential downside of the bundling strategy described earlier—using revenues from "profitable" projects to meet deficits elsewhere. So does the PA's work in rail transit. In the 1960s the PA agreed to take control of the money-losing Port Authority Trans-Hudson Corporation (PATH). In doing so, the PA deviated from its traditional criterion, which required that a project have the potential to break even financially in the long run. In exchange, Tobin secured approval to build the original WTC. PATH has required the PA to allot hundreds of millions annually to meet deficits.[59] The agreement that resulted in PATH and the WTC project established the precedent that "excess" agency revenues can be used for projects likely to generate permanent deficits (PATH) and for purposes outside its traditional focus (WTC). The PA began to support small-scale job-development efforts and agreed to underwrite building the Newark Legal Center. For many years a portion of the PA's funds was diverted to local officials to aid their economic-development plans; only in 2015, as demands for the agency to meet its central transportation goals increased, were these diversions ended.

Moreover, the flow of patronage positions at the PA greatly increased after Chris Christie became New Jersey governor in 2010, generating morale problems and diminishing the agency's effectiveness.[60] Christie's interventions forced the PA to hire more than sixty of his associates and divert funds to New Jersey's transportation needs, as well as finance parks and other amenities to reward supportive officials. The agency's leadership descended into chaos in 2013 when Christie's aides blocked traffic at the George Washington Bridge, in retaliation against a local Democratic mayor who declined to endorse his reelection. Soon after, two Christie appointees were forced to leave the agency. An investigation followed, and in April 2015 a Christie PA appointee pled guilty to conspiracy to commit fraud, while another was indicted, along with one of Christie's top aides. Meanwhile, Christie's mentor and appointee as PA chair pled guilty to using his position to coerce United Airlines to provide him special benefits.[61]

In 2014 Christie appointed a new chair who led the agency in a more professional direction. The PA Board of Commissioners and the two governors created a Special Panel on the Future of the Port Authority, which issued recommendations. A chief executive officer would be chosen by the board after a nationwide search; the diversion of PA funds to outside projects would end and patronage would be sharply curtailed.[62] In 2015–16 the board and senior staff implemented the reforms, restoring a sense of professional competence and independence.[63] However, with Christie chastened, New York's governor, Andrew Cuomo, pressed the PA to divert funds from a rebuild of the Port Authority Bus Terminal to upgrade LaGuardia and JFK airports. Most of the PA's board resisted, arguing that the bistate agency must make decisions based on professional judgments. In their view the Bus Terminal was a higher priority project, and funds must be safeguarded to construct a new rail tunnel under the Hudson.[64]

Port Environmentalism and Airport Regionalism at the PA

Environmental challenges are part of the PA's world as well. Responding to pressure from federal regulators and local communities, the PA sought to reduce air pollution from marine terminals. One notable effort is the creation of ExpressRail. Typically, containers arriving in Newark via rail off-load to trucks that navigate congested roads to reach the piers. To speed transfer, the PA constructed on-dock "double stack" rail facilities at Newark and Elizabeth. The ExpressRail project lays tracks from piers to the Eastern-seaboard rail lines and schedules the movement of large groups of loaded rail cars to blend with mainline operations. This $600 million project eliminates five hundred thousand truck trips each year.

The PA undertook other initiatives to reduce environmental damage. In 2008 the agency began giving toll reductions to low-emission vehicles. At seaport facilities the PA runs cooperative programs with environmental agencies. The agency report "Clean Air Strategy for the Port of New York and New Jersey" set out steps to reduce diesel and greenhouse-gas emissions, including replacing the oldest trucks, retrofitting switcher locomotives, and modernizing cargo handling. The PA set an ambitious agenda to become "carbon neutral" within a few years and reduce greenhouse-gas emissions by 80 percent by 2050 (from 2006 levels). These efforts yield reputational benefits. The PA also has pressed forward with regional solutions to growing air-traffic demands. In 2007 the Port Authority added Stewart Airport, sixty miles north of New York City, to its air-transport complex. The agency expects to expand the airport slowly, to take pressure off Newark and LaGuardia. The agency is investing heavily in Stewart and expects it will be a carbon-neutral airfield.

Regionalism's Reversal of Fortune

The LADOA, as a semiautonomous proprietary department, was ill suited to the role of regional steward. Through LAX, the agency handled the lion's share of air-passenger and cargo traffic. But with just 3,000 acres, LAX's ability to meet increasing demand was limited. LADOA took steps toward greater regionalism by acquiring Van Nuys Airport (1949) and signing a joint-powers agreement with the City of Ontario to take over their airport (1967), acquiring ownership in 1985. Anticipating that regional growth would require a larger facility to relieve LAX, the airport commission also agreed to issue airport revenue bonds to purchase 17,500 acres near Palmdale, north of Los Angeles.

Clifton Moore, LADOA's general manager, was a proponent of regionalization. In 1976 he proposed a regional airport forum through which airport operators could coordinate activities; and in 1983 the Southern California Regional Airport Authority (SCRAA) was formed with representation from Los Angeles, Orange, Riverside, and San Bernardino counties and the City of Los Angeles. Though granted expansive powers to own and operate any airport-related facility, and eminent domain, SCRAA floundered when the smaller counties refused to participate. Revived in 1999 by county supervisors interested in stopping LAX expansion, SCRAA disbanded in

2008.[65] Though addressing air-travel demand was urgent, the agencies operating Long Beach Airport, Bob Hope Airport in Burbank, and John Wayne Airport in Orange County were uninterested in seeing passengers diverted to their airports. Few actors were interested in participating in any initiative organized by their gigantic neighbor, Los Angeles.

The growing influence of community and environmental groups became evident when LADOA drafted a new master plan for LAX in 1989. The previous master plan was based on an annual target of forty million passengers. By 1989 traffic levels had exceeded this figure and were expected to grow. In 1996 LADOA initiated a public-review process to consider proposals for accommodating the projected increases in demand. In 1998 the agency, renamed Los Angeles World Airports, initiated the third phase, intended to choose an alternative, complete an environmental-impact report, and win approval from state and federal regulators. This third phase would be a wrenching affair, taking sixteen years and consuming two mayoral administrations with legal battles. Mayor Richard Riordan advocated privatizing LAX and was thwarted in diverting airport revenues to L.A.'s general fund. As opposition to LAX expansion mounted, Riordan fired the president of the airport commission—an unprecedented attack on its autonomy. The next mayor, James Hahn, opposed LAX expansion. Even Hahn's scaled-back plans failed to appease nearby communities. Hahn did win over some opponents with a community-benefits agreement for local groups, environmentalists, labor unions, and school districts. Under a third mayor, Antonio Villaraigosa, LAX undertook initiatives to reduce environmental pollution. In February 2006 the City of Los Angeles entered into a historic settlement agreement with the communities surrounding LAX to resolve the lawsuits surrounding the master plan. The agreement limited the number of gates at LAX and provided funding to impacted communities for noise mitigation, job training, and traffic improvements.

Meanwhile, airport regionalization receded into the background as local officials confronted the 2008 global recession. During the recession's first six months, air passengers at LAX declined by 20 percent; airfreight, by 25 percent. Ontario Airport, where LAWA spent more than $250 million to upgrade facilities, fared even worse.

Passenger traffic dropped from 7.2 million passengers in 2007 to less than 4 million by 2013. Focusing on improving LAX, LAWA did little to reverse the decline. In 2010 Ontario officials moved to sever the city's relationship with LAWA.[66] The first step was to create a locally controlled Ontario International Airport Authority (OIAA) to own and operate the airport. The second step was a lawsuit against Los Angeles, claiming that L.A. airport officials failed to abide by a 2006 agreement to develop a strategic plan to encourage passenger and cargo service at regional airports.[67] In January 2015 Los Angeles scored a temporary legal victory. However, after years of litigation, LAWA in October 2016 transferred ownership of Ontario Airport to the OIAA.[68] The OIAA has focused its initial efforts on streamlining operations, cutting administrative overhead, and contracting out services. Similarly, in July 2013 LAWA transferred operations at dormant Palmdale Airport to the City of Palmdale, which hoped to revive commercial service there.

In the postrecession era with LAX traffic rebounding, LAWA's efforts to appease community opposition to LAX modernization bore fruit. LAWA launched an access program that included new intermodal facilities with a planned light-rail extension to downtown and an automated people mover to carry passengers to the central terminal area. LAWA is also renovating existing passenger terminals and constructing a new Satellite Concourse with twelve new airport gates. Notwithstanding such improvements, LAX remains the only major international airport in the region, is highly constrained, and will eventually run out of capacity.

Greening L.A.'s Seaport Operations

By the early 2000s, the POLA and the POLB were playing defense against environmental groups and elected officials from nearby communities. In 2001 a challenge by the National Resources Defense Council delayed the opening of the China Shipping Container Line terminal at the POLA by a year and a half. In 2004 the city council of Long Beach refused to sign off on an environmental-impact statement for a project at Pier J, which would have added 115 acres to a 270-acre terminal, improving efficiency and reducing the number of idling trucks. The benefits notwithstanding, environmental groups were uninterested in projects that failed to address increasing emissions from the ports.

In October 2001 the L.A. Board of Harbor Commissioners directed port officials to hold emissions at or below their current levels and directed the POLA to address the concerns of surrounding communities. An advisory committee assessed the impacts of port development and in 2003 the POLA initiated a costly mitigation program. $23.5 million was earmarked for "community aesthetic" projects; $20 million, for air quality; and $10 million, for the Gateway Cities Council of Governments—an association representing cities in southeast L.A. County—to replace or retrofit diesel trucks. Similar developments occurred in Long Beach, where the POLB submitted a draft Green Port Policy, adopted in January 2005. The document establishes environmental stewardship, sustainability, community engagement, and education as guiding principles. In 2005 the POLB formed a Sustainability Task Force to integrate Green Port Policy into all aspects of operations.

Mayor Antonio Villaraigosa was elected in 2005 with a pledge to make Los Angeles "the cleanest, greenest big city in America." He selected an environmental lawyer and a labor official to serve on the harbor commission and appointed Geraldine Knatz as executive director at the POLA. Knatz had created Long Beach's Green Port Policy. In November 2006 the POLA and the POLB jointly approved the San Pedro Bay Ports Clean Air Action Plan (CAAP), the most far-reaching seaport environmental program ever undertaken. The CAAP directed the ports, in collaboration with public agencies and private industry, to adopt programs and technologies to reduce pollution by 45 percent over five years. The ports implemented a package of tariffs, lease requirements, grants, and incentive programs to curb emissions. Shippers were offered incentives to reduce the speed of vessels in San Pedro Bay. Truck drivers were required to retrofit vehicles to meet federal emissions standards. By 2012 the program had reduced port emissions from trucks by 80 percent. Under the CAAP all major terminals were equipped with shore-side electricity, so that vessels can shut down diesel-powered auxiliary engines and plug into electricity while docked.[69]

In 2010 the ports updated the 2006 plan, pledging further reductions in emissions. Between 2005 and 2015, port emissions of diesel particulate matter dropped 85 percent; nitrogen oxides, 51 percent; sulfur oxides, 97 percent; and greenhouse gases, 12 percent. The update also commits the ports to align with the California's Air Resource Board's Goods Movement Emissions Reduction Plan and federal standards.[70] In November 2016 the two ports released a draft 2017 CAAP with strategies to exceed local and state environmental goals. The latest CAAP pursues these goals through improvements in freight-system efficiency and deployment of zero-emission freight vehicles.

These initiatives illustrate the changing culture within L.A.'s transportation agencies. The programs are formally "voluntary" but necessary to forestall stricter oversight by state and federal regulators. They are also expensive. Indeed, L.A.'s transportation officials frequently negotiate side agreements to prevent lawsuits. In 2008 the POLA obtained approval to expand the China Shipping Container Line terminal. The project's benefits included doubling the size of the terminal and generating over 8,400 jobs. Attached were a host of environmental and "community beautification" initiatives.[71] Port officials are also involved in Los Angeles' ambitious L.A. Waterfront Investment Plan to provide new waterfront amenities, open space, and better infrastructure to the San Pedro and Wilmington communities.

Labor Disputes and Competitive Pressures at the L.A. and Long Beach Seaports

The governance challenges were on display in 2015 when a labor dispute between shippers and dockworkers slowed port traffic to a crawl. While local officials oversee daily operations, the performance of the San Pedro Bay ports depends on cooperative relationships with both the shipping companies and union members unloading cargo. Tense labor negotiations at the ports are nothing new. In the past, dockworkers represented by the International Longshore and Warehouse Union (ILWU) engaged in slowdowns to pressure shippers. The Pacific Maritime Association (PMA), which represents the shippers, responded by locking out union members. In 2002 President George W. Bush intervened with an injunction after a shutdown lasting ten days. Mindful of the impact that a pitched

battle might have on the competitive position of West Coast seaports, both sides pledged to avoid such tactics. The two sides worked
out agreements on health benefits and other issues. However, talks
broke down in the fall of 2014. The ILWU accused the PMA of decep-
tion, attributing congestion to chassis shortages and a preholiday
traffic surge. In December, after seven months of negotiations, the
PMA asked for federal mediation.

Fallout from the strike hit customers hard during the holiday
season as retailers scrambled to reroute shipments through East
Coast ports or transport goods by air at higher costs. Agriculture
producers asked President Barack Obama to intervene.[72] Officials
called on both sides to settle, to no avail. In February the PMA responded to union slowdowns by suspending weekend and holiday
operations. With container ships idling outside West Coast ports,
President Obama sent his labor secretary to meet with the two
sides. An agreement was reached on February 20, 2015. With a labor
agreement in hand, port officials worked with the union to clear the
backlog of cargo, though some industry officials believed that permanent damage had been done.[73] Hoping to forestall another costly
dispute, the PMA reached out to the ILWU with the goal of an early
agreement to extend the contract that was to expire in 2019.

The protracted dispute exacerbated other pressures, years in the
making. These include the need to upgrade and automate port facilities and to compete with East Coast ports and fast-growing ports
in Canada and Mexico. Years of financial struggles sparked efforts
among shippers to reduce costs. One response has been the construction of ever larger container ships, carrying more cargo on less
fuel. The container ships built today are three times larger than they
were a decade ago. When they arrive in port, they dump massive
container loads that clog the docks. This causes longer wait times for
other ships and truckers. Another response has been consolidation,
with shippers combining and using the same vessels and terminals.
Dockworkers must separate and sort these various shipments before
summoning truckers to pick them up.[74]

Fortunately, L.A.'s harbors are deep enough to accommodate today's container ships. A $1.3 billion project to upgrade the Gerald
Desmond Bridge is ongoing, and both ports are attempting to automate. The POLA opened its TraPac terminal, staffed almost entirely

by robots, including twenty-eight cargo-carrying machines and a fleet of self-driving vehicles. In 2016 the POLB opened its own automated terminal. When completed, port officials expect it to handle half the entire flow of traffic that moved through the port in 2015.[75] Meanwhile, ports on the East Coast and in Canada and Mexico are improving facilities to siphon off traffic from Los Angeles. Ports along the East Coast are investing in harbor dredging, bridge raising, and other projects to accommodate container ships. The widening of the Panama Canal facilitates these efforts, though the largest ships will still not fit the canal. Vancouver's Port Prince Rupert, closer to Asia and the deepest West Coast harbor, markets itself as a "congestion-free" alternative to L.A.'s ports. During the labor slowdown in 2015, some firms sent container ships to Vancouver only to find that its facility was overwhelmed. After the slowdown, container traffic surged at L.A.'s ports, an indication that confidence in their management was restored. Overall, these events suggest that L.A.'s port complex is unlikely to lose its status as a premier gateway for vessel cargo, but they underscore the pressures facing officials to modernize facilities and increase the relative efficiency of shoreside operations.

Our analysis of transportation agencies in the New York and L.A. regions highlights many unintended consequences that governance choices have for issues of interest to urban scholars and practitioners. Foremost is how the interests of local residents, elected officials, businesses, carriers, and others get represented in transportation policy-making. Local communities and mayors and other elected officials have much less influence in New York than in Los Angeles. The greater responsiveness of L.A.'s transportation agencies to local concerns is due, in part, to their local origin and single-purpose design. Equally important are other institutional features, such as the composition of the commissions that empower mayors, a tradition of "direct democracy" that makes voters influential, and administrative procedures that local communities can use to break open the process. In contrast, the PA is responsive mainly to the two state governors, although city and federal officials are influential when environmental issues and connection to local streets are involved.

To understand these regions' different approaches to the governance of transportation infrastructure, one must look beyond pluralist, elite-driven, and public-choice theories.[76] Though successes produced by executives and career staff in both regions generated positive policy feedback, their failings have also attracted public scrutiny. Both systems were set up to achieve efficient solutions to transportation deficiencies, unconstrained by short-term political pressures. Political configurations, however, dictated a regional approach in New York and a local one in Los Angeles. The conditions that shaped agency creation faded after the 1920s. Since then, other forces have enhanced the stability of existing arrangements, including interjurisdictional rivalries in Los Angeles, gubernatorial ambitions in New York, and the institutional interests and entrepreneurial strategies of transportation officials in both regions.

Our survey demonstrates that differences in governance influenced the performance and policy-making capacity of the transportation agencies. The PA had the more innovative design, and its leaders used its legal and financial flexibility to promote diverse projects. Its leaders adopted a risk-taking approach that resulted in a redesign of seaport facilities, leading to the containerization revolution.[77] L.A.'s transportation bureaucrats used direct democracy to enhance their authority and secure funds for port and airport upgrades. Its transportation agencies led the way into the jet age and were the first to recognize the opportunities of Pacific Rim trade. They since have been on the cutting edge of environmental-protection efforts.[78]

Our account illustrates the benefits of agency theory for understanding the complex governance arrangements that structure transportation at the subnational level. Delegation, whether to municipal departments, public authorities, or private-sector actors, is a fact of life for state and local governments. How elected officials (and, in California, voters) choose to arrange and manage these relationships determines what rights and influence they and other actors will have in future policy deliberations. In our two cases, elected officials initially delegated limited authority and resources to local transportation agencies. In time, these agencies acquired more of both. Indeed, their activities reflect a policy-making independence that confounds theories of strict legislative and executive control.

What explains the differences between our findings and studies of legislators and bureaucrats at the national level? One factor is the more sustained attention we give to appointed transportation officials. Our view is that these officials neither blindly follow orders from above nor scheme to undermine majority sentiment. Most appear to be public-spirited, though their actions do aim to influence both elite and public opinion. Differences between national and subnational settings that give rise to delegation are a second factor helping to explain our findings. At the federal level, relationships between elected and appointed officials are typically short term. In state and local settings, appointed officials have lengthy career horizons, and private-sector actors and even local public officials stay around a long time. In long-term relationships, the reputations of actors can be as important as their institutional constraints. In such settings, we believe that a historical-institutionalist approach, which emphasizes the effects of institutional choices realized over extended periods of time, can be especially useful.

Bureaucratic autonomy can indeed be inconsistent with democratic norms of representation and accountability.[79] As Gail Radford argues, by creating public authorities that rely on the income generated by their activities, state and local governments impel agencies to behave like private corporations.[80] They also limit public participation. We do not agree, however, that public authorities necessarily are disinclined to cultivate civic groups or build public support. We emphasize the incentives of bureaucrats, albeit selectively, to build political coalitions to support policy-making activities (and enhance their autonomy). Nor do we find that public authorities are unresponsive to noneconomic objectives, such as environmental protection and community stability. Agencies in both regions have elevated environmental objectives, often over the objections of private-sector customers. Transportation agencies will not always act as faithful stewards of the public good. Nonetheless, like Carpenter, we argue that the career and policy interests of bureaucrats can best be served by developing reputations for honesty and competence, which is a precondition for achieving and maintaining independent policy-making authority.[81]

Whether local and state governments should design agencies in order to achieve greater responsiveness to environmental groups, commercial interests, or local communities is a question that scholars will continue to ponder. The U.S. federal system gives states and local governments wide latitude in structuring the governance of transportation systems and thereby enables citizens to determine where to place their trust. As Justice Louis Brandeis argued, "A state may, if its citizens choose, serve as a laboratory, and try novel social and economic experiments without risk to the rest of the country."[82] As we have seen, the New York and L.A. regions have embraced innovative approaches to building and governing major transportation facilities. We have explained why particular governance choices were made, and how those early choices have shaped the policy-making capacity of local transportation agencies, while encouraging entrepreneurial behavior. However, our two cases cover just a small range of the diversity of approaches available to local governments. Future work in other settings and on other governance arrangements can inform both scholars' and practitioners' understanding of the forces that shape urban development.

Notes

The authors have drawn upon previous work, including portions of our essay appearing in David Halle and Andrew A. Beveridge, eds., *New York and Los Angeles: The Uncertain Future* (New York: Oxford University Press, 2013), 103–33.

1. See David C. Perry, Introduction to *Building the Public City*, ed. David C. Perry (Thousand Oaks, Calif.: Sage, 1995).

2. Joel A. Tarr, "The Evolution of the Urban Infrastructure in the Nineteenth and Twentieth Centuries," in National Research Council, *Perspectives on Urban Infrastructure* (Washington, D.C.: National Academies Press, 1984), 4–66.

3. On state entrepreneurship, see Mariana Mazzucato, *The Entrepreneurial State* (New York: Anthem, 2013); and Raymond Duvall and John H. Freeman, "The Techno-Bureaucratic Elite and the Entrepreneurial State in Dependent Industrialization," *American Political Science Review* 77, no. 3 (1983): 569–87.

4. Robert M. Fogelson, *Downtown: Its Rise and Fall, 1880–1950* (New Haven, Conn.: Yale University Press, 2003).

5. The Census Bureau defines special-district governments as "independent, special-purpose governmental units . . . that exist as separate entities with substantial administrative and fiscal independence from general-purpose local governments." U.S. Census Bureau, *2007 Census of*

Governments, Individual State Descriptions: 2007 (Washington, D.C.: U.S. Government Printing Office, 2012), vi. We use the terms "special district" and "public authority" interchangeably to refer to entities created by state and local governments with substantial administrative and fiscal independence.

6. Paul E. Peterson, *City Limits* (Chicago: University of Chicago Press, 1981).

7. Our analysis excludes agencies that focus exclusively on mass transit.

8. U.S. Department of Commerce, Bureau of the Census, *FT 920 U.S. Merchandise Trade: Selected Highlights* (Washington, D.C., December 2016).

9. Paul Pierson, *Politics in Time* (Princeton, N.J.: Princeton University Press, 2004); Joel Rast, "Why History (Still) Matters," *Urban Affairs Review* 48, no. 1 (2012): 3–36.

10. Peterson, *City Limits*.

11. John Hull Mollenkopf, *The Contested City* (Princeton, N.J.: Princeton University Press, 1983). See also *The Politics of Urban Development*, ed. Heywood T. Sanders and Clarence N. Stone (Lawrence: University Press of Kansas, 1987).

12. Susan E. Clarke and Gary L. Gaile, *The Work of Cities*, vol. 1 (Minneapolis: University of Minnesota Press, 1998); Ann O'M. Bowman and Michael A. Pagano, *Cityscapes and Capital* (Baltimore, Md.: John Hopkins University Press, 1997); and Bernard J. Frieden and Lynne B. Sagalyn, *Downtown, Inc.: How America Rebuilds Cities* (Cambridge, Mass.: Massachusetts Institute of Technology Press, 1989).

13. Mark Schneider, *The Competitive City* (Pittsburgh, Pa.: University of Pittsburgh Press, 1989); Robert L. Bish and Vincent Ostrom, *Understanding Urban Government* 20 (Washington, D.C.: American Enterprise Institute Press, 1973); Anthony Downs, *New Visions for Metropolitan America* (Washington, D.C., and Cambridge, Mass.: Brookings Institution and Lincoln Institute of Land Policy, 1994); John C. Bollens, *Special District Governments in the United States* (Oakland: University of California Press, 1957); and Christopher Berry, *Imperfect Union* (Cambridge, Mass.: Cambridge University Press, 2009).

14. Albert M. Sbragia, *Debt Wish* (Pittsburgh, Pa.: University of Pittsburgh Press, 1996).

15. David C. Perry, "Infrastructure Investment," in *The International Encyclopedia of Social and Behavioral Sciences*, ed. Neil J. Smelser and Paul B. Bates (Amsterdam: Elsevier, 2004).

16. Steven P. Erie and Scott A. MacKenzie, "Southern California's Crown Jewels," *Public Works Management & Policy* 14, no. 3 (2010): 205–45.

17. Michael N. Danielson and Jameson W. Doig, *New York: The Politics of Urban Regional Development* (Oakland: University of California Press,

1982); Alan Altshuler and David Luberoff, *Mega-Projects* (Washington, D.C.: Brookings Institution, 2003).

18. James N. Rosenau, "Governance, Order, and Change in World Politics," in *Governance without Government*, ed. James N. Rosenau (Cambridge, Mass.: Cambridge University Press, 1992); Jon Pierre, "Models of Urban Governance," *Urban Affairs Review* 34 (1999): 372–96; Jon Pierre and B. Guy Peters, *Debating Governance* (New York: Oxford University Press, 2000); Gerry Stoker, "Governance as Theory," *International Social Science Journal* 155 (1998): 17–27.

19. Gary J. Miller, "The Political Evolution of Principal-Agent Models," *Annual Review of Political Science* 8 (2005): 203–25.

20. William A. Niskanen, *Bureaucracy and Representative Government* (Chicago: Aldine-Atherton, 1971); Theodore J. Lowi, *The End of Liberalism* (New York: W. W. Norton, 1979).

21. Mathew D. McCubbins and Thomas Schwartz, "Congressional Oversight Overlooked: Police Patrols versus Fire Alarms," *American Journal of Political Science* 28 (1984): 165–79; and Mathew D. McCubbins, Roger G. Noll, and Barry R. Weingast, "Administrative Procedures as Instruments of Political Control," *Journal of Law, Economics and Organization* 3 (1987): 243–77.

22. William G. Howell and David E. Lewis, "Agencies by Presidential Design," *Journal of Politics* 64, no. 4 (2002): 1095–114; Terry M. Moe and Scott A. Wilson, "Presidents and Political Structure," *Law and Contemporary Problems* 57, no. 1 (1994): 1–44.

23. Daniel Carpenter, *Reputation and Power* (Princeton, N.J.: Princeton University Press, 2010); Daniel Carpenter, *The Forging of Bureaucratic Autonomy* (Princeton, N.J.: Princeton University Press, 2001).

24. Robert A. Caro, *The Power Broker* (New York: Vintage, 1974).

25. David C. Perry, "Urban Tourism and the Privatizing Discourses of Public Infrastructure," in *The Infrastructure of Play: Building the Tourist City*, ed. Dennis R. Judd (Armonk, N.Y.: M. E. Sharpe, 2003); Altshuler and Luberoff, *Mega-Projects*.

26. Bent Flyvbjerg, Nils Bruzelius, and Werner Rothengatter, *Megaprojects and Risk: An Anatomy of Ambition* (Cambridge, U.K.: Cambridge University Press, 2003).

27. Bent Flyvbjerg, Mette K. Skamris Holm, and Soren L. Buhl, "How (In)Accurate Are Demand Forecasts in Public Works Projects? The Case of Transportation," *Journal of the American Planning Association* 71, no. 2 (2005): 131–46.

28. Todd Swanstrom, *The Crisis of Growth Politics* (Philadelphia, Pa.: Temple University Press, 1988); Clarence N. Stone, *Regime Politics* (Lawrence: University Press of Kansas, 1989); and John R. Logan and Harvey

Luskin Molotch, *Urban Fortunes: The Political Economy of Place* (Oakland: University of California Press, 1987).

29. D. Roderick Kiewiet and Mathew D. McCubbins, *The Logic of Delegation* (Chicago: University of Chicago Press, 1992).

30. Carpenter, *Forging of Bureaucratic Autonomy*; Jameson W. Doig, *Empire on the Hudson* (New York: Columbia University Press, 2001).

31. Peter A. Hall and Rosemary C. R. Taylor, "Political Science and the Three Institutionalisms," *Political Studies* 44 (1996): 936–57; Robert H. Bates, Avner Greif, Margaret Levi, Jean-Laurent Rosenthal, and Barry R. Weingast, *Analytical Narratives* (Princeton, N.J.: Princeton University Press, 1998).

32. Grain, manufactured goods, and other products bound for European markets traveled by railroads to New Jersey–shore terminals, where they were loaded onto barges that shipped them to New York piers to be loaded onto ships. This process generated extensive delays and other costs.

33. This discussion draws upon Erwin W. Bard, *The Port of New York Authority* (New York: Columbia University Press, 1942); and Doig, *Empire on the Hudson*.

34. In the 1970s the agency's name was changed to the Port Authority of New York and New Jersey, reflecting its status as the creature of two states with equal voting power.

35. The state legislatures, controlled by Republicans, were wary of putting an important regional agency under local (Democratic) control.

36. See Doig, *Empire on the Hudson*, chapters 3–4; and Carpenter, *Forging of Bureaucratic Autonomy*.

37. See William Deverell, *Railroad Crossing* (Oakland: University of California Press, 1994).

38. Local control was cinched when the U.S. Army Corps of Engineers picked San Pedro as the preferred harbor site for a federally funded breakwater and dredging. Congress was also involved in the decisions.

39. Charles Queenan, *The Port of Los Angeles: From Wilderness to World Port* (Los Angeles: Los Angeles Harbor Department, 1983).

40. With this grant of franchise authority, the Harbor Department achieved proprietary status. Los Angeles had gained proprietary status in 1913. In 1925 Long Beach officials defeated an attempt to consolidate the neighboring ports.

41. Doig, *Empire on the Hudson*, chapters 5ff.

42. Steven P. Erie, *Globalizing L.A.* (Redwood City, Calif.: Stanford University Press, 2004): 53–63.

43. Erie, 67–72.

44. Erie, 67–72.

45. Thomas Romer and Howard Rosenthal, "Political Resource Allocation, Controlled Agendas and the Status Quo," *Public Choice* 33 (1978): 27–44.

46. The discussion below draws upon Doig, *Empire on the Hudson*, chapters 7–13.

47. Steven P. Erie and Scott A. MacKenzie, "Southern California's Crown Jewels," *Public Works Management & Policy* 14, no. 3 (January 2010): 205–45.

48. Raphael Sonenshein, *Los Angeles: Structure of a City Government* (Los Angeles: League of Women Voters of Los Angeles, 2006).

49. Erie, *Globalizing L.A.*, 34–39.

50. See Doig, *Empire on the Hudson*, 2001, chapters 11–12.

51. Doig, 259–81.

52. Doig, 374–76.

53. Erie, *Globalizing L.A.*, 90–92.

54. Erie, 89–90.

55. Erie, 157–62.

56. Carpenter, *Forging of Bureaucratic Autonomy*, 14–36.

57. Carpenter, 78, 109–10.

58. Doig, *Empire on the Hudson*, 399–401.

59. Doig, 382–85; Port Authority, *Annual Reports*, 2014–16.

60. Shawn Boburg and John Reitmeyer, "Dozens of Port Authority Jobs Go to Christie Loyalists," *The Record* (New Jersey), January 28, 2012; Jameson W. Doig, "Restore Integrity at the Port Authority," *New York Times*, February 28, 2012.

61. Mark J. Magyar, "Port Authority Scandal Is Result of Leadership, Patronage Mess, Analysts Say," *NJ Spotlight*, December 16, 2013; Amanda Terkel, "Top Christie Aides Found Guilty of All Charges in Bridgegate Scandal," *Huffington Post*, November 4, 2016.

62. From the 1990s until 2015, the governor of New York selected the executive director, and the governor of New Jersey chose the deputy executive director; although the primary loyalty of both officials was in theory to the Port Authority, each had a role in ensuring that the agency's work helped to achieve transportation improvements in his or her own state.

63. Port Authority of New York and New Jersey, Special Panel on the Future of the Port Authority, "Keep the Region Moving" (December 26, 2014); Jameson W. Doig, "Bridgegate, and the Lessons Learned," *Star-Ledger* (New Jersey), September 10, 2014; Martin Robins, "Port Authority Is Getting Back on Track," *The Record* (New Jersey), July 24, 2016.

64. Dana Rubenstein, "With Christie MIA, Cuomo Goes into Attack Mode at the Port Authority," *Politico*, November 29, 2016; Patrick McGeehan, "Governors Compromise on Port Authority Plan. Commissioners Don't Go Along," *New York Times*, December 8, 2016; Jameson W. Doig, "Cuomo's Crass Port Authority Play," *New York Daily News*, January 2, 2017.

65. Erie and MacKenzie, "Southern California's Crown Jewels," 231–32.

66. Dan Weikel, "Ontario Seeks to Take Control of Airport," *Los Angeles Times*, September 15, 2010.

67. Dan Weikel, "Ontario Seeks to Regain Control of Struggling Airport," *Los Angeles Times*, September 28, 2014.

68. Dan Weikel, "Ontario Officials Get Ownership of International Airport but Pledge More Flights and Services," *Los Angeles Times*, November 1, 2016.

69. Ports of San Pedro Bay, *Clean Air Action Plan* (Port of Los Angeles and Port of Long Beach, 2006).

70. Port of Los Angeles, "2005–2015 Air Quality Report Card," Port of Los Angeles, www.portoflosangeles.org/pdf/2015_Air_Quality_Report_Card.pdf.

71. Geraldine Knatz, "Looking Beyond Cargo and Cruise Ship," *Coastal Management* 41, no. 4 (2013): 314–26.

72. Suzanne Kapner and Laura Stevens, "Port Delays Leave Retail Goods Stuck in Transit," *Wall Street Journal*, December 18, 2014.

73. Joseph Bonney, "US Container Imports Surge as West Coast Backlog Cleared," *Journal of Commerce*, May 8, 2015, www.joc.com/port-news/us-ports/us-container-imports-surge-west-coast-backlog-clears_20150508.html.

74. Chris Kirkham and Andrew Khouri, "L.A., Long Beach Ports Losing to Rivals amid Struggle with Giant Ships," *Los Angeles Times*, June 2, 2015.

75. Natalie Kitroeff, "Competitors Are Eating into L.A. Ports' Dominance," *Los Angeles Times*, April 27, 2016.

76. Altshuler and Luberoff, *Mega-Projects*.

77. See Doig, *Empire on the Hudson*, 300–314, 374–76.

78. See Erie, *Globalizing L.A*, 172–232.

79. See Perry, "Urban Tourism," 28–30.

80. Gail Radford, *The Rise of the Public Authority* (Chicago: University of Chicago Press, 2013).

81. See Carpenter, *Forging of Bureaucratic Autonomy*; and Carpenter, *Reputation and Power*.

82. *New State Ice Co. v. Liebmann*, 285 U.S. 262 (1932).

5

Whetting Their Appetites

Privatization Schemes and the Case of Water

Ellen Dannin and Douglas Cantor

Why privatization? In 1981 Paul Peterson asserted that the primary concern of cities is "the maintenance and enhancement of their economic productivity."[1] American cities, in his view, were forced to struggle to achieve a delicate balance between, on the one hand, pursuing the ideal of pro-growth private enterprise policies and, on the other, providing for the needs of all citizens, regardless of their socioeconomic status. Peterson took the quest to establish this balance to mean that cities must focus solely on economic well-being, presupposing they not spend much on redistributive public services lest they alienate economic elites. The supreme imperative was to attract capital and wealth, not to improve social welfare. Peterson observed that while national government possesses the powers and the fiscal capacity to make improvements in welfare and housing programs, cities do not wield adequate resources for doing so.

Peterson argued that the multitude of competing demands for scarce resources within any city limit budgetary ambitions. While demands for redistributive policies and satisfactory basic services will be voiced by the wider electorate, and sometimes heeded, private economic elites must be served foremost. Cities get themselves into deep trouble if they attempt to mollify the former without also satisfying the latter. The best way for a city to solve this conflict is to promote robust pro-business policies and hope that the state and federal governments will address accompanying social welfare needs. Peterson readily allows that the maintenance of urban infrastructure is critical to the well-being of citizens because good infrastructure is central to growth and economic development.

This chapter deals with how local governments resolve or exacerbate problems that accompany infrastructure-privatization strategies. From transportation projects to urban infrastructure financing, this process in all its manifestations raises troubling questions for democratic governance with respect to public accountability. Our chapter, after a review of patterns of privatization, addresses perhaps the trickiest infrastructural subject: water. Water politics exemplifies the cumulative and characteristic drawbacks of privatization and illustrates the widespread worrying trend of divestment of municipal powers. While we contend that water is an exceptional policy area due to its being an indispensable daily human need, it is no exception to the need of researchers to understand who gets what, why, and when in urban politics.

Municipalities are increasingly constrained in ways to raise capital, provide infrastructure, and encourage economic development. When hard pressed, they will resort to expeditious ways to provide services, sometimes doing so in inept, overoptimistic, or incompetent fashion. The vast majority of Americans, roughly 87 percent, receive water through public utilities, with roughly 10 percent using piped services through for-profit companies, most of which serve small communities, concentrated in Idaho, New Jersey, and Massachusetts and throughout the Midwest.[2] Evaluations of water privatization by organizations such as Food & Water Watch and the American Water Works Association focused on cost, efficiency, and the growth of water privatization overall. Scholars are interested as well in the role local political entities play in striking balances between availing themselves of private sector expertise and, at the same time, maintaining a public-spirited concern for water as a public resource.

We take a different approach and instead discuss the questionable pragmatism of these public–private partnerships (P3s) and contracts. This chapter shows how and why water privatization has been framed inappropriately under the inflexible and injurious guidelines of other infrastructure privatizations, such as the privatization of bridges and tollways. Standard privatization frameworks generate not only gross inequalities in the distribution of financial risk between the public and private sectors but also a loss of power for local electorates, tendentious terms in privatization contracts, and a loss of public accountability. We begin with a discussion of the conceptual evolution of water politics. We then probe federal legislative efforts that favor water privatization and thereby alter relations between public and private entities so as to transform the local state. Next we outline resulting problems in a standard infrastructural area, such as transportation, with respect to public accountability. We conclude by arguing for public–public partnerships (PUPs). These are peer relationship–based collaborations between two or more public authorities or organizations (in some accounts, also including nonprofit organizations) forged around common objectives and values and case-specific contracts, which can help reconcile both dilemmas of accountability and the concerns of municipal governments for making water infrastructure available and affordable.[3]

Water as a Commodity

When the infrastructure on the auction block is water, it is both easy and dangerous to underestimate its distinctive importance because water provision seems similar to other forms of infrastructure that are privately acquired and administered. In the United States, transportation-related infrastructure includes parking meters, parking garages, roads, bridges, and airports. Historically, water provided transportation by rivers, lakes, and oceans for millennia. Water is used for drinking, cleaning, and growing crops. No other form of infrastructure serves so many uses that matter for sheer existence. David L. Feldman therefore proposes that water politics can usefully be broken into five themes: (1) a continuous growth in uneven distribution because of climate change and population growth; (2) pollutant hazards to water quality; (3) demand for fresh water exceeding supply; (4) competition over shared river and groundwater basins, resulting in disputes; and (5) the problem of finding solutions that promote equity, fairness, public acceptability, means of control, and confidence in institutions.[4]

We are concerned here especially with Feldman's fourth and fifth themes and with the nature of the political mechanisms through which solutions are decided. Feldman divides water politics into two basic forms: (1) cultural politics, which is "tied to socially constructed notions of nature," and (2) "community-based politics, [which] stresses how developing societies can harness modern technologies and methods" to "better manage their water needs." Our sights are trained on what Feldman defines as neoliberal water politics, which

> stresses the purported advantages of private sector investment, free trade, and globalization of ownership and control of water as means of promoting efficient, affordable, and safe water supplies. Embraced by market enthusiasts, neoliberals favor the growing trend toward privatization of water utilities and the increasing reliance on markets for moving water supplies from wasteful or inefficient practices to high-valued uses—as in parts of the western US and much of southeast Australia.[5]

Water then comes to be viewed as "just another" commodity, something to move and sell, like oil or copper, at whatever price merchants can make the market bear. Powerful international and domestic organizations, detecting profit opportunities, press for privatizing water and do so by setting down congenial conditions to promote water conservation. In April 2014 food-systems analyst Anna Lappé reviewed World Bank policy and found that it deemed privatization as virtually the sole solution to water crises, even though its own database showed a whopping 34 percent failure rate for private water and sewerage contracts between 2000 and 2010. Lappé notes that such efforts were financed through the International Finance Corporation, which had been promoting private water projects since the 1980s as "part of a broader set of privatization policies, with loans and financing tied to enacting austerity measures designed to shrink the state, from the telecom industry to water utilities."[6]

Recall that water supplies in many U.S. cities were initially managed privately. In New York, Philadelphia, and Los Angeles, joint-stock or other investor-owned enterprises "harvested groundwater, built surface water storage reservoirs, installed miles of pipelines, and connected households and businesses for a fee."[7] In rural areas, local farmers banded together and formed cooperatives in order to secure needed water. The subsequent shift from private to public management of water supply systems occurred as concerns about public health motivated municipalities to seek safe and affordable water-supply systems.

Private operators were not up to the task. U.S. cities have relied on public water utilities ever since, commonly as a special type of government district. In rural areas, water rights conflicts between the farmers' organizations "compelled the development of organizational alternatives that could provide the means to jointly control and share scarce water."[8] The success of these joint arrangements convinced other municipalities that they should regionalize water services. Bakker observes that, today, the debate over water privatization centers on the argument of proponents that private companies inherently "will be more efficient, provide more finance, and mobilize higher-quality expertise than their government counterparts."[9] Opponents such as Bakker counter that the cumulative evidence shows that government-run systems are far more "effective, equitable, and responsive; have access to cheaper forms of finance"; and perform as well as the private sector, specifically when it comes to water servicing.[10] Of added importance is the concomitant argument that it is unethical to profit from water because it is a basic necessity.

In 2010 only 12 percent of the world's population had privatized water or sewer service.[11] The very nature of water service as a public good and natural monopoly favors the public administration of water systems. Marketing water as if it were just another commodity will not promote shared responsibility for conservation. Food & Water Watch researcher Mary Grant observes that pricing alone cannot effectively promote conservation. Other demand strategies, such as rebates provided for installing modern lower-water-use equipment are more beneficial. "There is a cost to treating and delivering water, and no one is saying water service should be free. The question is how to allocate those costs."[12] Recent droughts in the West, especially in California, are drawing public attention to the importance of water and how it is delivered.[13] Extreme drought across the United States over 2012–14 contributed to tens of thousands of lost jobs, wildfires over millions of acres, and billions of dollars in property losses.[14] In 2012 an estimated 60 percent of the United States suffered severe levels of drought.[15]

Standard Contracts and Water

Applying the same standards for water contracts as are used for transportation is a misguided enterprise. Private contractors are typically allowed excessive leeway to demand compensation. From the point of view of the private contractor, of course, those rights are the basic core of conducting a guaranteed profit (as if profits are a right). The key advantageous contract right is "Adverse Action" claims, invariably found in infrastructure privatization contracts. Private contract terms gratuitously generate more value for investors who can claim they are injured by actions adverse to these private contractors' rights.[16] Two types of privatization—public services and government infrastructure—were championed during the Clinton administration. The Clinton–Gore team preferred the slightly stealthier term "commercialization" of government functions. Gore's influence in the National Performance Review resulted in replacing heavily freighted words and processes of governance, and thereby transformed "people" and "citizens" into "customers" and "consumers"—an ideological project still very much in progress. Such reframing of citizenship was not uncommon prior to Clinton. In 1988 Peter Eisinger foresaw shifts at the subnational levels of government, observing:

> Subnational economic development policy has undergone a recent shift from an almost exclusive reliance on supply-side location incentives to stimulate investment to an approach that increasingly emphasizes demand factors in the market as a guide to the design or invention of policy. The mastery of demand factors requires a sensitivity by the state to the structure and possibilities of the market, an entrepreneurial sensibility.[17]

Since then, infrastructure privatization has formed "standard" requirements, the major one being that the private sector builds infrastructure only if generous public guarantees are offered, as is the case under President Donald Trump's proposals. Earlier, in a 2014 congressional hearing on P3s, privatization proponents were asked by Congresswoman Eleanor Holmes-Norton how much private "partners" invested. The witnesses testified that the contractors' financing ranged from 3 to 20 percent, leaving the public to fill the 80–97 percent gap.[18] What, then, was the financial advantage of turning to the private sector?

Law professor Noah Hall observes that the main issue with viewing water solely according to market criteria is not how to value water but exactly *when* to charge a market-based rate. Because of the role of water as a necessary life resource, "no one really wants to make a pure market allocation; but if we don't make a pure market allocation, then who pays for it? Most common allocations still recognize basic human needs and then figure out who pays and how much."[19] While governments may rely on market-based rates for most infrastructure, doing so is dangerously myopic with respect to water. Recent events in Detroit provide an example of how fractious and fraught the issue is when it is treated according to blinkered market criteria.

In 2014 Detroit came under heavy fire for peremptorily shutting off the water of more than thirty-three thousand households with delinquent accounts. The shutoffs drew international attention, including condemnation from UN experts, arguing that shutoffs violated human rights. In reluctant response, Detroit enacted the Water Residential Assistance Program in 2015 to provide "up to $1,000 toward a monthly bill credit for residents across the region with income qualifications of 150 percent of the federal poverty level who use Detroit's water system."[20] Even though these events were not battles over privatization per se, they serve to illustrate the political barriers that a municipality can encounter when water is treated as a commodity.

Legislating the Weak Local State

Several recent legislative steps have been taken at the federal level to reframe water infrastructure within reigning notions of privatization. In 2014 the federal government enacted the Water Resources

Reform and Development Act (WRRDA). The massive bill had over-whelming bipartisan support, passing in the House 412–4 and in the Senate 91–7. On June 10, 2014, President Obama signed the bill. Among WRRDA's goals were decreasing the need for ground trans-portation, such as tanker trucks, and thereby addressing concom-itant problems of congestion and pollution, as well as developing post-Katrina infrastructure more resilient in the face of extreme weather and natural disasters.

But WRRDA also awarded considerable benefits to the financial industry, construction unions, legislators, the transportation in-dustry, and almost anyone or anything connected monetarily with water. WRRDA's Title I reforms attend to existing problematic water programs. Title II covers navigation and navigable waters. Title III concerns programs related to extreme weather events. Title IV ad-dresses issues with navigable rivers, rural Western water, and coastal areas. Title V provides public financing for privatized water projects. Finally, WRRDA updated the Clean Water State Revolving Fund, which provides financing for water infrastructure needs as loans are repaid. At a first superficial glance, these measures appear to be a responsible approach to looming problems. Disaster efforts appear to be streamlined, and water programs are reformed in the name of efficiency. However, with water policy, the funding details are, we ar-gue, what makes water infrastructure a vexing issue. One component of WRRDA was the Water Infrastructure Finance and Innovation Act (WIFIA), modeled on the Transportation Infrastructure Finance and Innovation Act. WIFIA provides limited funding through a revolving fund and loans for water infrastructure projects, including proposals dealing with flood control, wastewater, and drinking water.

As WIFIA loans are repaid, funds are lent to other water projects. And, according to the Associated Builders and Contractors Associa-tion, WWRDA creates "a Water Infrastructure PPP program that ex-pands the use of PPPs and allows the private sector to fund portions of public projects to ease the financial burden of taxpayers."[21] Our descriptions of previous problems with P3s in infrastructure pri-vatization predict how WIFIA will likely operate. If these preceding cases are the models there is ample reason for alarm. In a private–public partnership, one "partner" is allowed to invest as little as 3 percent in projected costs (real costs almost always run higher), while two others may provide 10–20 percent of the total projected investment. The private partners are not coming to the rescue of cash-strapped governments; rather, it is the other way around: cash-strapped governments aid highly resourced private entities. Research entities therefore urged caution with respect to WIFIA. A comprehensive investigation by the Public Services International Research Unit (PSIRU), a research organization at the University of Greenwich, in the United Kingdom, argues that the operation of privatized infrastructure reveals patterns that are not obviously in the public interest:

> In fact, restricted access to federal finance is the primary cause of the difficulties faced by local governments when it comes to investing in public water systems. Allowing private water corporations to access cheap federal finance via WIFIA could undermine the financial sustainability of the U.S. public water sector, because it could contribute to destabilizing the long-term financial viability of the municipal water operators that serve around 90 percent of major cities in the U.S. by further restricting their access to federal finance.[22]

In early 2017 the WIFIA program requested $20 million, and President Donald Trump accommodated the request in his budget proposal. President Trump's budget included a $4 million increase for the Environmental Protection Agency's State Revolving Funds, under which WIFIA operates, from the previous fiscal year.[23] WIFIA continues to enjoy broad support in Washington. For many Americans, a piece of legislation that obtains wide bipartisan support by promising disaster relief and increased efficiency appears inherently meritorious. It isn't. Our objection is that "quick fix" arrangements such as these do not come with protective stipulations or punitive consequences. In the WRDDA and WIFIA, the rules of the game conform to the rules of other forms of infrastructure financing, which should raise considerable concern. Highly likely are scenarios where local electorates are left responsible for the rash or myopic decisions of public partners if private institutions decide that their investments are no longer profitable enough. The remainder of this chapter outlines these problems.

Generic Predicaments of Infrastructural Privatization

Four problems daunt water privatization: (1) financing and risk inequality, (2) loss of influence for local electorates, (3) undetected or disregarded exploitative terms in privatization contracts, and (4) neglect of public accountability and access to information. The fundamental danger posed by structuring water privatization under standard P3s is a wide gap in financing, where opportunistic contractors are forced to foot only a tiny percentage. This disparity is not just about inequalities in finance but also about the maldistribution of risk for public and private agents. Under current structures, the burden of cost and risk is borne by the public, while control and underwriting of profitability favor private entities. For instance, in toll concessions, Randy Salzmann, associate editor for *Thinking Highways*, found that "private" money is usually less than 5 percent of total project cost. The role of that tiny percentage is to bait a hook, allowing a private toll or tunnel partner to then secure municipal bonds to guarantee the project. The bonds, guaranteed by Uncle Sam, eliminate all risk for the private entity:

> If and when the private toll road or tunnel partner goes bankrupt, taxpayers are forced to pay off the bonds while absorbing all loans the state and federal governments gave the private shell company and any accumulated depreciation. Yet the shell company's parent firms get to keep years of actual toll income, on top of millions in design-build cost overruns . . . Taxpayers are left paying off billions in debt to bondholders who have received amazing returns on their money, as much as 13 percent, as virtually all—if not all—of these private P3 toll operators go bankrupt within fifteen years of what is usually a five-plus decade contract.[24]

Most "private money" is actually loans, including government loans and "private activity bonds" backed by the state. Almost without exception, when the toll concessionaire goes bankrupt after collecting years of toll income, loans and private activity bonds are not repaid. Taxpayers are then left holding worthless notes that were sold to the most vulnerable entities—pension funds and retirement plans.

Another problem in privatization contracts is the ubiquitous noncompete clause, which forbids improving roads within a specific distance from a privatized road or bridge, for example. As a result, the contractor's goals include ensuring that nearby public roads will deteriorate so badly that the public will be forced to use private toll roads.[25] Yet another problem is that bankruptcy laws and serial privatization contracts are used to enable private contractors to walk away before they suffer the increased financial liability of upkeep of aging infrastructure.[26]

Onerous reimbursement terms make government the private contractor's insurer and guarantor and, in doing so, actually penalize the government if it dares to act in the public interest. In the case of water, such features can pose grave consequences for health and human safety, while forcing the public to cover the inevitably burgeoning bill, first in water rate hikes and later in buying back the infrastructure assets it principally funded in the first place. In privatizing public infrastructure, the influences of the global corporation are far-reaching. Local governments must proceed most carefully with respect to them. Applying standard infrastructure procedures to water privatization presents especially large risks for communities with respect to whom they hold accountable.

If a private corporation invests in a bottled water operation within an American municipality, there usually are international actors involved who control a water source or production site or operate under the license of local government. "Local authorities may have less influence over the operation of such enterprises than the countries in which these enterprises are based."[27] The transnational corporations, with legal liability protection that public governments lack, have proven highly problematic. Foreign corporations enjoy American bankruptcy protections. The case of the Indiana Toll Road provides a striking example of the consequences. In 2006 the state of Indiana, in fiscal crisis, leased the Indiana Toll Road, an east–west strip of highway that stretches from the Illinois to Ohio borders. The $3.8 billion lease deal went to Cintra-Macquarie, a Spanish-Australian consortium, and was slated to span seventy-five years. In a struggling economy, Indiana desperately needed money to shore up the state budget, and, at the time, this infrastructure privatization deal was the largest in history.[28] Less than a decade later, Cintra–Macquarie was the victim of a series of bad interest rate swaps in the wake of the 2008 financial crisis and was unable to fulfill the lease agreement, declaring bankruptcy. In 2015 Australia-based fund house IFM Investors purchased the Indiana Toll Road for $5.72 billion.[29]

Did the public have any say in the purchase? No, despite the fact that the public has seen rate increases upwards of 126 percent in the aftermath of IFM's purchase.[30] The bankruptcy was not unique. Other privately financed toll roads leased by foreign conglomerates suffered the same fate. San Diego's South Bay Expressway, for example, also operated by Macquarie, filed for bankruptcy protection in 2010.[31] Foreign corporations enjoy the privilege of masking their identities. In the case of the privatization of parking meters in Chicago, the city leased its parking meters for seventy-five years to Chicago Parking Meters LLC, an investment group led by New York–headquartered Morgan Stanley, German-headquartered Allianz Capital Partners, and the UAE-headquartered, state-owned Abu Dhabi Investment Authority.

However, journalist Matt Taibbi observed that, after the initial lease deal in December of 2008,

> Morgan Stanley sought new investors to provide additional capital and reduce their investment exposure . . . While a group of several Morgan Stanley infrastructure funds owned 100 percent of Chicago Parking Meters, LLC in December 2008, they had located a minority investor, Deeside Investments, Inc.—to accept 49.9 percent ownership. Tannadice Investments, a subsidiary of Abu Dhabi Investment Authority, owns a 49.9 percent interest in Deeside.
>
> So basically Morgan Stanley found a bunch of investors, including themselves, to put up over a billion dollars in December 2008: a big chunk of those investors then bailed out to make way in February 2009 for Deeside Investments, which was 49.9 percent owned by Abu Dhabi and 50.1 percent owned by a company called Redoma SARL, about which nothing was known except that it had an address in Luxembourg . . . According to my math, that still makes Abu-Dhabi-based investors at least 30 percent owners of Chicago's parking meters. God knows who the other real owners are.[32]

We stress that the bankruptcy of the Indiana Toll Road and the Chicago parking-meter ignominy should encourage the public not only to scrutinize water privatization contracts but to ask whether these deals should be done at all. The foregoing cases make for daily aggravation with respect to parking and tolls, but on the subject of water, similar activities may result in extremely dire situations with respect to public welfare. We next turn to the water privatization experiences of Allentown, Pennsylvania, and Flint, Michigan.

Privatization Contracts in Allentown

In August 2013, the city of Allentown, Pennsylvania, rented its water and waste systems for fifty years because it was cash-strapped. Allentown was not alone in turning to privatization to deal with cash-flow problems. Indeed, cities, counties, and states across the country privatize basic infrastructure built and paid for by prior generations. The challenges of drought and conflict were not the direct causes of Allentown's decisions; rather, Allentown leased its water and wastewater systems because it faced severe financial challenges. It had failed to fund its firefighter and police retirement accounts and, as with many other cities, to make critical repairs and upgrades to its water system. Allentown estimated that its minimum obligation to fund employee pensions would consume 25 percent of its budget. Indeed, finances were in such poor shape that it could not qualify for loans. The only option it could see was to treat its water infrastructure as a piggy bank. Allentown officials hoped to secure $100 million in an up-front payment by privatizing.[33]

Mayor Ed Pawlowski's announcement that he planned to privatize water drew strong criticism. Food & Water Watch pointed out that the public would be "taxed through the tap" and that an up-front payment was really just an extremely expensive loan.[34] The bidding attracted international bidders, but by summer 2013 Allentown found its white knight in the Lehigh County Authority (LCA), a public, nonprofit body in the county in which Allentown was situated. Even better, the LCA offered more than double the amount Allentown had hoped for—an up-front payment of $220 million and, starting in year four, an annual payment of $500,000. LCA also offered to hire Allentown's workers, maintain their pay and benefits, and recognize their union. In addition, the LCA was solvent and could borrow money at low terms. The LCA financed its up-front payment by issuing tax-free bonds that it planned to pay off in thirty years.

The LCA proposed a fifty-year contract, double what Allentown had proposed, but it is not surprising that Allentown accepted the bid. These governmental bodies were interdependent, with shared history and relationships. The LCA's offices were in Allentown, and Lehigh County had long depended on the city for water. As a result, the LCA's interests were largely aligned with those of Allentown. While other bidders might have taken this opportunity to increase revenues by lowering workers' pay and benefits and breaking their union, the LCA agreed to retain the city water workers and to recognize the union that represented them, an act that promoted a peaceful commencement to this new relationship. A 2012 Food & Water Watch report showed that Allentown's sewer and water charges were $425 a year, while charges for privatized Pennsylvania water and sewer operations were much higher. Aqua Pennsylvania charged $1,224 a year; Pennsylvania American Water charged $1,382; and the average price hikes for Pennsylvania cities that privatized their water was $516, an increase of 252 percent. Allentown and the LCA are public entities with many strong ties.

Does that mean that their public–public, fifty-year infrastructure privatization contract is different from public–private infrastructure contracts? The answer, surprisingly, is no. The 195-page LCA–Allentown contract includes the boilerplate language generally found in infrastructure privatization contracts. For example, the contract includes Article 14, the Adverse Action provision, a section that gives private contractors the right to reimbursement for claims. In this instance, the public partner has done something that deprives the private concessionaire of anticipated revenues, and the public partner is responsible for reimbursing the private partner. This is not the way true partners treat one another. So why did the LCA include such a clause in its contract, and why was it acceded to? Is the standard contract the only alternative? We argue that the LCA is an example of the larger problems observed throughout this chapter; that the LCA is symptomatic of water privatization's being framed under the same umbrella of other types of infrastructure privatization. In our concluding thoughts, we will offer solutions for how governments can proceed when making similar deals in the future, but the LCA–Allentown contract serves as a stern warning to municipalities with respect to contractual terms.

It is impossible to put a price on the value of public access to information about government activities. In practice, privatizing public infrastructure and services means losing public access to information and control. A recent example is Pennsylvania governor Tom Corbett's suppressing information about plans to privatize five thousand neglected, dilapidated, and dangerous Pennsylvania bridges and other transportation infrastructure, while also silencing concerns about the effects of privatization. Meanwhile, other public officials remained unaware of, or in denial about, how the public infrastructure would be paid for.[35] This neglect is encouraged in part through episodes of fierce antitax sentiment that even oppose federal, state, and local fuel taxes—those largely used to build and maintain highways—at the same effective level, taking inflation into account.[36]

These failures have been papered over by using reassuring but misleading terms such as "partner" or "partnership" in connection with privatization as a panacea.[37] As a result, average people assume that P3s mean equal sharing of burdens, benefits, and information. Instead, grossly unequal responsibility, liability, and lack of public access to information become the norm. Adjustments after a contract is signed either add costs to the public or lock the public partner into a long-term contract that hampers the state's ability to provide for the needs of its citizenry. Right-to-know laws are supposed to give the public the right to know what their government is doing, including the right to ask for public records. Information about privatized infrastructure is often, if not always, ruled confidential.

The Flint Crisis

Recent events in Flint, Michigan, highlight the importance of transparency with respect to water infrastructure. In 2011 the state of Michigan took over Flint's finances after projecting a $25 million deficit, including a water-fund shortfall of $9 million. The city switched water sources in 2014 from Lake Huron to the Flint River as a new pipeline connecting Flint to Lake Huron began construction. Despite residents voicing concern about the toxicity of the river for years, the city proceeded, with lead from aging service lines soon leaching into Flint's water supply. As more water test and research results indicating harm to public health were published, and lawsuits proposed, in October 2015, the governor signed a spending bill of $9.35 million to reconnect Flint to Detroit's water supply and provide health services for residents.[38] The damage was already done to the lead pipes, however. About half of the lines to Flint homes were made of lead, and the water turned brown because of the eroded iron water mains. In 2016 the governor asked for $28 million in federal aid to pay for bottled water and filters, the treatment of children, and other items. In April 2018 the governor announced the end of a free bottled water program in Flint as the water quality had been restored.[39] But the toxic effects persist and are irremediable.[40]

The remarkably insistent mishandling of the Flint water crisis drew widespread condemnation. State employees faced criminal charges after being found to cover up lead levels by downplaying them or simply lying. By February 2018 fifteen current and former state and city government officials were charged, and the most serious charge was involuntary manslaughter.[41] As a result of the mess, Flint successfully sued the state of Michigan. The state of Michigan and the city of Flint agreed to replace thousands of contaminated lead pipes over a three-year period. As per the court agreement, Flint will have replaced at least eighteen thousand lead or galvanized-steel water lines by 2020, and the state picks up the bill with state and federal money.[42] In 2016 Mayor Karen Weaver and the city of Flint launched the FAST Start pipe replacement program, organized in six phases running through 2019, with six thousand pipes replaced annually. During 2016–17, the program obtained $172 million funding, including $25 million in state funds and $100 million in federal funds.[43]

Flint's water still has a long way to go. In March 2017 Flint's mayor and the head of Flint's underground pipe replacement program said they "think it will be more than two years until residents can drink their tap water without filters."[44] Phase five of FAST Start was set in 2018. By September 13, 2018, 7,143 service lines were replaced.[45] First, as with Detroit, while the Flint case was not a failure of privatization arrangements, it was a failure that we can associate with viewing water solely as a fiscal property. More important, because public institutions were responsible, the electorate had immediate access to domestic entities to hold accountable for these institutions' failures. In the case of Flint, state institutions sought to suppress information after essentially poisoning residents and, because of public-information laws, were held accountable. The state government was forced to acknowledge its responsibility and is footing the bill for repairs. Would this have been the case if a private entity were responsible? If a foreign-based limited-liability corporation paves the road to toxicity, will the public have the ability to hold responsible parties accountable? No.

The terrible Flint incident happened because water was viewed only in terms of dollars and cents. The decisions made were enacted because a state economic manager was seeking in the most myopic manner to save money. The Flint incident thus illustrates the many delusions on which water decisions rest. When local residents are the victims of a one-sided parking meter deal, the results are an increase in complaints and lawsuits, fee hikes for citizens, and bad press for the city. With water, the penalties are simpler and more severe; lives are put at risk. Nonprofit philanthropic organizations, a recent study attests, also have proven to be significant alleviators, if not solvers, of the immense strains that Detroit and Flint have suffered over the last few decades, "but questions remain about the longer range recovery of the public sector."[46] The authors note that thirty more cities in Michigan alone are insolvent; nonprofits, they argue, can fill service gaps but cannot themselves be an adequate substitute for, or capacity builders of, a functioning public sector.

We do not wish to paint an unrelentingly grim picture of the future of water, nor do we assume that governments offer all the answers for water infrastructure, but it is worth noting that independent nonprofit organizations have taken notice in recent years and offered practical institutional alternatives to standard privatization practices. In 2012 Food & Water Watch released a study on a new structure for providing water through PUPs. Part of the impetus to create PUPs is dissatisfaction with P3s for their failing to provide quality water at stable and affordable prices. Food & Water Watch concludes that "proponents of privatization promised increased investment and efficiency, but privatization has failed to meet these expectations. Instead, it has often led to deteriorating infrastructure, service disruptions, and higher prices for poorer service."[47] The Public Services International Research Unit defines PUPs as

> the collaboration between two or more public authorities or organizations, based on solidarity, to improve the capacity and effectiveness of one partner in providing public water supply and/or sanitation services. PUPs are peer relationships forged around common values and objectives, which exclude profit-seeking . . . [and] allow public partners to invest all available resources into the development of local capacity, to build mutual trust that translates in long-term capacity gains, and to incur low transaction costs.[48]

Among other things, PUPs allow public water utilities and other organizations to share their resources and expertise. PUPs also allow the public to retain local control of existing water systems, as public utilities are responsible for most water and wastewater services.

PUPs keep water infrastructure within the public sector, which costs less. In 2014 Food & Water Watch conducted an analysis of the five hundred largest water systems in the United States, which showed that publicly owned water utilities "charge considerably lower rates than their private peers."[49] Specifically, private, for-profit utilities charged typical households 59 percent more than local governments charged for drinking-water service. "A typical household, using sixty thousand gallons a year, paid $316 for water service from a local government and $501 for service from a private company. That is, private ownership corresponds to about $185 extra each year for the average household."[50] In the United Kingdom, where water privatization is more widespread than in the United States, water privatization resulted in price increases upwards of 50 percent over the last two decades; and in France, the price of private water was "16 percent higher than public-sector-provisioned water."[51]

This chapter on water privatization focuses on the transformation of the local state into a pliant arm of private contractors. Lost, too, in the shuffle of conceptual arguments about privatization, or studies on cost, are the legal implications hidden within the minutiae of privatization contracts. If public officials are looking for a starting point for reforming privatization trends, the structure of agreements is a good place to begin. Ensuring potable water for all is a major global challenge that will increase over time. The United States is not exempt. The typical American household uses 260 gallons of water a day, making our nation's water footprint among the largest in the world. Indeed, the United States also faces the dangers of conflict, ecological disaster, and widespread suffering. Instead of utilizing contracting methods advocated by privatizers, which truly do put profits ahead of public needs, PUPs offer a way for state and local governments to protect the public and public employees in order to preserve this most vital of resources.

Notes

1. Paul E. Peterson, *City Limits* (Chicago: University of Chicago Press, 1981), 15.

2. Food & Water Watch, *The State of Public Water in the United States* (Washington, D.C., 2014), https://bit.ly/2HRDCYp.

3. David Hall, Emanuele Lobina, Violeta Corral, Olivier Hoedeman, Philip Terhost, Martin Pigeon, and Satoko Kishimoto, *Public-Public Partnerships in Water* (London: Public Services International Research Unit; Fermey-Voltaire: Public Services International; and Amsterdam: Transnational Institute, March 2009), https://bit.ly/2FN7xuX.

4. David L. Feldman, *Water Politics: Governing Our Most Precious Resource* (Cambridge: Polity, 2017), Kindle edition.

5. Feldman, *Water Politics*, Loc 963.

6. Anne Lappé, "World Bank Wants Water Privatized, Despite Risks," Al Jazeera America (website), April 17, 2014, http://america.aljazeera.com/opinions/2014/4/water-managementprivatizationworldbankgroupifc.html.

7. Feldman, *Water Politics*.

8. Feldman, *Water Politics*.

9. Karen Bakker, *Privatizing Water: Governance Failure and the World's Urban Water Crisis* (Ithaca, N.Y.: Cornell University Press, 2010).

10. Karen Bakker, "The Business of Water: Market Environmentalism in the Water Sector," *Annual Review of Environment and Resources* 39 (2014): 477.

11. Food & Water Watch, *State of Public Water.*

12. Mary Grant (campaign director, Food & Water Watch), interviewed by Ellen Dannin, 2014.

13. "California Drought Worst in at Least 1,200 Years," *Science News Magazine* 187, no. 1 (January 10, 2015): 16, https://bit.ly/2RShbTU.

14. Bobby Magill, "Climate Change Altering Droughts, Impact across the U.S.," Climate Central (website), June 22, 2017, www.climatecentral.org/news/climate-change-altering-droughts-us-21563. On the deleterious effect of budget cuts, see Jeffrey Mount, Ellen Hana, Caitrin Chappelle, Bonnie Colby, Richard Frank, Greg Gartell, Brian Gray, Douglas Kennedy, Jay Lund, and Peter Moyle, "Improving the Federal Response to Western Drought: Five Areas for Reforms," *California Journal of Politics and Policy* 8, no. 3 (2016): 1–35, www.ppic.org/content/pubs/report/R_216JMR.pdf.

15. Mount et al., "Improving the Federal Response." Also see Richard R. Heim, "A Comparison of the Early Twentieth-First Century Drought to the 1930s and 1950s Drought Episodes," *American Meteorological Society* 3 (January 2018), https://journals.ametsoc.org/doi/10.1175/BAMS-D-16-0080.1.

16. Ellen Dannin, "Crumbling Infrastructure, Crumbling Democracy: Infrastructure Privatization Contracts and Their Effects on State and Local Governance," *Northwestern Journal of Law & Social Policy* 6, no. 1 (2011): 47–105.

17. Peter Eisinger, *The Rise of the Entrepreneurial State: State and Local Economic Development Policy in the United States* (Madison: University of Wisconsin Press, 1989), 10.

18. U.S. Congress, House, Committee on Transportation and Infrastructure, *Overview of Public-Private Partnerships in Highway and Transit Projects*, hearings before the Committee on Transportation and Infrastructure, 113th Cong., 2nd sess., 2014.

19. Noah Hall (associate professor of law, Wayne State University), interviewed by Ellen Dannin, 2014.

20. Ryan Felton, "Detroit Water Shut-offs Resume—and Residents Continue to Struggle with Bills," *Metro Times*, July 6, 2016.

21. Ellen Dannin, "Water Privatization: Coming to a Century Old System Near You?," Truthout (website), June 18, 2014, https://truthout.org/articles/water-privatization-coming-to-a-century-old-system-near-you.

22. Public Services International Research Unit (PSIRU), "Troubled Waters: Misleading Industry PR and the Case for Public Water" (London, November 2014), https://bit.ly/2FM7MXa.

23. Becky Moylan, "Trump Administration Proposes Budget," *Infrastructure Report Card: 2017*, American Society of Civil Engineers, https://bit.ly/2rmMuep.

24. Randy Salzman, "A Blueprint for Bankruptcy," Truthout (website), October 16, 2014.

25. Dannin, "Water Privatization."

26. Ellen Dannin, "Why Anytown, USA, Privatizes Its Water System," Truthout (website), October 31, 2013.

27. Feldman, *Water Politics*, Loc 624.

28. Payton Chung and Angie Schmitt, "The Indiana Toll Road and the Dark Side of Privately Financed Highways," *Streetsblog USA*, November 18, 2014, https://bit.ly/2jw8eju.

29. Tribune Wire Reports, "Lease Sale Closes on Indiana Toll Road for $5.72B," *Chicago Tribune*, May 28, 2015.

30. CBS Chicago, "Many Indiana Toll Drivers Seeing Big Rate Increase," CBS (website), June 1, 2017, https://cbsloc.al/2HU20so.

31. Chung and Schmitt, "Dark Side of Privately Financed Highways."

32. Matt Taibbi, *Griftopia: A Story of Bankers, Politicians, and the Most Audacious Power Grab in American History* (New York: Spiegel & Grau, 2011), 169.

33. Ryan Holeywell, "How Allentown Leased Its Utilities to Fund Pensions," *Governing Magazine*, September 9, 2013, www.governing.com/blogs/view/gov-how-allentown-sold-its-utilities-to-fund-its-pensions.html.

34. Food & Water Watch, *Public-Public Partnerships: An Alternative Model to Leverage the Capacity of Municipal Water Utilities* (Washington, D.C., February 28, 2012), www.foodandwatereurope.org/reports/public-public-partnerships-an-alternative-model-to-leverage-the-capacity-of-municipal-water-utilities.

35. Associated Pennsylvania Constructors, *No April Fools' Day Joke: 5,050 of Pennsylvania's Bridges Need Structural Repair, New Analysis of U.S. Department of Transportation Data Finds*, April 1, 2015, www.prnewswire.com/news-releases/no-april-fools-day-joke-5050-of-pennsylvanias-bridges-need-structural-repair-new-analysis-of-us-department-of-transportation-data-finds-300059493.html.

36. Some works, for example, show how the frustrations of moderate income-earners seeking tax relief were fastened upon and adapted by affluent property and business owners to the benefit of the latter. Daniel A. Smith, "Peeling Away the Populist Rhetoric: Toward a Taxonomy of Anti-Tax Ballot Initiatives," *Public Budgeting and Finance* 24, no. 4 (December 2004): 88–110; and Clarence Y. H. Lo, *Small Property versus Big Government: Social Origins of the Property Tax Revolt* (Berkeley: University of California Press, 1990).

37. Eleanor Bader, "Secret Plans and Clever Tricks," Truthout (website), February 21, 2014.

38. CNN Library, "Flint Water Crisis Fast Facts," CNN, April 8, 2018, www.cnn.com/2016/03/04/is/flint-water-crisis-fast-facts/index.html.

39. CNN Library, "Flint Water Crisis Fast Facts."

40. Anna Clark, "Treating River Water Is Vastly More Complex Than Treating Lake Water," WBUR (website), July 10, 2018, www.wbur.org/2018/07/10/flint-water-crisis-poisoned-city.

41. Steve Carmody, "Officials Charged in Flint Water Crisis Back in

Court This Week, 2 Years After First Indictments," Michigan Radio (website), February 6, 2018, http://www.michicagnradio.org/post/officals-charged -flint-water-crisis-back-court-week-2-years-after-first-indictments.

42. Julie Bosman, "Michigan Allots $87 Million to Replace Flint's Tainted Water Piped," *New York Times*, March 27, 2017.

43. City of Flint, Michigan, "FAST Start Pipe Replacement Program," www.cityofflint.com/fast-start.

44. Jonathan Oosting, "Flint: 'All Clear' for Drinking Water Years Away," *Detroit News*, December 8, 2017.

45. Candace Mushatt, "Pipes Replaced at 6,957 Flint Homes to Date through Mayor Weaver's FAST Start Initiative," City of Flint, Michigan (2018), www.ityofflint.com/2018/08/20pipes-replaced-at-6957-flint-homes -though-mayor-weavers-fast-start-initiative.

46. Davia Cox Downey and Sarah Reckhow, "Unnatural Disasters: Can Nonprofit Governance Promote Recovery in Detroit and Flint?," Michigan Applied Public Policy Research Brief (2018), 2.

47. Food & Water Watch, "An Efficient, Effective Alternative to Water Privatization," *On the Commons* (blog), https://bit.ly/2KFUb7l.

48. PSIRU, "Troubled Waters."

49. Food & Water Watch, *State of Public Water.*

50. Food & Water Watch, *State of Public Water.*

51. PSIRU, "Troubled Waters."

6

The Role of the State in Public–Private Initiatives

Lessons from Great Britain

Alba Alexander

In 1965, when Andrew Shonfield published his landmark *Modern Capitalism: The Changing Balance of Public and Private Power*—note carefully that subtitle—he was confident that advanced industrial economies had achieved a new organizational phase that was immune to deep downturns and had the benefits of growth more evenly distributed. The point of "evenly distributed benefits" for Keynesians such as Shonfield was that the fiscal means for distributing the surplus assured demand growth and thereby guaranteed the smooth functioning of the economy, which otherwise was prone to capsize. Marxists and other critics therefore could bid underconsumption crises farewell. Assisted by Keynesian fine-tuning instruments and ancillary arrangements in public and private sector planning, a reformed economic paradigm emerged. The "bleak and squalid system," as Shonfield dubbed it, was finally tamed.[1] These mixed economy reforms succeeded in overcoming major defects of capitalism. In this upbeat verdict, he was joined by C. A. R. Crosland in the United Kingdom as well as by Daniel Bell, John Kenneth Galbraith, Ralf Dahrendorf, and others.[2]

Shonfield asked what changed capitalism from "the cataclysmic failure it appeared to be in the 1930s into the great engine of prosperity in the postwar Western world?" The answer lay in a political shift in the balance between public and private power, favoring the former, that orchestrated markets so as to promote steady growth, rising incomes and investment, and full employment. He argued that capitalism in its post–World War II form was superior to an older version that was conflict-ridden, myopic, and characterized by high joblessness, erratic growth, and upward capture of wealth. Shonfield's views comprised the political economic orthodoxy. The book heralded a Keynesian consensus, the prizing of deft state management and of its obligation to counter boom-and-bust cycles. The postwar period of growth and welfare state expansion ended in the Great Stagflation of the 1970s, marked by two oil price hikes, though it had additional causes.[3] Some analysts refer to the subsequent period as "permanent austerity," which it was for the average income earner, who never again saw a real rise in living standards.[4] This glum reality, however, gained little media traction in the United States and United Kingdom, where ascendant free market doctrines were portrayed as a sure cure.[5]

Shonfield's book exemplified the value of comparative analysis. Scholars who examined the period of the mid-1970s to the early 1990s focused on reasons why industrial democracies reached their peaks at distinct levels of market intervention and compensatory spending. Analysts such as Peter Katzenstein, Dietrich Rueschemeyer, Evelyn Huber, John D. Stephens, Peter Hall, and David Soskice, as well as many others, following Shonfield, have since characterized the United States and Great Britain as an ideal-type Anglo-American liberal (or market-friendly) welfare state, as compared to more social democratic continental European cases.[6] So this chapter focuses on the United Kingdom, where the shift away from the public sector was dramatic, in many ways matching that of the United States. Political leaders in the United Kingdom and United States entered office at the brink of the 1980s championing privatization—ceding of public power to private entities—as an essential part of a solution to their respective countries' economic problems.[7] The benign state interventionism Shonfield celebrated just a decade or so earlier was suddenly the source of all ills.

Britain since has been a pioneer in the use of "public–private partnerships" (P3s) to address shortfalls in the provision of infrastructure, deploying a form termed Private Finance Initiatives (PFIs).[8] More than 700 public–private projects are in effect.[9] Across the European Union, excluding Britain, between 2001 and 2007, governments approved 193 such projects worth over EUR 35 billion and procured an additional EUR 76 billion for new contracts.[10] An Organization for Economic Co-operation and Development (OECD) working paper observed that "many in the infrastructure industry see the United States as the next gold rush," with investors eager to transform all infrastructure projects into P3s.[11] How have revived market remedies actually performed in the provision of cost-effective infrastructure? I address the United Kingdom because it has extensive experience since 1992 with PFIs and P3s, encouraged by the Conservative government of John Major, in the wake of a wave of privatization of utilities and state-owned enterprises under Margaret Thatcher.

One inevitable casualty of austerity policies is infrastructure, which piles up a backlog of urgent needs. What do several decades now tell us about privatization schemes in infrastructure? Contrary to Grover Norquist's quest to shrink the state to a size that can be drowned in a bathtub, this objective of antistatist conservatives leads not to a lessening of public intervention but rather to a recrafting of relationships between public and private sectors, and in the latter's favor, which seems to be the real point.[12] Where private sector involvement is encouraged, it has been necessary first to build or repurpose other institutions to make private involvement attractive.[13] The motives for this transformed public role in infrastructure provisions have been questionable. Given the calls for transparency as part of the answer to problems arising from "partnerships," it becomes apparent that they were established to avoid transparency. When made transparent, one detects a "competition state" at work—that is, a state apparatus refashioning itself not to serve the citizenry at large but foremost to clear obstacles for major productive and financial actors.[14]

Hard times, Peter Gourevitch noted, brought this on, though, as he showed, not in the same way in every state.[15] In the Anglo-American cases, this rebalancing resulted in the private-oriented "workfare state," "network state," or "post-Keynesian state."[16] In recent renditions we behold the "submerged state" and the "delegated state."[17] Though the political rhetoric accompanying such partnerships in Britain stressed the imperative to shrink government, we find not a reduced state but rather a reoriented one serving privileged constituencies. The role of government as chief financier accordingly altered but never diminished, and likely was never intended to do so. Absent the resource guarantees by the central government, there would be few, if any, attractive infrastructure deals for private agents.[18]

I reconsider this shift in the balance of power between government and private actors, as well as its implications for future policy trends. When Margaret Thatcher in the United Kingdom and Ronald Reagan in the United States entered office, the largest cities in both nations were key bases of support for the opposition parties and therefore lost influence. In Britain, the central government increased its already considerable authority over local government.[19] Thatcher abolished the resistant Greater London Council in 1986 and sold off council (public) housing to build up instead an "ownership conservative mentality."[20] Reagan eliminated federal revenue sharing and was stinting in aid for urban needs.[21] Public agencies consequently were compelled to try to meet infrastructure needs in cash-strapped U.S. cities by increasingly resorting to P3s, a move foreseen by many advocates of this course.[22]

Privatization refers to the transfer of state-owned assets to private actors through sale, lease, or liquidation. Today, however, contractual agreements between government and the private sector to design, build, operate, maintain, or finance infrastructure are the key manifestations. ("Private–public partnerships" and "Private Finance Initiatives" in Britain are interchangeable terms.) The United Kingdom is considered a forerunner in developing infrastructure through P3s; hence, I explore lessons that the British experience may yield for the United States. Because these two countries operate increasingly according to similar economic doctrines, we might expect a similar trajectory in costs and benefits from P3 infrastructure development.

Governments always have "sold assets, contracted out services, and disengaged themselves from certain functions."[23] The distinctive aspect of public–private relationships now is that governments pursue them "with the explicit objective of significantly recasting the role and relations of state, market and civil society."[24] In the

United States, this process led to a proliferation of "special authorities" to accompany it.[25] In Britain, the counterparts are "quangos" (quasi-nongovernmental organizations), an unofficial term. Here I address indicative cases of P3s that, overall, deliver far fewer benefits than anticipated.

Has the relationship between public and private power, as delineated by Shonfield, been turned *permanently* on its head? Is the relationship less a symbiotic than a parasitic one?[26] To assess this policy trajectory, we need to understand why state actors resort to private sector collaborators.[27] The state, after all, need "not bow down easily to interest groups who approach it to seek handouts, rents, and unnecessary privileges like tax cuts," observes Mariana Mazzucato.[28] What is more difficult to achieve is the prescription that the state "should seek instead for those interest groups to work dynamically with it in its search for growth and technological change."[29] The P3 experience encompasses instances of both arrangements, so the question is, How does one generate more of the Mazzucato kind? Some analysts urge that we look at P3s merely as a policy tool.[30] This instrumentalist view disregards the political dimension and instead focuses on constructing capital works coalitions as if they are technical fixes. Are limits on political debate about intervention narrower today in the United States than elsewhere or at any previous time? Not more so than in the United Kingdom.

To summarize comprehensively for readers the current major competing perspectives on P3 development examined below, this chapter posits the following major perspectives: (1) P3s are superior to public action alone because they combine public and private efforts on the latter's terms; (2) P3s erode democracy but nonetheless get the job done; and (3) P3s are flawed and underperform, often scandalously so. While the first and second perspectives assume that these arrangements are at least cost effective, the third raises challenges as to routine claims of cost effectiveness.

Defining Terms: Public–Private Partnerships, Privatization, and Infrastructure

In the United States, a public–private partnership is any private involvement in the public sector, from taking a tiny part to taking over. Patrick Sabol and Robert Puentes concede that a "precise definition of a PPP for infrastructure is elusive."[31] They propose that a P3 be understood as any "legally binding contract between a public sector entity and a private company—typically referred to as a concessionaire—where the partners agree to share some portion of the risks and rewards inherent in an infrastructure project."[32] In Britain such a partnership "refers to agreements where the private sector designs, builds, finances, operates and maintains (also known as DBFOM) an infrastructure asset for a predetermined period of time. In exchange, the public sector provides a recurring payment based on the condition of the asset (known as an availability payment) or allows the private sector to collect tolls or fees generated from the project."[33] In the United States, the DBFOM type of public–private collaboration is the most comprehensive form, but it remains one of several possible arrangements.

The U.S. Federal Accounting Standards Advisory Board tried to craft a definition broad enough to capture P3 activities and different classes of assets in its pre-Trump effort to impose uniformity across federal agencies. The proposed definition seemed so expansive to discontented officials because it covered contracts that are not P3s at all. The draft definition suggested that the very formation of special purpose vehicles was an indicator that public–private partnership agreements assure the sharing of risks and rewards—even if one side bears all the risks.[34] So this tack proved quite unhelpful.

The International Monetary Fund (IMF) distinguished public–private partnerships from traditional public sector financing: "What defines a PPP is [not that they are involved in the contracting out of operations, construction or maintenance, but rather] that the government writes a contract with a single firm (usually a special purpose company [vehicle] that agrees to provide the service."[35] It is this relationship that distinguishes a PPP [or P3] from traditional public sector financing that contracted out projects. Uniform standards for implementation of partnerships are yet to be formulated. In the absence of a clear federal standard, it is not surprising that there is inadequate public institutional capacity to assess the maintenance costs of such deals.[36] The State Comptroller of New York alternately refers to P3s as either a "construction and financing technique" or as a "procurement technique."[37] Should we apply the same standards and measures to assessing a "construction and financing technique" as we do to a "procurement technique"? How do we weigh them against each other and against other pertinent factors in assessing an infrastructure deal? We have no agreed measures. New York, for example, is neither better nor worse in this regard than are other states (such as Washington, Ohio, Virginia, Pennsylvania, Florida, Indiana, California, Colorado, Kentucky, Texas, and New Mexico) that permit or are considering P3s. Some thirty states approved P3 laws since Virginia first passed one in the late 1980s.[38]

The balance between the public and private sector, expressed in the terms by which the jointly arranged production of goods and services occur, can be a useful focal point. To say privatization introduces private actors into the public equation tells us nothing about the terms. We can gauge this changing balance in the relationship between public and private power by examining the terms that public authorities aim to extract from private companies. I say "aim to extract" because aims differ from results. A corporate-friendly "competition state" is not going to drive hard bargains. Weber, Kass, and Hinkley, among others in this volume, provide a local illustration of why that is so in Chicago.

My privatization definition follows Paul Starr's: "Under traditional public procurement, the government borrowed to invest in new infrastructure, whereas the PFI instead establishes a long-term leasing arrangement, under which private consortia borrow the cash to build and run new [infrastructure] in exchange for annual fees."[39] Public authorities turn to the private sector to do the borrowing, a practice that differs considerably from arrangements Shonfield charted. There are "several types of PFIs but the most common requires the private sector to design, build, finance and operate facilities, usually for twenty-five to thirty-five years," Eric Shaw writes of the British case. "The private sector finances construction and is repaid by the state, in regular payments, for the use of the buildings and services."[40] Payments "are classified as revenue, not capital, and thus do no[t] count against public borrowing and do not commence until the building is completed." This approach therefore has enormous short-term political appeal, an appeal that may induce hard-pressed public authorities to overlook rather than oversee what unanticipated costs and effects transpire afterward.[41] That is the first lesson to be drawn from the British experience.

Public–Private Partnerships as Institutions

Partnership participants typically create a special organization to solidify the contractual agreements and provide "the basis for a continuing exchange within a set of mutually agreed rules."[42] These arrangements are not "transient relationships." While accountability and transparency are basic features of democratic political arrangements, the institutions created to consolidate the agreements between public and private sectors, known as special authorities or quangos, lack such features. Deliberately so, because these arrangements are designed to sidestep multiple veto points that critics claim hobbled or deterred earlier development deals.[43] P3s therefore take on a brisk "get things done" aura and have spread in popularity, at least among public authorities, precisely because they are deficient in accountability and transparency.[44] According to enthusiasts, the P3 relationship allows for "shared understandings of priorities . . . by the two (or more) actors," and that can only be a good thing.[45] At the top of the list of factors explaining the popularity of P3s is their "relative lack of visibility."[46] Because deals rarely reach mass attention, and supposedly, if they do, "private sector involvement is likely to make them more palatable to skeptics of the public sector."[47] This stealth aspect is advantageous because it bypasses potential public opposition. Still, voters have supported both "visible" and less visible infrastructure projects insofar as they understood them. The inherent stealthy character of these arrangements is another lesson to be drawn from British experience.

Unlike the United States, Great Britain had "no strong tradition of organizing public–private relations through joint participation in institutions."[48] In Britain, at the start of the twenty-first century, a debate commenced about how best to ensure that organizations, public or private, work in the public interest.[49] There has been a great deal of experimentation with public–private institutions, after which there has been a reappraisal. The trend toward P3s cannot be explained entirely in partisan terms. Their use arose under a Conservative government but continued apace under New Labour governments. Labour prime minister Tony Blair even praised PFIs for their "immense" contribution to the country's infrastructure.[50]

The IMF, however, expressed concern that what drives these

partnerships is that they "bypass spending controls and move public investment off budget and debt off the government balance sheet, while the government still bears most of the risk involved and faces potentially large fiscal costs."[51] A special Labour government commission in 2001 echoed the critique.[52] The IMF noted numerous loopholes in fiscal accounting and reporting conventions that create incentives to opt for P3s.[53] Because many P3 ventures approach major U.S. federal urban redevelopment projects in scale and visibility, they entice public officials concerned about voter approval. This state of affairs leads to diminished leverage by public officials over private actors and ultimately to disproportionate risks for the public. Several scholars ask, Why, despite ample evidence that large P3s often fail to deliver benefits, do public officials favor them? Bent Flyvbjerg poses the question starkly: Why do the worst projects get built? These projects hark to "Machiavelli's Formula," which requires that you "underestimate costs, overestimate revenues, undervalue environmental impacts, and overvalue development effects."[54] The McKinsey Global Institute projects global infrastructure spending at $3.4 trillion annually between 2013 and 2030, about 4 percent of total world GDP "delivered as large-scale projects."[55] The *Economist* dubbed this "the biggest investment boom in history": a need for repair and updating of infrastructure, as exemplified by the devastating levee breach in New Orleans, was anticipated to drive investment.[56] What's new about P3s is an outright "preference to use private finance arrangements."[57] "Even though there is a 19th century tradition of privately provided public infrastructure and even of private tolled roads and bridges, the United States still depends on the government for its public transport infrastructure."[58]

While Great Britain "financed $50 billion in transportation infrastructure via P3s between 1990 and 2006, the United States financed $10 billion."[59] The United States "will have to spend about $3.6 trillion on maintaining, expanding and updating infrastructure [needs] by 2020."[60] It has not happened. The use of P3s in the United States for "infrastructure increased fivefold between 1998 and 2006 and between 2008 and 2010."[61] Infrastructure has been built preponderantly through public direction and finance. Note the interstate highway system authorized as part of the Federal Aid Highway

Act of 1956. Nearly forty-eight thousand miles of routes were built through federal funds. Hence, another way to build major infrastructure projects is by a resumption of responsibility by the public sector, which in Trump's America went off the table. This remains curious because the United States cannot be credibly characterized as a poorer country than it was during the Eisenhower era.

Public-Private Collaborations in Britain

What are the motives, points of leverage, and institutional capacities behind the PFIs in Great Britain? Are public officials creatures of circumstances (austerity and tightened budgets) that compel the pursuit of particular options? The scale and scope of public provisions expanded in the United Kingdom following World War II and up to the 1970s.[62] In Britain a "framework for policy was created that proved durable."[63] State responsibilities enlarged, even if the growing welfare state never exceeded the warfare state, as widely imagined.[64] "Collective welfare provisions were extended through implementation of social security and the establishment of the National Health Service; public housing programmes were expanded, state education was restructured; and the government accepted new responsibilities for planning the economy and the environment."[65]

Like Republicans in the United States, Britain's Conservatives in the early postwar years learned to live with the welfare state, at least for the time being. The Tories accepted the "nationalized sector of industry, particularly in the areas of public utilities."[66] As Thatcher came to power in 1979 the social contract to promote common well-being was already unraveling. While both major political parties played a role in undermining the postwar settlement, during the 1970s the Labour government suffered internal turmoil for failing to devise a workable corporatist answer. Labour had relied on its relationship with the trade unions to fight inflation through spending cuts and wage restraints, resolving the 1970s economic crisis by driving down the living standards of its own supporters. Then Thatcher's Conservative government from 1979 to 1990, like Reagan's administration from 1980 to 1988, set out to reverse commitments to socioeconomic betterment through government intervention. Thatcher's Conservatives swept into office on a platform that, if short on specifics, promised a new direction for economic management, though it was tactically quiet about what Young calls "that most sacred of Tory obsessions, denationalization."[67] Thatcher's party called for labor union restrictions, less state intervention, less spending, and tax cuts. Thatcher undermined picketing, strike actions, and the closed shop. Through cutting taxes, Thatcher claimed to encourage entrepreneurship and investment.[68] Privatization—then called "denationalization"—was cited in the 1979 party manifesto but did not refer to "the big ones which happened after 1983."[69] Although by 1979, after a media campaign advocating market solutions, public favor for privatization rose to a high of 40 percent (from 21 percent a decade earlier), those in favor were still seriously outnumbered by the 43 percent who found the level just right, plus the 17 percent more who called for public ownership of more productive assets.[70] The previous year Thatcher aide Nicholas Ridley urged that denationalization "be approached cautiously and flexibly," but left no doubt that the nondefense public sector was targeted for extinction.[71]

In what became a standard salami-slicing tactic, Ridley suggested in 1978 that the telephone network remain nationalized for a while longer but that private telephone suppliers be given a larger role.[72] (This same graduated process is at work in the National Health Service today.)[73] So privatization policies "developed from a series of ad hoc decisions and experiments."[74] State enterprises, at least the profitable ones, had bull's-eyes on their backs so far as the Conservative government was concerned. By the late 1970s, nationalized industries "dominated the transport, communications, energy, steel and shipbuilding sectors," comprising 14 percent of investment and 8 percent of employment.[75] Thatcher's privatizations were viewed in conservative circles to be "fundamental to improving Britain's economic performance."[76] In 1979 nationalized industries accounted for "10.5 percent of GDP, by 1993 the figure fell to 3 percent and public sector employment fell by 1.5 million as a result of the sale of the industries."[77] By 1990 more than fifty state-owned companies (including British Petroleum, British Aerospace, Cable &

Wireless, Jaguar, Rolls Royce, National Freight Corporation, Water, British Steel, British Airways, Electricity, and British Gas) were sold or privatized, which enabled the Tories to legislate tax cuts geared to benefit the party's prime constituents.[78]

State companies were depicted by Conservatives as "poorly performing employment agencies, politically pressured to maintain and expand employment far beyond what was needed."[79] The state enterprises were purportedly unable to resist union pressure for higher wages, thus generating inflation. They also piled up losses.[80] This actual fact was in great part due to public enterprises fulfilling the original vision of the British Labour Party. A public official in the late 1940s heyday of nationalization explained, "The public corporation must be no mere capitalist business, the be-all and end-all of which is profits and dividends. Its board and its officers must regard themselves as the high custodians of the public interest."[81] Given the many supportive tasks these industries played in providing infrastructural aid to the overall economy, the tally sheet ought to differ considerably from that of a private enterprise. By the late 1970s, the high aspirations of Labour Party politicians for public corporations ironically made these organizations vulnerable to denationalization.

Thatcher's Treasury set up a committee chaired by Sir William Ryrie, to report on the role of private finance in public sector works. The 1981 report, known as "Ryrie Rules," established ground rules to promote public sector reduction, both to "stop Ministers from posting financial obligations into the future in order to get around budget constraints" and to "prevent Ministers from insulating private finance from risk."[82] The rules proved too stringent. "Privately funded projects had to be tested against a publicly funded alternative and shown to be more cost effective and that, save in exceptional circumstances, privately funded projects would result in equivalent reductions in public expenditure."[83] This twofold requirement yielded a dearth of qualified projects. Proof of cost effectiveness meant a public enterprise must be more economically run by the private sector. Given that much of the public enterprise sector was acquired precisely because private investors were incapable of running them efficiently and safely, privatization proved an awkward problem.[84] Further, the mark of a worthy project was that it would relieve public funding and guarantees. The limited pool of projects meeting the Ryrie Rules were mainly in transport: the Channel Tunnel in 1985, the Queen Elizabeth II Bridge Dartford Crossing in 1987, and the Second Severn Crossing in 1990.[85] The Tory solution was to relax standards, spruce up targeted state assets, and provide sweeteners.[86] Here is another lesson from Britain: market solutions require ample state support.

When it came to privatizing water, energy, and rail, in Thatcher's second and third terms (June 1983–November 1990), public funds were applied to render them attractive. An upsurge in privatized utility prices over inflation followed.[87] The rule that any project funded by private investment must result in public spending reduction was relaxed and in 1989 was abolished. The OECD detected that the Tory project of shedding public enterprises was accompanied by a "parallel process of centralization which progressively erased the autonomy of local government, intermediary institutions and professional associations turning the legislature into a rubber stamp for the executive."[88] The Thatcher administration, contrary to its rhetoric, strengthened the central state. The reasoning for this "seeming paradox is the government's attempt to neutralize mounting social opposition and escape accountability."[89] With extensive denationalizations under way, a network of practitioners was forged. Privatizations were managed by the sponsor department, within which a team of officials was set, advised by city merchant banks, accountants, and legal practices and with input from the Treasury and other departments. Each sale was supposed to lead to greater expertise, but as new teams worked on each privatization, there was an inevitable loss of knowledge when they disbanded. This led to a reinventing of the wheel every time for every privatization. This was so, even though some officials worked as members of more than one privatization team and despite Treasury oversight, the publication of guidance to departments, and resort to advice from what often were involved merchant banks and other city firms. A small number of city firms engaged repeatedly in privatization and developed their expertise but only after "many mistakes" were made, though to whose benefit the expertise was applied is open to question.[90]

Partnerships under John Major

Thatcher was compelled to leave office in 1990. While the conflicts over joining a single European currency, and the poll tax, precipitated her departure, there was a far longer list of accumulated discontents. Her privatization efforts included sale of over a million council-owned houses that in turn stoked continuous sharp rises in housing prices (with a brief interruption when the bubble burst in 2009). State subsidy of public housing continued to drop. From 1980 to 1984, sale of council houses actually "raised more money than the rest of the privatization program put together."[91] Unemployment shot up and poverty rates spiked from 13.4 percent in 1979 to 22.2 percent by the time she left office in 1990.[92]

In 1992 successor John Major was in search of a new means to enhance the private sector's role in the public sector. The introduction of the PFI in November 1992 followed the Maastricht Treaty earlier that year, which set public sector borrowing requirements for EU member countries. One treaty obligation was to keep "sound fiscal policies, with debt limited to 60 [percent] of GDP and annual deficits no greater than 3 [percent] of GDP."[93] Mark Hellowell affirms that resort to PFIs enabled Britain to bypass the Public Sector Borrowing Requirement "to provide the impression of prudent fiscal management."[94] The design of the contractual agreements to build roads, prisons, and hospitals meant that public sector payments to the private sector did not have immediate budgetary impact. The Conservative government's projections at the time anticipated a drop in public sector net investment from 1.6 percent of GDP to 0.75 percent of GDP by 2001.

The Major administration influenced the rival party to redefine itself as "New Labour" to regain power. The Labour Party staked out its ground on PFIs by raising the ante. In 1994 Labor Party leaders, like Bill Clinton's "New Democrats," set out to improve the party's relationship with elements historically hostile to Labour, "notably the financial institutions of the city of London and its advisers."[95] Labor Party leaders produced a critique of the Conservatives' PFI strategy, making "extensive use of the private sector's own reports." Management consultants, Ernst and Young and the Royal Bank of Scotland had "criticized the government's unwillingness to intervene in PFI to ensure its implementation (the Conservatives had preferred a 'hands-off' approach, consistent with their view that investment decisions ought to be made by the market and not by the government)."[96] Apparently, the Tories were taking market ideology far too seriously for market remedies to succeed. New Labour promised to be much less rigid about it. Just as Labour was on the brink of a landslide in June 1997, Labour leaders tied their own hands by announcing the Party would neither oppose PFIs nor raise income taxes nor exceed the borrowing rates under the Tories.[97]

New Labour reinterpreted the private finance of infrastructure in crimped Keynesian terms as a means to "put people back to work." Labour deemed as a fiscal virtue PFI's ability to "facilitate additional (rather than substitutional) public investment" through an "ability to hide expenditure from calculations of the U.K.'s national debt."[98] When the Conservatives announced in 1995, during John Major's administration, "a relaunch of the PFI with a [£9.4 billion] list of 'priority' projects," this news was recognized as a "tacit admission that PFI could not progress in the absence of government stewardship." Between 1990 and 1995, only three large contracts had been signed. The consequences of the capital works acquired political visibility as in the first PFI-funded public infrastructure in Skye, where the public paid £93 million for a £15 million bridge.[99] Between 1995 and the election in May 1997, twenty-four major deals would be signed amounting to £2 billion.[100] Purportedly, 1995 marked the breakthrough for PFI as "an effective financing mechanism," which Labour, too, embraced. "The public interest," as incoming Labour Party Chancellor of Exchequer Gordon Brown stated in 1997, "can be pursued either through government setting standards for the private sector or by the public sector working with the private sector to meet objectives."[101] Of course it could, but would public sector oversight by the Labour administration of Tony Blair have any teeth?

Government Stewardship of PFIs

When Tony Blair became Labour Party leader in 1994, he and his allies persuaded the Party to drop its nominal commitment to sweeping public ownership.[102] The 1997 Labour landslide still stirred hopes that Labour would "revive the social democratic agenda, both in terms of enhancing competitiveness and reconnecting politics with the interests and collective aspirations that were marginalized under Thatcher and Major."[103] Blair instead committed his image-conscious "Cool Britannia" government to privatization and reaffirmed PFIs as a "way of raising funds for public investment while keeping such borrowing off the government's balance sheet."[104] Labour more than doubled PFI deals—closing on twenty-eight worth about £2.3 billion in its first year and in its second year fifty-nine more for £2.4 billion.[105] Though Labour in opposition denounced PFI as "creeping privatization," Blair's government turned around to champion it as offering "value for the money." (A 2001 Labour Commission rejected the argument that PFIs enabled the government to undertake more projects because government money obviously underwrote such projects.) A review commissioned by Labour Trade Secretary John Hutton found no convincing evidence that private contracts were more economical or effective, but still concluded strongly in their favor.[106]

The promise was that "capital will be safe with Labour," Polly Toynbee and David Walker note. "Profits beckoned, as the state divested itself of air-traffic control and defense research, pushed contracting in health and IT, guaranteed returns for the companies owning water, nuclear and train companies and (though this changed later) soft-pedaled on competition inquiries in defense, communications and energy."[107] By his second term (June 2001–May 2005), Blair nevertheless declared PFI the key to "delivering modern, high quality public services and promoting U.K.'s competitiveness."[108] Because Labor's central criticism of the Conservatives' use of PFIs was its lack of "government stewardship" of projects, it is important to examine what institutional capacity Blair's government brought to bear. A PFI taskforce was created within Treasury to roll out PFIs with a "policy arm staffed by civil servants and a project arm staffed by private sector practitioners. This latter component of the taskforce was in 1999 reconstituted as a limited company, Partnership U.K. (PUK)." In 2000, "51 percent of the firm was sold to a selection of private companies—all of them large players in the PFI program." This company transformed into a "joint venture whose majority owners were financiers and active players in the PFI industry. PUK derives much of its income from fees, paid by public authorities, for delivery of projects."[109] The staff were drafted from financial institutions and management consultancies. While in theory PUK's role was implementation, not policy, in practice the line blurred. Labour softened the U.K.'s borrowing constraint since "the effect of using the PFI is to alter the timing of the debt principal and interest payments associated with the borrowing, not their magnitude."[110] In other words, the Labour government went easy on private actors. Chancellor Brown ordered that public authorities, such as the local councils and the National Health Service, build only under the PFI, and bidding standards were relaxed so that the lowest bidder need not win.[111] In a 1998 spending review, Brown said he expected that P3s would eliminate the need for public subsidies of these ventures by 2001, which was a grave miscalculation of eventual costs.[112]

The Treasury estimated the lifetime burden of Labour deals at £215 billion, for assets with a collective capital value of £55 billion to £65 billion.[113] The Labour "government's inability to understand the private companies' small print and fee structure, was to bequeath a legacy of financial poison for the Health Trusts that had been induced to enter into them," Peter Sinclair summarizes. "In the details, Blair's administration was blind and incompetent."[114] Expertise with skills to spot these badly structured small print deals is not difficult to acquire either by in-house encouragement or by consultancy hires, so why did this not occur beforehand? By 2003, as PFI shortcomings mounted and the details of many bad deals came to light, Chancellor Brown backtracked, at least verbally, admitting, "We risk giving the impression that the only kind of reform that is valuable is a form of privatization."[115] Yet the deals kept getting made right up to the 2007–8 financial crisis, because of evident institutional and ideological inertia.

Since the early 1990s, British governments negotiated half a billion pounds in PFI deals, with £154 million in the pipeline to 2020.[116] Publicly subsidized private companies built nearly all new British public infrastructure—roads, ports, bridges, tunnels, water treatment, airport, transit, school facilities, hospitals, and prisons.[117] The state, or else the consumers whose taxes subsidized them, increasingly became the renter of these assets under inflexible long-term contracts.[118] By March 2013 more than seven hundred PFI projects were operating, with a private sector investment value of £83.5 billion.[119]

The proliferation of quangos did come under fire, and ironically under the imposition of austerity, but reform measures scarcely touched quangos engaged in P3s. In 2010 some 902 bodies were reviewed, which led to proposals to abolish 202 bodies, merge 156, and reform 177.[120] The Public Bodies Bill, affirming these measures, became law in December 2011 but had no discernible impact on the privatization drive.[121] The mandate of a quango may be as narrow as a single task, or it can be involved in a variety of quasi-legislative and quasi-judicial functions within a specific policy domain. These organizations are not legally a part of government, "nonetheless they are publicly funded through budgetary allocations, taxes or fees." This form of delegation, notes Christopher Hood, was extremely popular in the U.S defense sector "as a device for administrative outflanking operations (that is the bypassing of congressional and to some extent, judicial scrutiny, civil service salary regulations and corrupt or inefficient state and municipal governments)."[122]

A Conservative–Liberal Democrat coalition eked into power in the United Kingdom in 2010. By this time the PFIs were receiving critical scrutiny in the media and in public debate, partly because private firms were not taking up government bids and banks were not lending.

In April 2011 the National Audit Office under coalition government of Conservative Party prime minister Cameron "issued the strongest health warning to date over use of PFI deals to build new schools and hospitals, saying the government should urgently find alternative ways to invest in major infrastructure projects after some costs spiraled out of control."[123] The report stated that PFIs have "become increasingly expensive since the credit crisis," and the government should consider slowing down the number of deals it enters into. Given reports since the financial collapse of 2007–8 of "excess" investible capital readily available, with few outlets except speculative ones, governments ought to be in an excellent bargaining position—private investors need investment outlets as much or more than the state needs them—which makes the state's concessionary bargaining all the more mystifying.[124]

On Comparisons

Back in the United States, Steven Erie, Vladimir Kogan, and Scott MacKenzie reject the argument that P3 "efficiency" can be determined by considering what local government would spend if it "constructed the project in house" and they do so on the grounds that large-scale projects "cannot be undertaken with local government resources alone." They suggest instead measuring the contributions of public and private actors against public benefits.[125] What are the foregone benefits of using land, labor, and capital by P3s? Flyvbjerg, however, points out that if one starts with key characteristics of projects, they are not unique at all. Identify the reference class of past similar projects and look at measures of their performance. In a recent analysis of U.S. states pushing P3 enabling legislation, the authors found that "appropriate institutional frameworks are necessary for PPP success," but that is easier said than done (which is another lesson from the British case). Erie and coauthors depict San Diego's redevelopment P3 as a "story of failed delegation, not municipal leadership."[126] Private developers captured most benefits, while cost overruns were borne by the public. The city shouldered risks in up-front costs through land procurement and financing. Project monitoring was assigned to a redevelopment agency whose mission was depicted as "developer friendly." Further oversight was allotted to an executive from a private development company, which only served to limit the role of the mayor and city council. The city possessed real leverage that it was unwilling to exercise for concern about being blamed for "wreaking havoc downtown." A succeeding mayor, to save the failing project, provided alternative financing derived from hotel tax revenues "earmarked for civic and cultural purposes."[127] Every detail here echoes British experiences.

Privatized British Energy had to be restored, expensively, into public keeping. The collapse of Metronet, a private player in running London's Underground, cost the public purse several hundred million pounds.[128] Regarding the financialization that Rachel Weber, Amanda Kass, and Sara Hinkley explore elsewhere in the volume, British PFIs generated a lucrative secondary market. Refinancing enabled the shareholders of Octagon, a private hospitals investor consortium, to increase share value from 15 percent to

60 percent almost overnight.[129] The NHS Trust garnered less than a third of £115 million in gains from refinancing. Heavily subsidized train routes resulted in steadily hiked fares over inflation in the most expensive public transport network in the world. In the NHS the good news is that so-called Independent Sector Treatment Centres, which provide standard surgeries for knees, hips, and cataracts, relieved pressure on wait times, but operations cost 11 percent more than NHS ones did. Monbiot cites cases where authorities in the health and education sectors were encouraged by central government to undertake public projects "which would make money for private companies, rather than proposing one which would better meet the needs of people."[130] "Our analysis of these data for one group of schools shows that PF2 [PFI upgrade in 2012] costs are around forty per cent higher than the costs of a project financed by government borrowing," wrote the U.K. National Audit Office analysts in 2018.[131] "The Treasury Committee undertook a similar analysis in 2011, which estimated the cost of a privately financed hospital to be 70% higher" than public–private partnerships. The government went on regardless for its own reasons.

Concepts such as the "entrepreneurial city" characterize a moment when the capacity of the state to solve the problems of local governments is dismissed.[132] Current trends can be "rebalanced" in the other direction. The pendulum can swing again, if not all the way. In developmental economics, even at its most statist, Michael Lind explains, the government is not the enemy of the private economy but its sponsor and partner, rather than an easy mark.[133] The polity is the proper unit of analysis, and should treat "the private and public sectors as collaborators in a single national project of maximizing the military security and well-being of the community by means of technological modernization," for which purpose the "market is good to the extent that it helps necessary industries."[134]

Creative partnerships have been sought among various levels of the state, business, and labor, though not always including all.[135] If we focus on expenditures alone, we miss the changeable roles of these actors. The ensuing typology encompasses forces engaged in changing public–private relations: (1) an interventionist strategy is when government attempts to correct market failures; (2) a competitive strategy is when P3s are competing with public provision of goods and services; and (3) a negotiated strategy occurs when public resistance to and expert dissent about the terms of major projects are resolved as part of a new understanding of public–private interactions. The U.S. state actually has an exemplary record of infrastructure construction. Shonfield's work reminds us that we take for granted the delegation of authority to the private sector to build infrastructure while neglecting to ask why we are not restoring (after decades of upper-level tax cuts) taxation on those who formerly were tapped to fund it. Most of the P3s examined here were instances of partial government disengagement, where they "pay for but do not operate services, own but do not manage productive assets, or sell off some ownership but retain a controlling interest."[136] To characterize this phenomenon as a contraction of the state overlooks the increased public spending that a shift to private production entails. While the reduction in the state role in the economy was the overt motivation during the Thatcher and Major years, "there was less progress in permanently reducing state spending and taxation." The size of government did not shrink. In 1980 government expenditure accounted for 43 percent of GDP. It fell marginally during the 1980s to 42 percent by 1990, but then rose to 45 percent by 2005.[137] That a political project, such as privatization, may persist that had little to do with proclaimed efficiency aims is another lesson we can draw from Britain.

Changing Relations of Public and Private

Shonfield's work provides a template by which to measure shifts between public and private power. In what forms do the power of the state and of private actors best combine in the interest of the society they operate in? How do we engage in economic activities that benefit citizens and also satisfy private investors? A multitude of public authorities—quasi-public agencies—have been created with independent administrative, financial, and legal authority operating at arm's length from citizen input and from the governments that create them.[138]

What would Shonfield say about the contemporary use of public authorities? These quasi-public entities are beholden to bondholders who seek surefire revenue streams.[139] They do so when the state bargainers opposite them are forced to face a Hobson's choice: "This or nothing." There is no alternative, as Margaret Thatcher told the British people. Many believed it, if only as a short-term reality to be made the best of. The results in the British case are not appealing ones when "health and school authorities are prisoners of bad contract drafting and extraordinary naiveté on the part of Blair's ministers, civil servants and/or advisors."[140] One "consequence is that some older hospitals, not encumbered with PFI obligations, and in a stronger financial position, were threatened with closure to stem the losses of PFI hospitals."[141] In 1997 Labour Health Secretary Alan Milburn ruled that in (self-imposed) straitened economic conditions, it was "PFI or bust."[142] Here we are, as Orwell put it, "inside the whale."[143]

What is outside? The disparaged choice, until recently, is revival of preponderantly public projects. Shonfield explained national patterns of policy in terms of domestic institutions that specify useful rules of interaction. He evaluated the extent to which domestic arrangements help or hinder the state, and subnational actors, in achieving economic goals. Measuring state privatization in terms of spending is insufficient because it fails to take account of externalities and how the balance of power between public and private is recast. Privatization does not assure expenditure reduction, but is synonymous with a transformation of the state. Public sector service cutbacks under imposed austerity result in a deterioration in quality. Limits on access and degraded quality diminish political support for services, thereby creating an environment in which more reductions are likely. What else is there?

Two interweaved visions of relations between government and business emerged from the New Deal: one emphasized collaboration to achieve common ends; the other underscored public supervision of private enterprise. The Public Works Administration, Gail Radford notes, "functioned to channel state and local economic activism into the public authority model as we have come to know it, not to develop alternate visions." She attributes this choice to fiscal conservatives who were "attracted by the prospect of reducing unemployment and building needed infrastructure without fully paying the cost through direct federal outlays."[144] Two success stories of public ownership are Detroit's power generation plant and Cleveland's Municipal Light.

Radford poses these as "counterexamples to the common refrain that only by taking such functions out of the control of politicians, and plac[ing] them in institutions insulated from the electorate, can goods and services be provided efficiently."[145]

This does not mean one rotely follows 1930s programs and procedures, which were trimmed back at the time to serve racist ends and regional power circles. The Green New Deal that has hit headlines of late is an upsurge of environmentally sensitive and popularly attuned programs for a fourth or fifth (depending on who's counting) industrial revolution.[146] Proponents do tend to see relationships between public and private sectors as needing to return to the balance at play during the FDR era in order for the ambitious programmatic vision to go into action.[147] Quite likely the turning point will require another financial crash, to chasten major private actors, and a new Democratic administration, unwilling to bail out "too big to fail" firms. Short of that, progress may occur on many hitherto small fronts. The latest is the swelling call for the introduction of free public transport in major cities, with Luxembourg and Estonia actually starting the experiment.[148]

In Britain the Labour Party, despite being defeated in the 2019 election by its own internal Brexit split, maintains its commitment to restoring rather than further cutting taxes on the rich and taking utilities back into public control. Indeed, in the 2017 election, in which it forced a hung Parliament, Labour under then leader Jeremy Corbyn demonstrated that alternatives suddenly can become viable virtually overnight when long-smoldering discontents find political voice.[149] In January 2018 came the collapse of the huge U.K. firm Carillion—a major PFI participant—with pension liabilities of nearly £1 billion and owing £2 billion to subcontractors. The state will take on the pension liabilities, while most subcontractors are excluded. Not a single official bothered to meet with Carillion, or its subsidiaries, in the year running up to its sudden collapse, despite awarding it four major contracts worth £1.5 billion.[150] Labour, to wide approval, vowed to end these private schemes. Finally, under immense pressure, on October 28, 2018, Conservative Party chancellor Philip Hammond abolished PFIs altogether.[151]

In a poll of the U.S. Conference of Mayors, "respondents overwhelmingly endorsed spending as an important priority for all levels of government. 'Fixing infrastructure, including roads, bridges, water and sewage systems' should be a high priority for a city mayor, 65 percent said."[152] Still, in states headed by Republican administrations, there is well-placed ideological opposition to federal spending on infrastructure.[153] "What is needed," Mazzucato argues in her defense of the mixed economy, "is a functional risk-reward dynamic that replaces the dysfunctional 'socialized risk' and 'privatized rewards' characterizing the current economic crisis and evidenced in modern industry as well as finance."[154] We were unlikely to come up with such a scheme in the Trump years, when the president's infrastructure "plan" was a doubling down on all the worst aspects of recent experiences, but it is worth bearing in mind.[155]

Notes

1. Andrew Shonfield, *Modern Capitalism: The Changing Balance of Public and Private Power* (New York: Oxford University Press, 1965), 3.

2. Daniel Bell, *The End of Ideology* (Glencoe, Ill.: Free Press, 1960); John Kenneth Galbraith, *The Affluent Society* (New York: Houghton Mifflin Harcourt, 1958); C. A. R. Crosland, *The Future of Socialism* (London: Macmillan, 1956); Ralf Dahrendorf, *Class and Class Conflict in Industrial Society* (Stanford, Calif.: Stanford University Press, 1959).

3. Robert Pollin, *Contours of Descent* (London: Verso, 2003), 22–24.

4. Mark Blyth, *Austerity: The History of a Dangerous Idea* (New York: Oxford University Press, 2015); John Stephens, "Revisiting Pierson's Work on the Politics of Welfare State Reform in the Era of Retrenchment Twenty Years Later," *PS: Political Science & Politics* 48, no. 2 (2015): 274–78.

5. Nicole Hemmer, *Messengers of the Right* (Philadelphia: University of Pennsylvania Press, 2016); Donald T. Critchlow, *The Conservative Ascendency* (Cambridge: Harvard University Press, 2007); Timothy P. R. Weaver, "By Design or by Default: Varieties of Neoliberal Urban Development," *Urban Affairs Review* 54, no. 2 (March 2018).

6. Peter Katzenstein, *Small States in World Markets* (Ithaca: Cornell University Press, 1985); Dietrich Rueschemeyer, Evelyn Huber, and John D. Stephens, *Capitalist Development and Democracy* (Chicago: University of Chicago Press, 1992); Peter Hall and David Soskice, eds., *Varieties of Capitalism* (New York: Oxford University Press, 2001); Mark Blyth, *Great Transformations* (New York: Cambridge University Press, 2002); John Myles and Jill Quadagno, "Political Theories of the Welfare State," *Social Service Review* 76, no. 1 (March 2002): 34–57.

7. James R. Kurth, "A History of Inherent Contradictions: The Origins and End of American Conservatism," in *American Conservatism*, ed. Sanford Levinson, Melissa S. Williams, and Joel Parker (New York: New York University Press, 2016), 53.

8. For a critique of PFI, see House of Commons Treasury Committee, "Private Finance Initiative" (July 2011), https://publications.parliament.uk/pa/cm201012/cmselect/cmtreasy/1146/1146.pdf.

9. H. M. Treasury, National Audit Office, "PFI and PF2" (January 2018), https://bit.ly/2DoSA5c; Organization for Economic Co-operation and Development, "Review of Public Governance of Public-Private Partnerships in the United Kingdom" (December 2015), https://bit.ly/2IkIwwv.

10. Mike Raco, *State-Led Privatization and the Demise of the Democratic State* (Burlington, Vt.: Ashgate, 2013), 67.

11. George Inderst, "Pension Fund Investment in Infrastructure," *OECD Working Papers on Insurance and Private Pensions*, no. 32 (2009): 5, www.oecd.org/finance/private-pensions/42052208.pdf, cited in Raco, *State-Led Privatization*, 67.

12. "I don't want to abolish government. I just want to reduce it to the size where I can drag it into the bathroom and drown it in the bathtub." Mara Liasson, "Conservative Advocate," National Public Radio, *Morning Edition*, May 25, 2001.

13. Paul Starr, "The New Life of the Liberal State: Privatization and the Restructuring of State-Society Relations," in *Public Enterprise and Privatization*, ed. John Waterbury and Ezra Suleiman (Boulder, Colo.: Westview, 1990), 22.

14. Philip Cerny, "Paradoxes of the Competition State: The Dynamics of Political Globalization," *Government and Opposition* 32, no. 2 (April 1997): 251–74.

15. Peter Gourevitch, *Politics in Hard Times* (Ithaca: Cornell University Press, 1986).

16. Jamie Peck, *Workfare States* (New York: Guilford, 2001); Martin Carnoy and Manuel Castells, "Globalization, the Knowledge Society and the Network State," *Global Networks* 1, no. 1 (January 2001): 1–18; Neil Brenner, *New State Spaces* (New York: Oxford University Press, 2004).

17. Suzanne Mettler, *The Submerged State* (Chicago: University of Chicago Press, 2011); Matthew Flinders, *Delegated Governance and the British State* (Oxford: Oxford University Press, 2008); Kimberly Morgan and Andrea Louise Campbell, *The Delegated Welfare State* (New York: Oxford University Press, 2011).

18. Michael Meecher, "If You Think Privatisation and Outsourcing Are Sacred, Read This," *The Guardian*, June 24, 2013. Also see Colin Samson, "The Three Faces of Privatisation," *Sociology* 28, no. 1 (February 1994): 79–97.

19. Michael Parkinson, Bernard Foley, and Dennis Judd, eds., *Regenerating the Cities* (Manchester: Manchester University Press, 1988); Paul Pierson, *Dismantling the Welfare State* (New York: Cambridge University Press, 1995); Mark Mowbray, "What Became of the Local State? Neo-liberalism, Community Development, and Local Government," *Community Development Journal* 46, no. 1 (January 2010): 132–53.

20. Desmond King, "Political Centralization and State Interests in Britain," *Comparative Political Studies* 21, no. 4 (January 1989): 467–94.

21. Peter Eisinger, "City Politics in an Era of Federal Devolution," *Urban Affairs Review* 33, no. 3 (January 1998): 310–11; Demetrios Caraley, "Washington Abandons the Cities," *Political Science Quarterly* 107, no. 1 (Spring 1992): 1–30.

22. See for example, David Stockman, *The Triumph of Politics: Why the Reagan Revolution Failed* (New York: Harper & Row, 1986).

23. Starr, "New Life of the Liberal State," 28.

24. Starr, 28.

25. Dennis R. Judd and James M. Smith, "The New Ecology of Urban Governance: Special Purpose Authorities and Urban Development," in *Governing Cities in Global Era*, ed. Robin Hambleton and Jill Gross (Hampshire, U.K.: Palgrave Macmillan, 2007).

26. Mariana Mazzucato, *The Entrepreneurial State* (London: Anthem Press, 2013), 5.

27. Elisabeth S. Clemens, "Lineages of the Rube Goldberg State: Building and Blurring Public Programs, 1900–1940," in *Rethinking Political Institutions*, ed. Ian Shapiro, Stephen Skowronek, and Daniel Galvin (New York: New York University Press, 2006), 380.

28. Mazzucato, *Entrepreneurial State*, 193.

29. Mazzucato, 193.

30. B. Guy Peters, "With a Little Help from Our Friends," in *Partnerships in Urban Governance: European and American Experience*, ed. Jon Pierre (New York: St. Martins Press, 1998), 11; Patrick Sabol and Robert Puentes, "Private Capital, Public Good: Drivers of Successful Infrastructure Public–Private Partnerships" (Washington, D.C.: Brookings Institution, 2014).

31. Sobel and Puentes, "Private Capital, Public Good," 3.

32. H. M. Treasury, "A New Approach to Public-Private Partnerships" (December 2012), quoted in Sobel and Puentes, "Private Capital, Public Good," 3.

33. Treasury, 4.

34. Federal Accounting Standards Advisory Board, "Public Private Partnerships" (2016), www.fasab.gov/public-private-partnerships.

35. Katja Funk, Tim Irwin, and Isabel Rial, "Budgeting and Reporting for Public-Private Partnerships," International Transport Forum, OECD, Discussion Paper (2013), https://bit.ly/2wmbUhk.

36. Caitlin MacLean and Dale Bonner, "Public-Private Infrastructure Financing Solutions" (Santa Monica, Calif.: Milken Institute, November 2014).

37. New York, Office of the State Comptroller, "Controlling Risks Without Gimmicks" (January 2011), https://bit.ly/2jxsvFx; and New York, Office of the State Comptroller, "Private Financing of Public Infrastructure: Risks and Options for New York State" (June 2013), https://bit.ly/2rmvzsf.

38. Virginia, Office of the Secretary of Transportation, "Virginia's Public-Private Partnership Program" (Summer 2008), https://bit.ly/2rq7JLt.

39. Paul Starr, "The Meaning of Privatization," Yale Law and Policy Review 6 (1988): 6–41.

40. Eric Shaw, "The British Labour Government and the Private Finance Initiative in the National Health Service," Innovation Journal: The Public Sector Innovation Journal 8, no. 3 (2003): 2–21.

41. Dexter Whitfield, "Private Finance Initiative and Public-Private Partnerships" (Tralee, Ireland: European Services Strategy Unit, 2001).

42. Peters, "With a Little Help," 11.

43. George Tsebelis, Veto Players (New York: Russell Sage Foundation, 2002).

44. Peters, "With a Little Help," 18.

45. Peters, 19.

46. Alan S. Altshuler, ed., Governance and Opportunity in Metropolitan America (Washington, D.C.: National Academy Press, 1999).

47. Peters, "With a Little Help," 19; Matthew Flinders, "The Politics of Public-Private Partnerships," British Journal of Politics and International Relations 7, no. 2 (May 2005): 215–39.

48. Alan Harding, "Public-Private Partnerships in the U.K.," in Partnerships in Urban Governance: European and American Experiences, ed. Jon Pierre (London: Palgrave Macmillan, 1998), 72.

49. Suzanne Kapner, "British Reopening the Debate over Privatization," New York Times, August 29, 2002; and Richard Wachmann and Tim Webb, "Have We Reached the End of the Line for Privatisation?" The Guardian, July 5, 2009.

50. Richard Alleyne, "Blair Defends PFI as NHS Trust Face Bankruptcy," The Telegraph, June 26, 2012.

51. International Monetary Fund, Fiscal Affairs Department, "Public-Private Partnerships" (March 2004), 5, https://bit.ly/2wfbIjD.

52. Rajiv Prabhakar, "New Labour and the Reform of Public Services," in Governing as New Labour, ed. Steve Ludlam and Martin J. Smith (London: Palgrave Macmillan, 2004), 175.

53. International Monetary Fund, Fiscal Affairs Department, "Public-Private Partnerships," 22–26.

54. Bent Flyvbjerg, "What You Should Know about Megaprojects and

Why: An Overview," *Project Management Journal* 45, no. 2 (April/May 2014): 6–19.

55. McKinsey Global Institute, "Infrastructure Productivity: How to Save $1 Trillion a Year" (McKinsey and Company, January 2013), quoted in Flyvbjerg, "What You Should Know."

56. "The Cracks Are Showing: Infrastructure," *Economist*, June 26, 2008, cited in Flyvbjerg, "What You Should Know."

57. G. A. Hodge, C. Greve, and A. E. Boardman, introduction to *International Handbook on Public-Private Partnerships*, ed. Graeme A. Hodge, Carsten Greve, and Anthony E. Boardman (Cheltenham, U.K.: Edward Elgar, 2012), 3.

58. Eduardo Engel, Ronald Fischer, and Alexander Galetovic, "Public-Private Partnerships to Revamp U.S. Infrastructure" (Washington, D.C.: The Brookings Institution, February 25, 2011), 5, www.brookings.edu/wp-content/uploads/2016/07/02_partnerships_engel_fischer_galetovic_paper.pdf.

59. Engel, Fischer, and Galetovic, 9.

60. American Society of Civil Engineers, "2013 Report Card for America's Infrastructure" (2013), https://bit.ly/1k1cHTQ.

61. Engel, Fischer, and Galetovic, "Public-Private Partnerships," 30.

62. See Myles and Quadagno, "Political Theories of the Welfare State."

63. Andrew Gamble, "Privatization, Thatcherism and the British State," *Journal of Law and Society* 16, no. 1 (1988): 1–20.

64. See David Edgerton, *Warfare State: Britain 1920–1970* (Cambridge: Cambridge University Press, 2005).

65. Edgerton, 2.

66. Edgerton, 2.

67. Hugo Young, *The Iron Lady* (New York: Macmillan, 1989), 130.

68. Earl A. Reitan, *The Thatcher Revolution* (Lanham, Md.: Rowman and Littlefield, 2002), 11.

69. David Edgerton, *The Rise and Fall of the British Nation* (London: Allen Lane, 2018), 581n27.

70. Leo Panitch and Colin Leys, *The End of Parliamentary Socialism* (London: Verso, 1997), 130.

71. Charles Moore, *Margaret Thatcher* (New York: Knopf, 2013), 11.

72. Moore, *Margaret Thatcher*, 11.

73. George Monbiot, *Captive State* (London: Pan, 2001), 62–63.

74. Gamble, "Privatization, Thatcherism and the British State."

75. David Parker, *The Official History of Privatization: Vol. II* (London: Routledge, 2012), 1; Alistair Osborne, "Margaret Thatcher: One Policy That Led to More than 50 Companies Being Sold or Privatized," *The Telegraph*, April 8, 2013.

76. Parker, *Official History of Privatization*, 3.

77. Parker, 23.

78. Young, *The Iron Lady*, 537.

79. Young, 537.

80. Daniel A. Yergin and Joseph Stanislaw, *Commanding Heights* (New York: Touchstone, 1998), 144.

81. Herbert Morrison, quoted in John Vikers and George Yarrow, *Privatization: An Economic Analysis* (Cambridge, Mass.: MIT Press, 1988), 127. For public corporations in the United States, see Christopher Decker, *Modern Economic Regulation* (Cambridge, U.K.: Cambridge University Press), 45.

82. Deborah Phillips and Gary Whannel, *The Trojan Horse* (London: Bloomsbury Academic, 2013), 881; William Ryrie, *Report of the National Economic Development Council Working Party on Nationalized Industry Investment* (London: H. M. Treasury, 1981).

83. Frederik D. Pretorius, Berry-Fong Chung-Hsu, Paul Lejot, and Douglas Arner, *Project Finance for Construction and Infrastructure* (London: Wiley-Blackwell, 2008).

84. John Westergaard and Henrietta Resler, *Class in a Capitalist Society* (London: Heinemann, 1975).

85. Pretorius, Chung-Hsu, Lejot, and Arner, *Project Finance*.

86. David Miller and William Dinan, "The Rise of the PR Industry in Britain, 1979–98," *European Journal of Communication* 15, no. 1 (2000): 5–35.

87. Organization for Economic Co-operation and Development, *Infrastructure to 2030* (Paris: OECD Publishing, 2007).

88. Antonino Palumbo, "From Thatcherism to Blairism," *Osterre* 4 (2004): 14.

89. Palumbo, 14.

90. Parker, *Official History of Privatization*, 6.

91. Richard Vinen, *Thatcher's Britain* (New York: Simon and Schuster, 2010).

92. Simon Rogers, "How Britain Changed under Margaret Thatcher," *The Guardian*, April 8, 2003.

93. Mark Hellowell, "The U.K.'s Private Finance Initiative: History, Evaluation, Prospects," in *International Handbook on Public-Private Partnerships*, ed. Graeme A. Hodge, Carsten Greve, and Anthony E. Boardman (Cheltenham, U.K.: Edward Elgar, 2012), 308.

94. Hellowell, 308.

95. Hellowell, 308.

96. Hellowell, 308.

97. Robert Peston, *Brown's Britain* (London: Short Books, 2005), 164.

98. Hellowell, "U.K.'s Private Finance Initiative," 309.

99. George Monbiot, "A Scandal of Secrecy and Collusion," *The Guardian*, December 28, 2004.

100. Hellowell, "U.K.'s Private Finance Initiative," 309.

101. Peston, *Brown's Britain*, 164.

102. Peston, 146.

103. Martin Rhodes, "Desperately Seeking a Solution: Social Democracy, Thatcherism and the 'Third Way' in British Welfare," in *Recasting European Welfare States*, ed. Maurizio Ferrera and Martin Rhodes (New York: Routledge, 2000), 161–86.

104. Bob Jessop, "New Labour or the Normalization of Neo-Liberalism," *British Politics* 2, no. 3 (2007): 282–88.

105. Hellowell, "U.K.'s Private Finance Initiative," 310.

106. Polly Toynbee and David Walker, *The Verdict* (London: Granta, 2010), 267–68.

107. Toynbee and Walker, 71–72.

108. H. M. Treasury, "Public-Private Partnerships: The Government's Approach," quoted in Shaw, "British Labour Government," 3.

109. Hellowell, "U.K.'s Private Finance Initiative," 311.

110. Hellowell, 210.

111. Toynbee and Walker, *Verdict*, 268.

112. Toynbee and Walker, 268.

113. Toynbee and Walker, 268.

114. Peter Sinclair, "The Treasury and Economic Policy," in *Blair's Britain*, ed. Anthony Seldon (Cambridge: Cambridge University Press, 2007), 212.

115. Peston, *Brown's Britain*, 336.

116. H. M. Treasury, "Private Finance 2," (2014), https://bit.ly/1quLwXy.

117. H. M. Treasury, "Private Finance 2."

118. Ben Joravsky and Mick Dumke, "Fail, Part One: Chicago's Parking Meter Lease Deal," *Chicago Reader*, April 9, 2009; "Fail, Part Two: One Billion Dollars!" *Chicago Reader*, May 21, 2009; and "Fail, Part Three: The Insiders," *Chicago Reader*, June 18, 2009.

119. H. M. Treasury, "Private Finance 2."

120. Cabinet Office (U.K.), *Public Bodies Reform—A Proposal for Change* (London: H. M. Government, 2011).

121. Nigel Hawkes, "Body Politic: This Is No Way to Cull the Quangos," *British Medical Journal* 341, no. 7777 (2010): 341.

122. Christopher Hood, "A Public Management for All Seasons?" *Public Administration* 69, no. 1 (1991): 3–19.

123. Polly Curtis, "PFI Projects Not the Best Value for the Money Says Watchdog," *The Guardian*, April 27, 2011.

124. Adam Davidson, "Why Are Corporations Hoarding Trillions?" *New York Times Magazine*, January 20, 2016; Robert Picard, "Too Much Cash Becomes Serious Business Problem," *Forbes*, August 8, 2011; George Magnus, "Why Are Corporations Sitting on So Much Cash?" *Prospect Magazine*, May 24, 2016.

125. Steven Erie, Vladimir Kogan, and Scott MacKenzie, "Redevelopment, San Diego Style," *Urban Affairs Review* 45, no. 5 (2010): 644.

126. Erie, Kogan, and MacKenzie, 658.

127. Erie, Kogan, and MacKenzie, 658.

128. Toynbee and Walker, *Verdict*, 56.

129. Toynbee and Walker, 56.

130. George Monbiot, "Could This Be Labour's Poll Tax?" *The Guardian*, October 1, 2001.

131. "PFI and PF2s," HC 718, Sessions 2017–2019, National Audit Office, H. M. Treasury (January 18, 2018), 15.

132. Tim Chapin, "Beyond the Entrepreneurial City," *Journal of Urban Affairs* 24, no. 5 (Winter 2002): 565–81.

133. Michael Lind, *Land of Promise* (New York: HarperCollins, 2012), 13.

134. Lind, 13.

135. Thomas Frank, *The Wrecking Crew* (New York: Henry Holt, 2008), 361.

136. Frank, 28.

137. Christopher Pierson, *The Modern State* (London: Routledge, 2011).

138. Gail Radford, *The Rise of the Public Authority* (Chicago: University of Chicago Press, 2013), 155–66.

139. Radford, 155–66.

140. Sinclair, "Treasury and Economic Policy," 206.

141. Sinclair, 207.

142. Monbiot, *Captive State*, 63.

143. George Orwell, *Inside the Whale and Other Essays* (London: Gollancz, 1940).

144. Radford, *Rise of Public Authority*, 110.

145. Radford, 160.

146. For some of the earliest inklings, see Christopher Freeman, John Clark, and Luc Soete, *Unemployment and Technical Innovation: A Study of Long Waves and Economic Change* (London: Greenwood, 1982).

147. Thomas L. Freidman, "The Green New Deal Rises Again," *New York Times*, January 8, 2019; and Robinson Meyer, "The Fist Fight over Democrats Climate Green New Deal," *The Atlantic*, January 1, 2019.

148. Andrea Lo, "Luxembourg Makes All Public Transport Free," CNN, January 15, 2019.

149. Richard Seymour, *Corbyn: The Strange Rebirth of Radical Politics* (London: Verso, 2016); and Alex Nunns, *The Candidate: Jeremy Corbyn's Improbable Path to Power* (London: OR Books, 2017).

150. Rob Davies, "Frank Field Demands Answers over Reckless Running of Carillion," *The Guardian*, January 19, 2018.

151. Rob Davies, "Hammond Abolishes PFI Contracts for New Infrastructure Projects," *The Guardian*, October 29, 2018.

152. Kristen Capps, "Poll: Spending on Infrastructure Is a Top Priority for Americans," *The Atlantic*, City Lab, January 21, 2015, 1–4.

153. David A. Graham, "How Mayors Became America's Infrastructure Mavens," *The Atlantic*, March 24, 2015.

154. Mazzucato, *Entrepreneurial State*, 182–83.

155. Alba Alexander and Kurt Jacobsen, "Donald Trump, American Political Economy, and *Terrible Simplificateurs*," in *Trumponomics: Causes and Consequences*, ed. Edward Fullbrook and Jamie Morgan (New York: World Economics Association, 2017).

Part III

The Fiscal Politics of the
New American Local State

7

Financing Urban Infrastructure and Services under the New Normal

A Look at Special Assessments

Shu Wang and Rebecca Hendrick

According to the National League of Cities, financial officers from cities around the United States reported in 2014 that the financial condition of their governments had improved greatly since the Great Recession but had not yet returned to prerecession levels.[1] They also reported being greatly concerned about the fiscal future of their governments. They expected current and impending infrastructure and pension obligations to claim a much greater share of government resources in the near future, due in part to long-term underfunding of these obligations. They also reported being threatened by declining levels of state and federal aid and legal and political constraints in raising taxes, especially property taxes that many local governments rely on heavily. The phrase "new normal" has been used to describe the continued slow growth of the economy since the 2008 recession and the type of economic conditions that all sectors are likely to face for many years.[2]

Not surprisingly, local governments have been turning to nontax and creative sources of revenue to finance operations and capital spending in response to these conditions. For the past two decades, cities have increased fees and charges for services to boost revenues, and they are increasingly looking to the private sector to help them cover the costs of capital projects.[3] Maintaining and increasing capital spending at all levels of government will be essential to reduce the "infrastructure deficit" that exists in this country and raise its cumulative grade-point average for infrastructure above D+.[4] This research contributes to the field of public finance by examining the use and usefulness of special assessments (SAs) for local governments to finance capital and even operational spending. Although SAs will not alleviate the problems of the new normal economy or resolve the infrastructure deficit, we believe that SAs are an underutilized tool in many local governments.

According to common vernacular, SAs are a method of funding improvements to properties and sometimes services that benefit only property owners within a designated area, called a special assessment district (SAD), rather than all property owners or citizens within a jurisdiction. These districts have different names, including community facilities districts (Arizona), assessment districts (California), special service areas (Illinois), special improvement districts (Ohio), and local improvement districts (Washington). All SADs are the creatures of the local government (municipal, township, county, special district) that created them and are not independent special district governments as defined by the U.S. Census Bureau. Although some SADs can have boards appointed by the parent government and a level of fiscal sovereignty, such as the power to change or maintain, or both, an SA levy and issue debt, the parent government still has significant control and oversight of the SADs, and the SADs do not have corporate authority separate from the parent government. Instead, the U.S. Census Bureau considers SADs to be "dependent" or "subordinate" agencies to the parent local government because of their more limited legal authority.[5]

SAs usually take the form of additional property taxes that are added to the general property tax levy or bill on each parcel within the SAD. The additional taxes may be ad valorem or based on the physical characteristics of the parcels and, therefore, non–ad valorem. Oftentimes the SADs are residential, but they can be commercial or industrial. Business improvement districts (BIDs) that are used by many municipalities to finance economic development projects and other services to commercial and industrial areas within their boundaries are often financed with SAs. SAs are a form of land-secured financing and, similar to SADs, have many other names in different states.[6]

From several lines of inquiry that are implicit within questions about the value and appropriateness of SAs, this research will assess whether these tools can be used to a greater degree. For instance, levying taxes according to benefits received is considered to be desirable according to the tenets of public finance. Benefit-based taxes function similarly to prices and allocate public goods and services more efficiently than taxes levied using a different basis.[7] However, not all government goods and services can be provided in this manner. This is especially true for goods and services in which benefits cannot be uniquely assigned to individuals or measured easily. There are also legal barriers to SAs' use and costs. States have different requirements for how SAs are used and created by local governments, requirements that greatly affect the ability of local governments to use these tools and how costly they will be to establish and implement.

To assess whether SAs can be used more by local governments, this research will examine the pros and cons (benefits and costs) of SAs from both a theoretical and practical perspective. Our knowledge of many of the practical costs and benefits of SAs comes from extensive qualitative data from suburban municipalities in the Chicago metropolitan area. In 2015 we interviewed municipal finance officials in twenty-six specifically chosen governments and the executive director of one council of government in the region about governments' use of SAs and officials' opinions about these financing mechanisms. (Many of those interviewed drew from their experiences with SAs in other governments.) We also obtained information about SA use from financial documents from the governments where we interviewed officials and thirteen additional municipal governments in the region that were not interviewed.

Our research will also report on state statutory requirements that affect whether and how SAs are used and their costs in twenty-one states. Although the question of whether governments *should* use these tools is separate from whether governments *can* use them, the first question is irrelevant if the answer to the second is no or only under limited circumstances. The field also has little knowledge about the actual level of SA use by local governments in the

United States. Our information about state statutes on SAs comes from many online sources, including the LexisNexis legal database. Data on actual use of SAs come from the U.S. Census of Governments for 2007 and 2012, data downloaded from state government websites, and multiple data sources in Illinois. We have very extensive data on SA use by Chicago suburban municipal governments from 1988 to 2012, and financial, demographic, and socioeconomic data in a more limited time period (from 1998 to 2012) for the same municipalities. (See Appendixes B and C for details on quantitative and qualitative data and methods.)

Important Characteristics of SAs

As a financing mechanism, SAs follow the benefit principle, which means they are levied according to the benefits received from the goods and services provided by government. In his theory of government finance, James M. Buchanan emphasized the advantages of financing government goods and services based on the benefits received by individuals, instead of based on social or public utility.[8] He argued that, compared to the principle of social utility that is often ill-defined and unstable, the individual and aggregate outcomes of benefit-based financing are closer to what is observed for private goods and services. In the private sector, customers pay for goods and services based on their personal demand and perceived benefits, compared to public goods and services in which the amount taxed and the level provided is determined by the government. Thus, as Buchanan and others have argued, benefit-based financing of government goods and services is desirable because it provides government with signals about citizens' willingness to pay, allows public goods and services to be valued or priced at marginal cost, makes the use of government resources more efficient, and promotes "client-responsive" management by government.[9]

As with private goods and services, benefit-based financing of government goods and services only works when benefits can be clearly established and are not shared with others. In this case, it is the ability to exclude people from benefiting from publicly provided goods and services and to allocate costs according to individual benefit that makes the provision of some goods and services amenable to direct-benefit financing.[10] Direct-benefit financing of public goods and services can take many forms, but the most common is charges for services such as water, sewer, and garbage collection. Although the actual charge may be a flat fee per household rather than a charge that reflects the benefit received (e.g., the amount of garbage collected), it is possible, at least in theory, to identify distinct, nonshared benefits that individual households receive from many services such as clean water, adequate sewers, and timely garbage pickup. These goods and services are more on the private end of the public–private continuum compared to services such as national defense and disease control in which the use of direct-benefit financing is difficult.[11] Direct-benefit financing is especially appropriate for property-based goods and services, including capital improvements to public facilities, in which the value of the improvements is capitalized into property values.

The critical factors that distinguish SADs and SAs from other financing mechanisms are, first, that the benefits financed by the SA can be measured and assigned uniquely to the entities paying the tax; and, second, that the amount levied by the SA to each entity should accurately reflect the benefits received.[12] SAs, in this case, are simply a subset of the entire set of mechanisms that governments can use to finance goods and services that have proprietary and direct benefits. In addition to property values and improvements to property values, SAs can be levied based on property characteristics such as lot size, frontage of the property to the improvement, or proximity of the property to the improvement.[13] They can also be levied based on marginal or average costs similar to charges for services.

Increases in property values due to government goods and services is considered to be an ideal representation of direct benefits of property taxes and a good basis for assigning tax liabilities when the properties are dissimilar.[14] As discussed in the next section, some states specify that SAs must be levied based on the expected increase in market value of properties that benefit from public goods and services. Compared to ongoing services, however, the direct benefits of onetime capital expenditures are probably easier to distinguish and measure and, therefore, more appropriate for benefit-based financing. When the properties within an SAD are similar or when ongoing goods and services are being financed with SAs, direct benefits can be measured with property values. In this case, the additional ad valorem property tax being levied on properties within the SAD could be viewed as a user charge for public goods and services, and the special benefits received by properties within the SAD (and not by others in the jurisdiction) are considered to be borne in proportion to property values.[15]

SAs in municipalities, counties, and even special district governments are different than charges and general taxes in that SAs are not levied on the entire jurisdiction of the parent government. Rather, SAs apply only to a designated geographic area within the jurisdiction. It is also not unusual for local governments to have multiple SADs within their boundaries. Thus, property owners and others within a jurisdiction may be taxed or charged different property tax rates based on the particular benefits they receive from government goods and services that are delivered to their SAD only. Additionally, SAs are often levied for a limited time period to fund specific capital improvements compared to special district governments that levy taxes in perpetuity for goods and services that are provided continuously. There are numerous examples, however, of SADs, such as BIDs, in which taxes or charges are levied every year for ongoing services that are not received by residents or businesses in other parts of the jurisdiction. Thus, whether the taxation is short term or long term is not a good test of whether a financing mechanism is an SA.

When Does Using SAs Make Sense?

As noted previously, use of SAs makes sense for property-based goods and services and capital improvements because the benefits can be assigned more easily to individual properties than to other government goods and services in which the benefits are diffuse and shared by all. Local governments, but especially municipalities, have many property-based services for which it is not practical to apply charges based upon marginal or average costs, either because the government is not able to determine these costs or because what is being delivered cannot be measured in terms of level of usage or consumption. For instance, use or consumption of services such as water and garbage collection can be measured in terms of water delivered or volume of garbage collected. But charging for services such as alley repaving, installation of municipal water services to replace private wells, and maintenance of facilities that provide special benefits to a subset of the population of the jurisdiction (e.g., retention ponds in subdivisions) is more difficult because the costs per property (unit costs) are not clear and are variable in some cases. As a tool for financing public goods and services, however, SAs are very appropriate in these instances because the beneficiaries are relatively distinct and clearly defined geographically.

Some of the officials we interviewed in the Chicago suburban municipalities also believed that it made sense to use SAs to deliver goods and services that are "outside the norm" of what is provided to the general population. Examples of such services that their governments financed with SAs include the maintenance of brick streets in downtown residential neighborhoods, special lighting and infrastructure features in residential or commercial areas, and upgrade of basic infrastructure in neighborhoods not built to municipal standards prior to annexation. Many Chicago suburbs where we interviewed officials or gathered online information about use of "backup" SAs to provide the same services that would be provided by a nonprofit homeowners' and business-owners' association, such as street maintenance, plowing, landscaping, and maintenance of naturalized areas within the boundaries of the development. Such dormant SAs, which are created when land is first developed, have been used by many suburbs in the region and become active only when the association fails. In some cases, we observed that the city and developer agreed to use SAs to have the municipality provide services to the common areas of the subdivision, shopping center, or business park in perpetuity instead of establishing a voluntary association to handle this responsibility.

Figure 7.1 shows a map of the number of active ad valorem special service areas (SSAs) in 265 municipalities in the Chicago metropolitan region with the boundaries of the six counties also shown. Darker jurisdictions have more of these SSAs, and lighter areas have none. The figure shows a pattern of higher use of SSAs in less urban and less dense areas of the region that have experienced significant growth and development since the 1990s. Although SSA use in Will County is an exception to this pattern, correlations confirm that

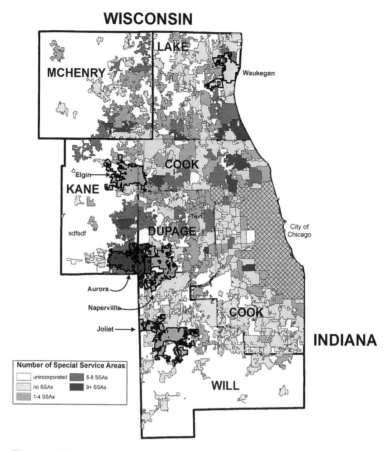

Figure 7.1. Chicago Municipalities and Counties: Number SSAs, Avg. 2006–12.

municipalities in more recently developed areas farther away from the City of Chicago have more ad valorem SSAs than municipalities closer to the city.[16] Nonactive or dormant SSAs are not shown on the map. Our qualitative data suggest that dormant SSAs, which are established by the developer in agreement with the municipality as part of the planned urban development, are very common in all counties except Cook and Will and cover the entire residential area of many suburban municipalities. As such, maintaining the common areas of subdivisions, shopping centers, and business parks is expected to be the most widespread use of SSAs in this region.

We conclude from our observations that clear boundaries, similar land use, and comparable property values facilitate the process through which proprietary benefits are accrued from public service provisions. Jurisdictions with more recent growth and development have more of the former characteristics because of the prevalence of residential subdivisions, shopping centers, and business parks within their boundaries. By comparison, older jurisdictions are more likely to be laid out on a grid and have residential, commercial, and industrial uses mixed within the same block. In the former case, the only difference between an ad valorem SA for the purpose of maintaining common areas in a subdivision and a general ad valorem property tax to provide similar services to an entire jurisdiction is that the SA applies only to the SAD and not to the rest of the jurisdiction. Thus, we might say that the benefits from special services to each taxpayer in these types of SADs are shared by taxpayers within the SAD but localized compared to the rest of the jurisdiction.

Although most governments in the Chicago region and elsewhere, as shown in the next section, use SAs to provide capital improvements, many states, including Illinois, allow their local governments to use SAs to provide services. In fact, ongoing services are commonly financed by SAs in BIDs and in place of owners' associations, but what about core services such as police? Theoretically these services could be financed, at least in part, through SAs, as was demonstrated in one Chicago suburb in which the government proposed using an ad valorem SA levied on property owners of eighteen multifamily complexes for additional police protection and other services. The village, which consists mostly of single-family homes, believed that the apartment area was not being maintained by the owners and was requiring an "inordinate" amount of services compared to the rest of the village. The government had already established an SAD in one of its single-family neighborhoods to raise money for a private security force, but that SAD was requested by a majority of the residents in that neighborhood.

Another important factor that affects governments' ability and incentive to use ad valorem and non–ad valorem SAs in Illinois, as is true of SADs in many other states, is that these taxes are not subject to the state-imposed tax and expenditure limits (TELs). Because

SAs in most states are not subject to state-level TEL restrictions, local governments can increase property taxes and other sources of revenue in the SADs beyond these restrictions. California courts, for instance, pronounced that SAs are not subject to Proposition 13 and thus enabled local governments to increase property taxes while circumventing two-thirds public approval by voters.[17] Other scholars have concluded that growth in SADs is a logical outcome of TELs in California and Florida.[18] In contrast, our research on SADs in the greater Chicago area does not show that non-home-rule municipalities, which are subject to TELs, use SAs more than do home-rule municipalities, which are not subject to TELs.[19]

When Does Using SAs Not Make Sense?

Using SAs does not make sense for public goods and services where there are significant spillovers of benefits and costs, especially in densely populated areas. For instance, inadequate sewer connections or systems on one side of a street may create sewer backups on the other side of the street after rainstorms, and good garbage pickup may lower the rat population for the entire neighborhood. For this reason, benefit-based financing of goods and services may be more appropriate and straightforward in less dense and nonurban areas. An exception to this rule, however, is demonstrated in the Chicago region, where SAs are often used to provide stormwater management and flood prevention, services that can generate more significant spillovers than are often acknowledged. The Chicago region has a geography and weather pattern that requires good stormwater management, and there is often flooding from a major river that runs north and south through the entire west side of the region. In this case, good stormwater management and flood prevention in one area affects drainage and flooding in other areas, so the use of SAs is less appropriate, yet many municipal governments in the region use SAs to finance these services.

In addition to spillovers, one must also consider economies of scale in assessing whether public goods and services can be financed through SAs. In the case of fire services, which are property based, the application of the benefit principle is such that if the fire department were to charge only those who received their services, the costs (and benefits) would be prohibitive and few property owners could afford it. The issue of fairness and ability to pay is also an important factor in deciding whether to finance publicly provided goods and services with SAs or through general taxation. The practical issues surrounding perceptions of fairness of SAs for governments that implement them, which is related to questions about whether the benefit is proprietary and how benefits are defined and measured, is discussed more in another section. But we did observe some Chicago governments that subsidized capital improvements in neighborhoods and for individual properties with SAs as a way of promoting these improvements and increasing the affordability of these projects for property owners.

Using SAs for Economic Development

There is one use of SAs that should be discussed separately because its function is somewhat different than what has been described for SAs previously. Specifically, many SAs in the Chicago region and elsewhere in the United States are used to repay bonds that the municipality issues to build basic infrastructure (e.g., streets, water, and sewer) to support new commercial, industrial, and residential development. When development occurs in municipalities, there are three primary alternatives for financing the basic infrastructure for the development: (1) the developer pays out of personal funds and secures borrowed money for which only the developer is obligated; (2) the municipality finances the infrastructure and assumes obligation for the borrowed money; or (3) the developer leverages land-secured financing in which all property owners in the development become obligated to pay some portion of the borrowed money.[20] In the case of the third option, the municipality issues bonds for the basic improvements that are secured by the SA on the property. Initially, the developer is liable for those bonds, but as the properties are sold, the obligation for the debt is transferred from the developer to the new property owners and repaid through the collection of a separate property tax.

Theoretically, the cost and resale price of properties affected by the SAs should be reduced by the SA liability, but there is little clear evidence to support this outcome. Additionally, there is a lot of confusion among property owners about these types of SAs and significant issues of accountability, especially in Florida where much of the hypergrowth and development in the 1990s and 2000s was financed with this mechanism.[21] We also observed more than a few reports about homeowners in the Chicago region having to pay off their SA debt to facilitate the sale of their home and instances in which the total set of SA taxes was higher than the total set of general property taxes on some properties.

But, on balance, using SAs in this manner is beneficial for both the developer and the government, and, therefore, for tax payers in the long run. It reduces the up-front capital and interest costs for developers and thus improves their cash flow and reduces debt on their balance sheets after the properties are sold.[22] In fact, governments and others view SAs as one type of incentive strategy in the arsenal of economic development tools used by local governments.[23] Governments like SAs for this purpose because they are not liable for the debt, but they can seek new ownership of properties within an SAD for which SA property taxes are not paid. The flexibility of ownership gives governments some recourse if a developer becomes insolvent and cannot finish a development. Using SAs for this purpose also allows governments to follow their policy of requiring "new development to pay for itself," and it has been cited as an example of public–private partnerships in several redevelopment plans we examined for governments in the Chicago region.

Statutes Affecting the Use of SAs

Although it might theoretically make sense to use SAs to a greater degree in the provision of public goods and services, as with all matters pertaining to local governments, state law determines how local governments create and use SAs. State law determines how SAs are authorized, their purposes, and how they are financed. On the basis of our investigation of the literature that documents state statutes affecting the adoption and implementation of SAs and SADs and our other qualitative evidence, we identify the following five factors that significantly affect whether and how local governments use these tools in each state.

Purpose of SAD: Is the use of SADs limited to capital improvements, or can they be used for ongoing services?

Initiation and adoption: What number and type of petitioners are required to bring the SAD up for consideration?

Value basis: What is the basis for assessing the value of the benefit to the beneficiary and levying the tax?

Bonding: May governments issue bonds guaranteed by the SAs, and what types of bonds may be issued?

Bond liability and nonpayment: Who is liable for the bonds, lien priority, and resolution for nonpayment of SA?

Table 7.2 (Appendix A) shows how the first three characteristics are defined in twenty-one states that all have populations greater than five million. To construct this table, we first conducted a general search on Google and identified the key words referring to SADs and SAs in these twenty-one states. We then used these key words to conduct a Boolean search on LexisNexis legal database and collected state laws pertaining to SAs and SADs. We relied on law reviews and reports by cities that utilize SADs to interpret the application of these laws. Our search results are consistent with previous studies in this area but provide additional information.[24]

Our review of these statutes and others show that there is tremendous variation in legislation pertaining to SAs and SADs across states, which makes it hard to generalize about their features for local government in the United States overall. The consensus in the literature seems to be that all fifty states allow their local governments to use SAs, but there is no systematic investigation or documentation of enabling legislation in all states.

Most states in Table 7.2 have one row because they have only one form of SA, but six states have two forms of SAs and so have two rows in the table. We documented SAs separately when they have different names and other significant differences in one or more of the other categories in the table. In Illinois, for instance, one SA is called a special assessment and the other type is called a special service area (SSA). The tax bases for SAs in Illinois are property characteristics such as foot frontage or size of the property, but the tax basis for special service areas are property values (ad valorem). As discussed previously, whether the basis for taxation is ad valorem or something else (usually property characteristics) can significantly affect the costs of implementing SAs for the parent government. The costs of implementing SAs are also greatly affected by the adoption requirements. The adoption requirements examined for Table 7.2 suggest that the critical factor for executing an SA is whether it must be approved by some portion of those affected by the SA or whether the parent government can adopt the SA unless some portion of those affected veto it. In Illinois, for instance, a special service area can be established by counties and municipalities unless it is vetoed by 51 percent of both the property owners and residents in the proposed district. In Pennsylvania, an SAD can be vetoed by only 40 percent of the property owners, which makes vetoing SAs easier there than in Illinois. Most states, however, require that a designated percentage of beneficiaries of the improvements or services initiate (through petition) and ultimately consent to the SAs.[25] Because gaining approval of a majority of beneficiaries is more difficult than avoiding a veto, one would expect SA use to be lower in states where local governments must gain approval from property owners. Column one in Table 7.2 documents whether the SA documented is beneficiary approval, beneficiary veto, unilateral creation by government, or other.

Considering the twenty-one states examined here, it seems that most states restrict the use of SAs to financing the acquisition, construction, and maintenance of public infrastructure. Illinois is one of eight states that allow SAs to be used for services, but our investigation of municipalities in the Chicago region suggests that SAs are used much more for capital improvements and infrastructure maintenance than for services such as special police protection. Although it is not shown in Table 7.2, there is evidence that all states allow local governments to issue bonds that are secured by the SAs, although state law varies greatly as to whether the bonds can be general obligation (GO) or some other type (e.g., alternate GO bond in Illinois). It also appears that the local governments issuing the bonds are not liable in the event of nonpayment of the SAD bonds, at least technically. Rather, the property owners are liable, but the government may feel a moral or strategic obligation to become involved if debt service on SAD bonds and assessments are not paid. Additionally, most state-enabling statutes generally provide that the SAs bear the same priority for collection as general property taxes do, and may be enforced in the case of delinquency or nonpayment in the same manner as the collection of delinquent property taxes are.

Actual Use of SAs by Local Government

Unfortunately, there is not a lot of empirical research on SA use by local governments, except for research on BIDs nationwide and on the use of SAs in Florida and California. From this research, we know that SAs were not widely used throughout the United States before the 1980s.[26] Some speculate that SA use has increased in the United States overall because of tax and expenditure limitations imposed by states on local governments, such as by California with Proposition 13.[27] In Florida, however, increase in SA use is more closely linked to growth in development and the use of SAs to finance new construction.[28]

National data on the use of non–ad valorem SAs are available from the U.S. Census of Governments that reports the dollar value of these SAs plus impact fees collected by local governments every five years.[29] Table 7.1 shows the sum of SA revenue (code U01) collected by all municipalities in each state as a percentage of all capital (F codes) and construction (G codes) expenditures by these governments in 2002, 2007, and 2012. Although municipalities are usually the biggest users of SAs, counties also use them a great deal, and many states allow special district governments to use them as well. The table includes municipalities from all states in Table 7.2 and all states in which the percentage of non–ad valorem SA use by municipalities was greater than 3 in 2012. The states are sorted according to level of percentage in 2012, and the last column shows the change in percentage of SA use from 2002 to 2012. States in Table 7.1 that are not in Table 7.2 are highlighted in bold.

Table 7.1 shows that most of the states with the highest use of non–ad valorem SAs by municipalities are not in Table 7.2. In this case, many of the high-use states have smaller populations. States from Table 7.2 with the highest non–ad valorem SA use by municipalities are Illinois, Minnesota, Florida, and Ohio. Municipalities in

Table 7.1. Non–Ad Valorem SAs as Percent of Capital and Construction Spending for All Municipalities in States from Table 7.2 and States with Total Values Greater than 3 Percent in 2012

	2012	2007	2002	Absolute Change
MT	29.79	31.73	58.64	−28.85
ND	28.71	29.36	24.96	3.75
IL	17.82	10.30	4.17	13.65
KS	16.37	6.19	11.77	4.61
MN	15.91	15.99	16.19	−0.28
FL	13.02	10.26	6.23	6.79
DE	9.13	6.94	0.08	9.06
ID	6.59	8.03	2.03	4.56
UT	6.01	2.87	1.60	4.41
WV	5.86	17.73	14.02	−8.16
RI	5.57	0.00	0.00	5.57
CA	5.48	4.54	5.40	0.08
OH	5.44	4.81	4.93	0.51
WA	4.82	2.02	2.41	2.40
WI	4.57	5.92	6.10	−1.53
TN	3.92	5.87	1.55	2.37
MI	3.92	2.43	1.44	2.48
AZ	3.72	3.00	3.26	0.46
TX	3.14	2.79	1.43	1.72
CO	2.91	7.76	5.67	−2.76
PA	2.67	0.63	1.73	0.94
MO	1.62	1.96	0.80	0.82
MD	1.32	0.70	1.15	0.17
VA	1.04	2.23	1.13	−0.09
NC	0.98	0.76	0.70	0.29
NJ	0.62	0.16	1.00	−0.38
GA	0.60	0.16	0.13	0.47
NY	0.10	0.13	0.16	−0.05
IN	0.01	1.75	1.19	−1.17
Total U.S.	3.92	3.75	3.10	0.81

Source: U.S. Census of Governments: code U01 / all F + G codes.

Illinois and Florida also experienced a higher increase in the use of these types of SAs from 2002 to 2012 than any other state except Delaware.

We also compared spending, revenue, and non–ad valorem SA data for 2012 for the 265 municipalities in the Chicago region with that for other municipalities in the State of Illinois. Interestingly, the use of these SAs by the 265 municipalities in the Chicago region (minus the City of Chicago) was only 0.57 percent of capital and construction spending in 2012 compared to almost 44 percent for the City of Chicago. Additionally, we compared Census data on non–ad valorem SAs with data on ad valorem SAs that are available from the State of Illinois for the 265 municipalities in the Chicago region for 2012 (see Appendix B). We found that the dollar value of non–ad valorem SAs is only 11 percent of the dollar value of the ad valorem SAs for these municipalities. This finding is consistent with our qualitative findings that non-ad valorem SAs have lower transaction and administrative costs and are used much more than ad valorem SAs in the region.

To determine if this ratio of ad valorem SA to non–ad valorem SA use was similar in other states, we investigated financial data on SA use in municipalities that were easily available online from the state governments. Unfortunately, none of the states for which we found data allowed SAs to be levied on an ad valorem basis. On the other hand, this data showed that the level of non–ad valorem SA values for most of the states for which state-level data was available were similar to what was reported by the Census Bureau.

Contrary to our argument that the use of SAs for many types of infrastructure improvements and even some ongoing services makes sense in many circumstances, Table 7.2 demonstrates that the actual use of non–ad valorem SAs by municipalities in most states is not very high. In the United States as a whole, non–ad valorem SA use by municipalities in all states was only about 4 percent of capital and construction spending in 2012, according to the U.S. Census of Governments. As shown in Table 7.1, these percentages were above 10 percent in only six states, and four of these six states were below 20 percent. For all counties (not shown in the table), use of non–ad valorem SAs was also only 4 percent of capital and construction spending in 2012. Even if we add the ad valorem SAs levied by Chicago municipalities as reported by the state and the non–ad valorem as reported by the census, total SA use as a percentage of capital spending (as reported by the State of Illinois) and capital and construction spending (as reported by the U.S. Census of Governments) is only about 8 percent and 5 percent, respectively, for municipalities in the Chicago region.

Although the use of non–ad valorem SAs is low overall, Table 7.1 also shows that the use of these tools has risen in many states and 0.81 percent in the United States as a whole since 2002. Assuming that local governments continue to be motivated to find other sources of revenue besides property taxes, we expect them to rely more on SAs and other benefit-based financing sources, including charges and fees, in the future than they have in the past. Reported trends show that charges as a percentage of total general revenues in all local governments in the United States have increased from 14.4 percent in 1992 to 15.3 percent in 2007 to 17.5 percent in 2012.[30]

Practical Issues in Using SAs

Compared to the previous section that relates the theoretical reasons why and when SAs should be used, this section relates conditions and practical issues that we observed to affect SA use in Illinois and elsewhere. Possibly the biggest factor that may explain the low use of SAs among local governments in the United States is lack of knowledge and understanding of SAs by government officials, citizens, and others. From the government officials we interviewed in the Chicago region, it was apparent that SAs are simply not one of the options they have considered for financing capital expenditures other than for economic development. Either the staff has never made the elected officials aware of these tools, or the staff is not aware of all the possible uses of SAs and the relative ease with which ad valorem SAs can be established and implemented in Illinois. Many officials' statements in the interviews and in the online material we obtained also contain inaccurate claims about both types of SAs in the state. However, one cannot overlook the administrative difficulties, transaction costs, and other practical difficulties involved in implementing SAs in other states and the non–ad valorem SA in Illinois. These practical difficulties are directly related to the tax basis of the SAs, requirements for SA approval, and perceptions of fairness of the tax. Tax basis and requirements for approval are noted in the last two columns in Table 7.2.

Tax Basis of SAs

One practical problem that exists for using SAs is how to define or determine benefits accurately in order to levy taxes in proportion to the benefits received.[31] Most state legislation requires that the amount of taxes or charges, or both, and assessments imposed on properties located within the SAD bear a reasonable relationship to the value of the benefits accruing to the affected property. It is often difficult, however, to determine and differentiate the special benefits that actually accrue to property owners from public improvements and government services (as distinct from general benefits to all), and it is difficult to measure these benefits accurately and in a way that can be translated into a financial assessment. Some states, such as Florida, Colorado, and Illinois, allow local governments to levy SAs based on property values (ad valorem), but doing so requires SA benefits and property values to be correlated. SAs in many other states are not ad valorem; in other words, the amount of SAs is calculated based on a mathematical formula that takes into account other property characteristics such as lot size, frontage, and proximity to improvement.[32] Table 7.2 also shows that California, Washington, and Minnesota define special benefits as the increase in property values after the SAs have been established, but the actual increase in property values will not be known until some time after the SA has been established. In this case, local governments must also rely on formulas based on physical property characteristics to predict the future capitalization of public improvements that are to be financed with SAs.[33]

From our qualitative evidence from municipalities in the Chicago region, we found that determining special benefits using a mathematical formula based on physical property characteristics is more difficult to calculate and defend to property owners than special benefits based on property values are. Non–ad valorem SAs are costlier to implement because the parent government bears the entire cost of administration and enforcement. In Illinois the administration and enforcement of ad valorem SAs (called special service areas in Figure 7.1) is simply folded into the counties' responsibilities to administer and enforce general property taxes for all local governments.[34] By comparison, if the SAs are not ad valorem (called special assessments in Table 7.2), then the parent local government needs to prepare and maintain a separate tax roll, generate and deliver tax bills, collect revenues, and enforce payments. In this case, it is not surprising that the vast majority of SAs among Chicago municipal governments are ad valorem.[35] California has a similar situation in which their assessment districts are also implemented through the county property tax bills, whereas the Mello-Roos districts are implemented independently by the local government.[36]

The Transaction Costs of Approving SAs

The last column of Table 7.2 documents what is probably the second biggest factor affecting the use of SAs, which is the rules for establishing them. Although there are exceptions, the state-level rules presented in Table 7.2 can be divided into three basic categories based on different levels of transaction costs for the government and, hence, likelihood of establishing SAs. Special assessments in the first category, called *beneficiary approval*, can only be created if a majority of the SAD (defined as registered voters, property owners, total assessed value, or land area) petition for or vote in favor of, or both, the SA.[37] The creation of SAs in the second category, called *beneficiary veto*, does not require the petition or approval by a majority of the SAD. Rather, the SA can be created by the parent government, unless some portion of the beneficiaries veto it. In the third category, *government creation*, the parent government can create an SA without majority approval from beneficiaries, and there is no apparent way for beneficiaries to prevent the SA from being established.

From the parent government's perspective, it is more difficult to obtain voluntary approval for a tax increase from a set of beneficiaries than it is to avoid cancellation of a tax once it is in place. Many people refer to these difficulties as transaction costs. Broadly speaking, transaction costs are the costs of exchanging goods and services, whether across markets or within organizations.[38] In this case, transaction costs are the bargaining and decision costs associated with the formation of any contractual relationship or establishing the terms of agreement between a set of parties.[39] If a city or a minority of property owners in an area of a city want to create an SA in a jurisdiction in which a majority of property owners must agree to this action, either through petition or voting, then the city or minority of property owners must get many others to agree to the SA and actively vote on the matter. On the other hand, if the city or a minority of property owners can simply establish SAs unilaterally, then property owners who disagree with this action must bear the transaction costs of getting others in the SAD to reject the SA through voting.

Compared to beneficiary approval and veto, however, government creation without approval or avoidance of a veto has the lowest transaction costs. Thus, one would expect to see the highest use of SAs in states that have been classified as government creation in Table 7.2 and the lowest use of SAs in states that are beneficiary approval. This would not necessarily be true, however, if the SA is established to build basic infrastructure on land that is entirely owned by the entities who are financing the development. In this case, to establish an SA, the government must negotiate the terms of the SAD with only a few developers who have similar interests rather than with a large group of property owners with diversified needs and demands.[40]

Looking at the twenty-seven SA entries in Table 7.2, sixteen can be classified as beneficiary approval (Arizona, California [2], Colorado, Georgia, Michigan [2], Maryland, Minnesota, Missouri, New York, North Carolina, Ohio [2], Texas [2], and Virginia) and only five are beneficiary veto (California, Illinois, Pennsylvania, Washington, and Wisconsin). Another four SAs in Table 7.2 are government creation (Colorado, Florida, Indiana, and New Jersey), and the remaining three SAs use some other requirement for establishing them (Illinois, Minnesota, and Tennessee). Even within these categories, however, there are different levels of transaction costs for establishing SAs. In the case of New Jersey and Colorado, for instance, SAs are created entirely by the government without approval or opportunity for veto by the beneficiaries. Indiana, on the other hand, requires petition by at least 25 percent of the beneficiaries and so is costlier than the other two states. But 25 percent is far less costly to approve than a majority of beneficiaries, so establishing an SA in Indiana is much less costly for the government than for governments in states that require majority or greater beneficiary approval. For the SAs in the other category, those in Tennessee have the lowest transaction costs because they are government created yet can be vetoed through the circuit court. In Illinois, non–ad valorem property taxes are created by the circuit court, which requires litigation by the local government, and SAs in Minnesota can be created in some cases with a supermajority in the council.

Perceptions of the Fairness of SAs

Although many people would agree that taxation according to benefits received is an equitable and fair method, we found that both governments and citizens in the Chicago area have broader perceptions of fairness than the principle of benefits received. We also found that fairness depends on the tax basis, how benefits are measured, and other factors. For instance, it became apparent from several interviews and documentation of public hearing and case law in Illinois that the ad valorem form of SAs is considered to be more appropriate and fairer for properties that have similar value and physical features, such as lot size, whereas non–ad valorem SAs are considered to be more appropriate and fairer for properties with dissimilar characteristics. There is also a great deal of debate and case law covering how to measure benefits and assign costs with the non–ad valorem form of SA, demonstrating that the fairness of this method is not always evident to governments or beneficiaries.[41]

We also found that many of the governments we examined had similar and favorable views about using SAs in particular situations. This was especially true for using SAs in unincorporated areas to bring the infrastructure up to the standards of the government as a condition of annexation. Many governments interviewed also expressed the opinion that it was fair to use SAs to provide higher quality infrastructure to one area compared to other areas of the jurisdiction, or to install infrastructure that does not exist elsewhere in a jurisdiction. Similarly, it is not considered to be fair for some properties within a jurisdiction to pay for improvements or services through SAs that have already been provided to others in the jurisdiction through general property taxes.

We encountered more than a few references in our qualitative evidence about the need to consider what level and quality of goods and services have been provided using SAs versus general taxes in the past in order to judge whether the use of these tools is fair in particular cases. For this reason, debates about whether SAs are fair with respect to improvements to areas that are already developed and where land use has been established seem to occur quite often when considering whether to use an SA. These debates seem to be particularly contentious in jurisdictions that have been developed at different times and, therefore, have varying qualities of infrastructure. In these cases, questions about what constitutes a unique benefit for properties in an SAD relative to the rest of the jurisdiction and even past time periods are more difficult to resolve to everyone's satisfaction.

We also encountered some governments that believe that providing higher levels or quality of goods and services to some areas of the jurisdiction and not to other areas is not fair under most circumstances because it shows favoritism and, in some cases, may be contrary to precedence and the government's view of what constitutes a basic public good. Additionally, we found many governments that would create SAs only when they were approved by a majority of property owners, although Illinois statute allows local governments to create SAs unless the SA is vetoed by a majority of both property owners and voters.

Few people deny that the fiscal policy space of local governments has shrunken greatly because of the passage of TELs by states beginning in the late 1970s and continuing through the 2000s, the recession in 2001, and the Great Recession in 2008. The additional pressures of increasing obligations for public pensions, higher health-care costs, and deteriorating capital infrastructure have motivated local governments to craft innovative financial tools. Studies of the impact of TELs and these fiscal pressures strongly suggest that local governments will continue to find and lobby for new revenue sources. The purpose of this study is to develop a more comprehensive and accurate picture of SAs as a tool for financing capital improvements and even operating expenditures in order to assesses whether they are an appropriate and viable source of new revenue.

To accomplish this task, this study examines the benefits and costs of or problems with SAs on the basis of public finance theory, and it shows that SAs are justified by the benefit principle for certain types of goods and services.[42] From an efficiency perspective, it is better to have property owners pay for government goods and services according to the benefits they receive, but this is not always feasible. Many goods and services delivered by government have characteristics that make them more public than private, but the benefit principle only works for goods and services that have more private characteristics. Benefit-based financing is also more appropriate for goods and services that have few spillover effects or for areas where spillover effects are minimized. Compared to rural and suburban areas with less population density and more single-purpose land use, spillover effects for all government goods and services will be greater in urban areas. On the other hand, SAs are considered to be one of the easiest funding techniques to defend in the minds of those who benefit and pay for government goods and services, especially for capital improvements.[43] Thus, it makes sense for governments to use SAs in many circumstances and areas of the country.

This study also reports on the laws that determine the feasibility and costs of SA use in the twenty-one largest states in the United States (twenty-seven SAs). The study finds that state laws regarding the tax basis of SAs and how they must be established vis-à-vis beneficiaries or taxpayers greatly determine the costs of creating and maintaining the SA and SAD. The study found that ad valorem SAs were much less costly than non–ad valorem SAs for municipalities in Illinois because administering and enforcement of property taxes are the responsibility of the counties in the state. Although it is not known how many states administer and enforce ad valorem SAs through their county property tax systems, it is likely that ad valorem SA costs are greatly reduced for municipalities in the eleven states that allow ad valorem SAs (and where the county is responsible for the property tax system) compared to the ten states that do not allow ad valorem SAs. State laws that specify how SAs must be established also greatly affect the transaction costs for local governments. The study showed that SAs can be grouped into three primary categories of higher to lower transaction costs based on whether beneficiaries must approve of the SAs (twelve states), whether beneficiaries must veto the SAs (five states), or whether the local government can create SAs unilaterally (four states). Illinois's laws place the state in the second category for ad valorem SAs, but in the fourth category of "other" for non–ad valorem SAs.

This study also reports on the actual use of non–ad valorem SAs by municipalities nationwide and ad valorem SAs by municipalities in the Chicago metropolitan region. The results show that municipal governments in most states use SAs very little in terms of the proportion of municipalities that have one SA and the total dollar value of SAs relative to total revenue and capital infrastructure improvements. On the basis of the qualitative and quantitative data, the study also finds that ad valorem SAs are used to a far greater extent than non–ad valorem SAs in the Chicago region, a finding that is consistent with expectations of differences in the transaction costs of these two tools. This finding also suggests that overall SA use across states is likely to be higher than what is indicated by the non–ad valorem SA data available from the U.S. Census Bureau. Unfortunately, no data could be found on ad valorem SA use in states with these types of SAs. Thus, it is impossible to accurately judge the extent to which SAs are used in states that allow ad valorem SAs.

Finally, this study assesses the benefits and costs of or problems with SAs on the basis of factors affecting the use of SAs as reported by or about municipal governments in the Chicago metropolitan area. Although many of the conclusions drawn about these tools are from the experiences and perceptions of government officials and reports from only one area of the country, these conclusions are grounded within the state-level legal framework within which SAs operate. To a large degree, the benefits and costs of and problems with SAs are determined by this framework, but other issues, such as the efficiency of benefit-based financing in different contexts, apply nationwide.

One finding from interviews and reports on SAs in the Chicago region that has potentially significant implications for the understanding of government behavior and the practical use of SAs is that these tools are not often well understood by public officials. This lack of understanding likely precludes many governments from using SAs appropriately or to their fullest extent, even in states such as Illinois that do not require approval from property owners or others who benefit from the delivery of proprietary government goods and services. This finding also challenges claims about government's ability to take advantage of citizens' fiscal illusion about tax prices to increase tax rates and service levels beyond what taxpayers desire.[44] In this case, governments cannot pursue their Leviathan desires if they have incomplete or inaccurate knowledge of the tools that allow them to take advantage of this fiscal illusion. However, even when government officials in the Chicago suburbs have good knowledge of SAs, they report a sensitivity to taxpayers' perceptions of SAs and a reluctance to use these tools, although Illinois has weaker legal constraints against their use than other states. In conjunction with the findings that the use of SAs is relatively low nationwide and in the Chicago region (even considering ad valorem SAs), one might conclude that the Leviathan is tamed with respect to SAs. In conjunction with the other findings of this study, we conclude that SAs could be used to a greater degree if transaction costs are reduced and the public becomes more familiar with and knowledgeable about SAs as a tool for financing capital improvement.

Appendix A

Table 7.2: Characteristics of SADs in States with Populations Greater Than Five Million

	Term	Authority	Separate Political Entity?	Uses	Tax Basis	Beneficiary Approval / Veto / Appeal
Arizona ** Beneficiary approval	Community facilities districts	Counties and municipalities	Y[1]	Capital improvements and enhanced services related to public infrastructure	• Costs associated with the benefits received, or ad valorem	• Petition by 25 percent of property owners • Approval: a majority of votes of qualified electors in the affected district weighted by the acreage of land in district • Property owners can appeal in courts
California ** Beneficiary approval	Community facilities districts (Mello-Roos)	Municipalities, counties, and special districts	N	Public-capital facilities and services (developing areas and areas undergoing rehabilitation)	• Not ad valorem (measure of benefit not required)	• Petition by not less than 10 percent of landowners or registered owners, or request signed by two members of the legislative body • Approval: ⅔ of votes in favor • Veto: Disapproval from 50 percent or more of the registered voters or 50 percent or more of the owners
California ** Beneficiary Approval	Assessment districts	Municipalities, counties, and special districts	N	Capital improvements only, including public-infrastructure projects, public-transit facilities, and related maintenance	• Benefit measured based on mathematical formulas that take into account how much each property will benefit from the installation of the improvements • Each parcel is responsible for a fixed percentage of the total district debt	• Creation by local government based on owners' petition • Majority protest exists if ballots submitted in opposition to the assessment exceed ballots submitted in favor. Ballots weighed according to proportional financial obligation of the affected property
Colorado Creation by government	Special or local improvement district	Counties and municipalities	N	Capital improvements only	• Cost-based methods, such as the front-foot method, the area method, the per-lot method, or other methods that equitably allocate the burden of the assessment upon the benefited properties	• Through government initiative • Allows hearing on objection

[1] Community-facilities districts are governed by the board of directors of the district composed of the members of the governing body of the municipality or county, ex officio, or, at the option of the governing body, five directors appointed by the governing body.

Table 7.2 (continued)

	Term	Authority	Separate Political Entity?	Uses	Tax Basis	Beneficiary Approval / Veto / Appeal
Colorado Beneficiary approval	General, public, or business improvement district	Counties and municipalities	Y[2]	Public improvements, economic development, and business-related services (only with BIDs)	• Ad valorem • Cost-based methods, such as the front-foot method, the area method, the per-lot method, or other methods that equitably allocate the burden of the assessment upon the benefited properties • Fees or charges for services	• For GID/PID: Petition signed by the lesser of 30 percent or two hundred property owners • For BID: Petition signed by property owners of at least 50 percent of assessed values in the district
Florida ** Creation by government	Community development district	Counties and municipalities	Y	Capital improvements only	• Ad valorem, or • Apportionment of costs based on special benefits received, measured by front footage, area, property values, or any other reasonable unit	• Creation by local government based on owners' petition
Georgia Beneficiary approval	Street improvements	Municipality	N	Capital improvements related to street maintenance	• Lineal frontage of streets	• By municipalities' resolution • Need approval from a majority of electors
Illinois ** Other	Special assessment	Counties and municipalities	N	Capital improvements only	• Apportionment of costs based on special benefits received, measured by front footage, area, property values, or any other reasonable unit	• Circuit court confirms, rules against, or dismisses
Illinois ** Beneficiary veto	Special service area	Counties and municipalities	N	Mostly capital, but may do services	• Ad valorem	• Veto: by 51 percent of voters and property owners

[2] Improvement districts take different forms in Colorado, including special improvement districts (SIDs), general improvement districts (GIDs), local-improvement districts (LID), public improvement districts (PIDs), and business improvement districts (BIDs). SIDs and GIDs are established by cities and towns, whereas LIDs and PIDs are organized by counties. SIDs and LIDs are not separate political subdivisions and do not have independent corporate existence. GIDs and PIDs are separate political subdivisions with their own board of directors, and the governing body of the organizing government (city council, board of trustees, or board of county commissioners) is the ex officio board of directors of a GID or PID. In addition, municipalities can also organize BIDs. There are four different forms of BIDs' governing bodies: ex officio board; appointed board by municipalities, overlapping with other entities; elected board; or electors.

State	Name	Administrative body		Purpose	Cost measurement	Initiation
Indiana Creation by government	Barrett Law Funding; Improvement districts	Counties and municipalities	Y[3]	Capital improvements and redevelopment	• Increases in assessed property values	• Petition by at least 25 percent of the parcels of real property in the proposed district
Michigan Beneficiary approval	Public Improvement districts	Townships	N	Capital improvements and services	• Based on benefits received; statutes do not specify the measurement of benefits	• Petition by owners of land constituting at least 50 percent of the total land area or by owners of land constituting more than 50 percent of the total frontage, depending on the purpose of the improvement district
Michigan Beneficiary approval	Special assessment district	All local governments	N	Capital improvements only	• Increases in the market value of property	• Petition by owners of land constituting at least $\frac{2}{3}$ of the total land area
Maryland ** Beneficiary approval	Special taxing district	Municipalities and selected counties	N	Capital improvements only	• Ad valorem, or • Apportionment of costs based on special benefits received, measured by front footage, area, property values, or any other reasonable unit	• Petition by $\frac{2}{3}$ of property owners • Council approval only
Minnesota Beneficiary approval and other	Special assessment	Municipalities and special districts	N	Capital improvements only	• Capitalization measured as the increase of property value	• Petition by 35 percent of property owners; do not need majority vote for initiation by council • 51 percent approval for petition-initiated projects, or $\frac{4}{5}$ council approval for council-initiated projects • To veto, property owners subject to proposed SAs can sign a written objection and file it before or at the assessment hearing, and appeal to the district court

[3] The works board is the administrative body in counties. At the municipal level, owners within the improvement district may establish an association of fifteen persons who are the owners of at least fifteen separate parcels and at least 20 percent of the surface area of the real property within the district.

Table 7.2 (continued)

	Term	Authority	Separate Political Entity?	Uses	Tax Basis	Beneficiary Approval / Veto / Appeal
Missouri Beneficiary approval	Community improvement district	All local governments	Y	Capital improvements and services	• Ad valorem • Reasonable measurement of benefits correlated with costs • Sales or use tax	• Petition by owners of more than 50 percent by assessed value, or more than 50 percent of the owners of all property in the district • Home-rule cities with more than four hundred thousand residents located in first-class counties can initiate the establishment
New Jersey Creation by government	Special improvement district	Municipalities	Y	Capital improvements and services for economic development	• Apportionment of costs	• By government initiative
New York ** Beneficiary approval	Improvement district	Municipalities[4]	Y[5]	Capital improvements only	• Ad valorem or benefits-based (laws do not provide guideline of how to measure benefits)	• Petition by owners whose properties aggregate at least one-half of the total assessed values in the district
North Carolina Beneficiary approval	Special assessment authority	Counties and municipalities	N	Capital improvements only	• Apportionment of costs based on special benefits received, measured by front footage, area, number of lots, increased property values, or any combination of the above	• By petition signed by at least the owners who represent at least 66 percent of the assessed value of all real property to be assessed
Ohio Beneficiary approval	Special improvement district	Municipalities	Y	Capital improvements and services	• By a percentage of the tax value of the property assessed • In proportion to the benefits • By the front foot of the property	• Created by petition of owners of at least 60 percent of the front footage or owners of at least 75 percent of the land area • Repeal initiated by a petition signed by property owners of at least 20 percent of the assessed value

[4] Towns can establish improvement districts that perform functions related to various capital projects. In this case, the districts will be named based on the particular function to be carried out, such as water, sewage, energy efficiency, resource conservation, and the like. In addition, municipalities, including cities, towns, and villages, can establish BIDs.

[5] Improvement districts are usually governed by towns, unless the law that creates a district specifies the establishments of a board of commissioners.

Ohio Beneficiary approval	Special assessment	Municipalities and special districts	N	Capital improvements and services	• By a percentage of the tax value of the property assessed • In proportion to the benefits • By the front foot of the property	• Petition by owners of 60 percent of the front footage of property abutting upon a street, road, or other improvements, or by owners of 75 percent of the area to be assessed for the improvement
Pennsylvania ** Beneficiary veto	Neighborhood improvement district[6]	Municipalities	Y	Capital improvement and services; downtown commercial developments	• Benefit measured as physical characteristic (no information from laws)	• Initiated by businesses or residents, or both • Veto: by 40 percent of voters and property owners
Tennessee Other	Special assessment	Municipalities, counties, and special districts	N	Capital improvements only	• Cost allocated based on the ratio of the assessed value of individual property to the total values of all properties • Apportionment of costs based on special benefits received, measured by front footage, area, property values, or any other reasonable unit	• By ordinance • Property owners can protest at the public hearing before the adoption of ordinance and appeal to the district court
Texas ** Beneficiary approval	Public improvement district	Counties and municipalities	Y[7]	Capital improvements only	• Ad valorem, or • Apportionment of costs based on special benefits received, measured by front footage, area, property values, or any other reasonable unit	• Petition signed by more than 50 percent of the assessed value of the real property

[6] Neighborhood improvement districts include business improvement district (BID), residential improvement district (RID), industrial improvement district (IID), institutional improvement district (INID), and mixed-use improvement district (MID) depending on the type of district established.

[7] The governing body (counties or municipalities) can appoint an advisory board to develop and recommend an improvement plan to the governing body.

Table 7.2 *(continued)*

	Term	Authority	Separate Political Entity?	Uses	Tax Basis	Beneficiary Approval / Veto / Appeal
Texas Beneficiary approval	Municipal management district	Municipalities	Y	Services to enhance economic development	• Ad valorem	• Petition by the owners of a majority of assessed value of the real property or by fifty persons who own real property within the district
Virginia ** Beneficiary approval	Community development authority	Municipalities, counties, and special districts	N	Capital improvements only	• Ad valorem	• Petition by 51 percent of land area or assessed value • Council approval only
Washington Beneficiary veto	Improvement districts	Municipalities, counties, and special districts	N	Capital improvements only	• Ad valorem: the difference between the fair market value of the property before and after the special benefits have attached, or • Benefit measured with mathematical cost-distribution formulas based on physical characteristics	• Petition or resolution initiated by the city council • Approved by bond counsel • Veto: protested assessments should amount to 60 percent or more of the dollar amount of preliminary assessments • Veto may be overridden by council
Wisconsin Beneficiary veto	Special assessment	Municipalities	N	Capital improvements only	• Benefit measured as physical characteristic	• By ordinance • Property owners can appeal to circuit court within ninety days of the notice

Note: All States with Population > 5 Million (N = 21).
**Reviewed by Orrick and Datch.

Appendix B. Quantitative Data on Municipal Governments in the Chicago Metropolitan Region

Data on special service areas in Illinois, which are one of two forms of SAs allowed in the state, come from the Illinois Department of Revenue and are available for 1988 to 2012. We have data on the number of active special service areas in all 265 municipal governments in the Chicago region, the level of assessment on each district, the regular property tax levy (called the extension in Illinois), and the equalized assessed value (EAV) of the jurisdiction. We also have extensive financial data on these governments from the Illinois Office of the Comptroller, the U.S. Census, and other sources, but these data are available only for 1998 to 2012. We define the use of this tool in these governments in three ways: (1) whether governments have at least one special service area; (2) the number of active special service areas in the jurisdiction; (3) the total special service area levy for all areas divided by EAV, expenditures, or revenues. The State of Illinois collects information about special service areas because revenues generated in these areas are ad valorem based on property values as are general property taxes in this state. The state does not collect data on the other form of SA allowed in Illinois (called a special assessment), which is not ad valorem and not implemented or enforced by the municipal government. Illinois also does not collect data on dormant special service areas.

Appendix C. Qualitative Data on Municipal Governments in the Chicago Metropolitan Region

Our qualitative data consist of interviews with officials from twenty-five governments, one of which is just outside the six-county region, and one interview with the executive director of the primary council of government in DuPage County on the use of SADs in their governments or other governments in the region. Many persons interviewed had worked in other governments in the region, and most of the officials interviewed were finance directors, but many were village or city managers and several were directors of economic development. We have also collected financial documents (budgets, CAFRs, and official statements) and other sources of information available online that discuss both forms of SADs used by these governments and thirteen other governments in the region that were not interviewed. Thus, we have qualitative data on SAD use by thirty-eight governments and by the council of government for one county. All qualitative data have been coded, and we have conducted much preliminary analysis on the primary purposes of the SADs and motivation for using or not using them.

The interviews were conducted from late January to late August 2015. They were unstructured and geared toward what we knew about the governments from the online information and quantitative data. Below is a listing of areas of questioning for all governments interviewed.

- The accuracy of the quantitative data about SSA use
- Uses of SSAs and SAs: residential, commercial, economic development, BIDs, development, infrastructure improvement, maintenance of common areas, other uses (e.g., marketing, special events, public safety)
- Specific uses such as stormwater management (flooding and drainage), alleys, lighting, water, parking, etc.
- Issuance of bonds for infrastructure improvements and whether the government is responsible for the bonds
- Adoption, implementation, and administration
- Perceived costs and benefits
- Policies regarding SSAs and SAs

We used a two-stage, discriminate sampling strategy to identify jurisdictions and governments for investigation. First, we chose governments to interview on the basis of seven classifications of jurisdictions according to characteristics that we believe are factors affecting the use of these tools, such as population, population growth, percentage of residential EAV, county in the region, home-rule status, and the extent to which the jurisdiction is built out. We then proceeded to request interviews from two or more governments from within these groups that had been relatively high users of SSAs from 2006 to 2012 and two or more governments that had been low or nonusers of SSAs during the same time period. After conducting sixteen interviews, we were able to identify four primary uses or purposes of these tools plus an "other" category. In stage two of our sampling strategy we went back to our seven groups of jurisdictions to identify more governments to interview in order to get a more complete picture of the four primary purposes. Our strategy in this stage was to interview within these groups until we no longer encountered new information from our interview questions.

Notes

1. Christiana McFarland and Michael A. Pagano, *City Fiscal Conditions* (Washington, D.C.: National League of Cities, 2014).

2. Lawrence Martin, Richard Levey, and Jenna Cawley, "The 'New Normal' for Local Government," *State and Local Government Review* 44, no. 1-suppl (2012): 17S-28S.

3. McFarland and Pagano, *City Fiscal Conditions*; Zhirong J. Zhao and Kerstin Larson, "Special Assessments as a Value Capture Strategy for Public Transit Finance," *Public Works Management and Policy* 16, no. 4 (2011): 320–40.

4. American Society of Civil Engineers (ASCE), "2013 Report Card for America's Infrastructure" (2013), www.infrastructurereportcard.org.

5. Carol Jean Becker, "Self-Determination, Accountability Mechanisms, and Quasi-Governmental Status of Business Improvement Districts in the United States," *Public Performance & Management Review* 33, no. 3 (2010): 413–35.

6. Dean J. Misczynski, "Special Assessment in California: 35 Years of Expansion and Restriction," in *Value Capture and Land Policies*, ed. Gregory K. Ingram and Yu-Hung Hong (Cambridge, Mass.: Lincoln Institute of Land Policy, 2012): 97–119; Marcus T. Allen and Harry C. Newstreet, "Smoothing Wrinkles in the Spread: Special Assessment Issues," *Appraisal Journal* 68, no. 2 (2000): 201–8.

7. Richard W. Tresch, *Public Finance: A Normative Theory* (Cambridge, Mass.: Academic Press, 2014); Geoffrey Brennan and James M. Buchanan, *The Power to Tax: Analytical Foundations of a Fiscal Constitution* (Cambridge, Mass.: Cambridge University Press, 1980).

8. James M. Buchanan, "The Pure Theory of Government Finance: A Suggested Approach," *Journal of Political Economy* 57, no. 6 (1949): 496–505.

9. Richard M. Bird, "User Charges in Local Government Finance," in *The Challenge of Urban Government*, ed. R. Stren and M. E. Freire (Washington, D.C.: World Bank Institute, 2001): 171–82; Richard M. Bird and Thomas Tsiopoulos, "User Charges for Public Services: Potentials and Problems" (Toronto: Centre for the Study of State & Market, Faculty of Law, University of Toronto, 1996).

10. Louis M. Rea, Glen W. Sparrow, and Dipak K. Gupta, "Direct Benefit

Financing: An Opportunity for Local Government," *Public Administration Quarterly* 7, no. 3 (1984): 29–43.

11. Paul A. Samuelson, "Diagrammatic Exposition of a Theory of Public Expenditure," *The Review of Economics and Statistics* 37, no. 4 (1955): 350–56.

12. Allen and Newstreet, "Smoothing Wrinkles."

13. Zhao and Larson, "Special Assessments as a Value Capture Strategy."

14. William A. Fishel, "Municipal Corporations, Homeowners, and the Benefit View of the Property Tax," in *Property Taxation and Local Government Finance*, ed. Wallace E. Oates (Cambridge, Mass.: Lincoln Institute of Land Policy, 2001): 33–77.

15. Fred J. Giertz, "The Property Tax Bound," *National Tax Journal* 59, no. 3 (2006): 695–705; George R. Zodrow, "Capital Mobility and Source-Based Taxation of Capital Income in Small Open Economies," *International Tax and Public Finance* 13, no. 2 (2006): 269–94.

16. Our qualitative evidence suggests that low use of SAs in Will County compared to other rural counties is due to the experiences of several municipalities in the county and nearby with developers defaulting on bonds secured by SAs during the 2001 and the Great Recession.

17. Terri A. Sexton, Steven M. Sheffrin, and Arthur O'Sullivan, "Proposition 13: Unintended Effects and Feasible Reforms," *National Tax Journal* 52, no. 1 (1999): 99–111.

18. Robert Cervero, "Paying for Off-Site Road Improvements through Fees, Assessments, and Negotiations: Lessons from California," *Public Administration Review* 48, no. 1 (1988): 534–41; Theodore J. Stumm and Pamela Pearson Mann, "Special Assessments in Florida Cities and Counties: Dodging Amendment 10?," *Journal of Public Budgeting, Accounting & Financial Management* 16, no. 2 (2004): 171–87.

19. Rebecca Hendrick, Ayman Bari, Shu Wang, and Dody Hutabarat. "Use of Special Taxing Districts by Municipal Governments in the Chicago Metropolitan Area: Is Leviathan Dead or Merely Sleeping?" (paper presented at the Annual Conference of the Association for Budgeting and Financial Management, Washington, D.C., October 2–4, 2015).

20. Sarah Ayers, Robert Eger, and Ken van Assenderp, *Community Development Districts: Financial and Accountability Issues* (Tallahassee: Leroy Collins Institute, Florida State University, 2014); Misczynski, "Special Assessment in California."

21. Gina Scutelnicu and Sukumar Ganapati, "Community Development Districts: An Innovative Institutional Framework for Financing and Managing Infrastructure in Florida?," *Economic Development Quarterly* 26, no. 4 (2012): 361–72.

22. Scutelnicu and Ganapati, 361–72; John R. Orrick Jr. and Demetrios M. Datch, "Special District Financing for Infrastructure: Sharing the Credit

with Local Government," *Journal of Taxation and Regulation of Financial Institutions* 29, no. 2 (2008): 47–76.

23. Jeffrey L. Osgood Jr., Susan M. Opp, and R. Lorraine Bernotsky, "Yesterday's Gains Versus Today's Realties: Lessons from 10 Years of Economic Development Practice," *Economic Development Quarterly* 26, no. 4 (2012): 334–50.

24. For example, Orrick and Datch, "Special District Financing."

25. The percentage of beneficiaries is usually from 51 to 100 and can be based on land area, assessed valuation, number of residents, or number of property owners within the SAD.

26. Jerry Mitchell, "Business Improvement Districts and the Management of Innovation," *American Review of Public Administration* 31, no. 2 (2001): 201–17; Rea, Sparrow, and Gupta, "Direct Benefit Financing"; Gina Scutelnicu, "Special Districts as Institutional Choices for Service Delivery: Views of Public Officials on the Performance of Community Development Districts in Florida," *Public Administration Quarterly* 38, no. 3 (2014): 284–316.

27. A. Quang Do and C. F. Sirmans, "Residential Property Tax Capitalization: Discount Rate Evidence from California," *National Tax Journal* 47, no. 2 (1994): 341–48; Jeffrey Chapman, "Proposition 13: Some Unintended Consequences," Occasional Papers (San Francisco: Public Policy Institute of California, 1998); Christopher Hoene, "Fiscal Structure and the Post-Proposition 13 Fiscal Regime in California's Cities," *Public Budgeting and Finance* 24, no. 4 (2004): 51–72; Misczynski, "Special Assessment in California."

28. Scutelnicu and Ganapati, "Community Development Districts"; Stumm and Mann, "Special Assessments."

29. The U.S. Census of Governments reports only non–ad valorem SAs. The figures reported do not include ad valorem SAs and, therefore, exclude SAs in which property values are the basis of taxing and valuing of the amount to be levied. In *Classifications Manual*, 4–10 and 4–38.

30. Rebecca Hendrick, "Non-Tax Revenue," in *Management Policies in Local Government Finance*, 6th ed., ed. John Bartle, W. Bartley Hildreth, and Justin Marlowe (Washington, D.C.: International City/County Managers Association Press, 2013): 219–50; and U.S. Census Bureau, Census of Governments, *Individual State Descriptions: 2012* (Washington, D.C.: U.S. Government Printing Office, 2013).

31. Rea, Sparrow, and Gupta, "Direct Benefit Financing"; Misczynski, "Special Assessment in California."

32. Zhao and Larson, "Special Assessments."

33. Allen and Newstreet, "Smoothing Wrinkles."

34. Thomas P. Bayer, Michael T. Jurusik, Patrick A. Lucansky, and J. Allen Wall, "Special Assessments, Special Service Areas, and Business Districts," in *Illinois Municipal Law: Financing, Tax, and Municipal Property*,

ed. Illinois Institute for Continuing Legal Education (Springfield, Ill., 2012): 1–100.

35. Michael E. Bell, "Real Property Tax," in *The Oxford Handbook of State and Local Government Finance*, ed. Robert D. Ebel and John E. Petersen (Oxford: Oxford University Press, 2012): 271–99.

36. Fieldman & Rolapp Associates, *Overview of Community Facilities Districts vs. Assessment Districts*, www.fieldman.com/PDFs/Chart_2_ADvs CFDsnapshot.pdf.

37. Some states accept majorities of different bases. For instance, the creation of Michigan special-improvement districts requires a petition by landowners of at least 50 percent of the total land area of the SAD *or* 50 percent of the total frontage to the improvement.

38. Oliver E. Williamson, *Market and Hierarchies: Analysis and Antitrust Implications* (New York: Free Press, 1975).

39. Ronald Coase, *The Firm, the Market, and the Law* (Chicago: University of Chicago Press, 1988).

40. Cervero, "Paying for Off-Site Road Improvements"; Orrick and Datch, "Special District Financing."

41. Bayer, Jurusik, Lucansky, and Wall, "Special Assessments."

42. Allen and Newstreet, "Smoothing Wrinkles."

43. Denvil Duncan, John Graham, Venkata Nadella, Ashley Bowers, and Stacey Giroux, "Demand for Benefit Taxation: Evidence from Public Opinion on Road Financing," *Public Budgeting & Finance* 34, no. 4 (2014): 120–42.

44. Brennan and Buchanan, *Power to Tax*.

8

Devolution and Debt

Financing Public Facilities in an Age of Austerity

Rachel Weber, Amanda Kass, and Sara Hinkley

Starting in the early 2000s, municipalities across North America began leasing existing infrastructure assets to global investment consortia and relying on "structured finance" instruments and techniques to build new assets. The uptick in new instruments, cash flows to monetize, and financial-engineering techniques was motivated partly by capital supply: the flow of global funds into urban infrastructure occurred as investors searched for alternative outlets in the face of stock-market fizzles and historically low interest rates. It was also motivated by fiscal stress experienced by local governments, who were burdened with increased spending responsibilities but wanted to keep their tax rates low and bond ratings high.

These processes created a context for highly leveraged infrastructure ventures in the 2000s that diverge from the classic public–private partnership model favored by entrepreneurial governments in the previous century. Specifically, the adoption of these instruments and techniques are evidence of a trend some have called "financialization." Financialization refers to both the increasing size of financial markets and institutions and the increasing role of finance in nonfinancial sectors.[1] In the case of urban policy, the degree of financialization is reflected in the increase in local debt for development purposes, the privatization and securitization of public assets, the size and complexity of the financial services available to city governments, and the investor orientation of policies affecting collective consumption and public goods.

Much of the recent literature on urban policy as a target for financialized restructuring examines how banks, financial intermediaries, and the logic of shareholder value are capable of diminishing the authority of states over economy and society.[2] These authors assume that as the power of finance increases, municipalities experience a concomitant loss of local autonomy. In contrast, we propose that governing capacity is critical to attracting global finance to local assets and that, in turn, finance can enhance rather than limit the capacity of that regime. In other words, local governments "construct the powers, networks, and contractual frameworks to work with, through, or against finance."[3]

Examining the use of auction-rate securities paired with interest-rate swaps by the Chicago Public Schools (CPS; sometimes referred to as "the district"), we demonstrate how local governments were hit by the one-two punch of devolved responsibility and constrained taxing authority and subsequently sought deliverance through exotic financial instruments. Strong mayoral control over Chicago's school district was celebrated by the bond market and enabled a reinforcing cycle of cheap debt and ambitious capital plans. Other large urban school districts such as Denver's and smaller ones in states such as New Jersey, as well as numerous water, housing, and airport authorities, gravitated toward similar kinds of securities and financial-engineering techniques during this period, but in Chicago such experiments were the norm rather than the exception. Chicago, therefore, offers an opportunity to examine an extreme, and therefore illustrative, example of policy financialization.

Local indebtedness is a critical piece of the devolution story that has not received much scholarly attention. Government borrowing is not new and not always a problem; it makes sense to borrow, for example, when governments, whose beneficiaries include future generations, need to fund long-term capital expenses. As debt markets have become more volatile and the instruments more opaque, however, riskier forms of financialized urban policy have emerged. We examine the school district's use of auction-rate securities and derivatives, which exacerbated and exposed CPS' financial precarity when this market imploded in 2008. In the context of devolution, taxing limitations, and investors' search for reliable yields, government actors and their private partners became desensitized to the risks, assuming they could be managed through technical means and strong political control.

Whereas these techniques have not garnered much attention when used by investment banks, they have set off alarm bells when used by the public sector for the purpose of financing K–12 education. Perhaps the incongruity of innocent schoolchildren, complex debt instruments, and pinstripe-clad bankers touches a nerve. In this chapter, however, we heed Brett Christophers' warning about studying the financial logics themselves, not just their use in strange places.[4] Indeed, one of the intentions of this chapter is to demonstrate that financial rationality has become so deeply entrenched as the conceptual framework for contemporary urban governance that the use of exotic instruments imported from Wall Street now appears normal.

Innovations in Infrastructure Finance: The Mechanics of Structured Financial Instruments

The markets for both public and private debt have displayed immense creativity in their search to avoid taxes and regulation and to manage risk. Every few years a new instrument or technique is devised to exploit interest-rate differentials, circumvent trading caps, or increase liquidity.[5] The evolution and normalization of complex or "structured" financial instruments in an area previously considered a sleepy backwater—state and local government finance—is evidence of this innovative capacity.[6]

Over the past fifteen years, the use of interest-rate swaps and variable-rate debt by public entities has grown significantly. For example, auction-rate securities (ARSs) were created in the mid-1980s, but their use by governmental entities skyrocketed during the 2000s.[7] In 1988 there was only one municipal ARS issuance, but by 2004, the number reached 438.[8] At its peak in 2004, ARSs accounted for 10.3 percent of the entire municipal market.[9]

ARSs are variable-rate bonds whose interest rates are periodically reset during Dutch auctions, when bondholders choose to hold or "auction" their holdings off to other investors. The use of ARSs

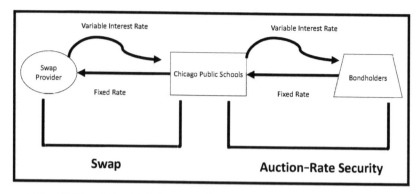

Figure 8.1. The relationship between auction-rate securities and interest-rate swaps.

in conjunction with interest-rate swaps is intended to provide savings to issuers by permitting them to convert floating or variable-rate bonds (preferred by investors to protect against interest-rate fluctuations) into fixed-rate loans. When an ARS is paired with an interest-rate swap, it is referred to as "synthetic fixed rate debt," and contains two distinct parts: (i) the ARS, whereby the local government receives a fixed amount of money from the bond sale and in turn pays bondholders a variable interest rate; and (ii) a fixed-rate swap, in which the government pays a fixed interest rate to a counterparty, who pays the government a variable interest rate. Figure 8.1 depicts the two parts of this type of debt product.[10]

In theory, the variable interest rate paid on the ARS and the variable rate paid on the swap cancel each other out so that the issuer pays an "artificial" fixed interest rate. For issuers, debt derived from variable-rate securities is often cheaper than conventional fixed-rate debt (and other forms of variable-rate debt) because, if it works, the swap arrangement can manage the risk that interest rates fluctuate.[11] The relatively lower cost of ARSs is also due to their lack of a "put option."[12] While ARSs are long-term debt obligations, they trade as short-term debt, making them attractive to investors.[13] During the 2000s, most ARS debt carried triple-A ratings and, because of the insurance they carried, attracted high-net investors and corporate treasuries.[14]

Variable-rate debt does come with less obvious costs and risks.

Most notable for ARSs is the question of short-term liquidity. Local governments and bondholders face the prospect of the market freezing up if no one wants to purchase the instruments. In such cases, interest rates skyrocket for the issuer, and investors "are unable to liquidate them at or near face value, having to absorb substantial losses to get out of their investments."[15] There are also the risks of costly swap terminations and a mismatch between the swap and the bond interest rates.

Reasons for Their Adoption

Why do local governments adopt such complex and risky financing techniques?[16] The popular press has painted a picture of public officials falling prey to the compelling sales pitches of investment brokers, who stood to gain from the use of these instruments.[17] In that narrative, gullible public administrators were motivated to take on excessive risks because of the chicanery of these relatively unregulated middlemen. While these portrayals have some basis in truth, they often ignore the internal pressure on public entities to be entrepreneurial and financially innovative.

The critical political economy perspective similarly perceives a deliberate shifting of risk and rents from the private to public sector in the use of these kinds of debt, one that is an essential attribute of neoliberal urbanism and austerity.[18] As a core strategy used to dismantle the welfare state, financialization creates a legal imperative to protect bank and bondholder interests over those of the citizenry.[19] The increasing importance of municipal debt also gives more power to financial actors, such as credit rating agencies, to enforce the norms and policy preferences of institutional investors.[20] Financial disintermediation and federal devolution have removed important buffers between the local state and financial capital.

Deepening these understandings, we argue that the expanded use of debt also reflects a straightforward and growing need for capital as states and the federal government cut funding for infrastructure. A drawn-out process of devolution, starting in the 1970s and 1980s, forced cities to develop their own strategies and find own-source revenues to address significant capital needs and hold on to footloose firms.[21] Few were able to compensate for the loss of federal and state funds, even as they faced growing demands by the electorate for infrastructure and services. The desire to fund capital projects while minimizing the perceived cost to current voters led local governments to prioritize strategies that did not require public ballot measures or raising taxes.

Facing limited revenue-raising options, cities sought to fund urban development and operations through borrowing and leveraged revenue streams.[22] The municipal securities market came to fill the funding vacuum left in the wake of rollback neoliberalism; the amount of new, annual municipal debt issuances increased from $169.1 billion in 1986 to $498.6 billion in 2010.[23] This deepening dependence on credit reflects both legal constraints on raising taxes and regulations provided by higher scales of government. It also reflects the growth in capital supply as cities' need for funding coincided with the deregulation of derivative markets and low or volatile returns in the other economic sectors investors were considering.

Before the 2000s, financing infrastructure with conventional bonds was common, interest rates held steady, and defaults were rare. More recently, local governments have shifted toward variable-rate products and revenue bonds. Financial innovation has led public issuers to seek out new income streams to pay creditors and bondholders. For example, cities pledge liens on overdue property tax bills and the rights to a stream of future property tax revenues (i.e., tax increment financing, or TIF) as security for borrowing.[24]

Not all local governments have access to these complex instruments. The ratings agencies restrict access to the rated and therefore less risky segment of capital markets; they only sanction borrowing for those entities that demonstrate sufficient commitment to protecting bondholder interests. As evidenced by the case of TIF in Chicago, the bond market rewards those governments with a strong "risk management" apparatus in place.[25] The local state must demonstrate its ability to exert sufficient control to fend off challenges on the property tax base and transfer payments from claimants other than investors (public sector unions, parents' groups) by enrolling opponents in the project of maximizing growth, cutting deals with them, and pressuring them into concessions. Indeed,

for a struggling local government to even sell promissory notes requires enough political strength and professional capacity so that
investors accept the instrument as legitimate and the promises of
the public sector as credible. In addition to these differences in capacity, there is variation in the fiscal and political pressure to pursue these financialized approaches. Not all local governments have
experienced the same degree of fiscal stress or chosen to address
financing gaps through debt-based solutions.

The Impact of Policy Financialization

To examine the detailed workings of financialization as a policy
project, we do not start with the assumption that local governments lose autonomy over decision-making and planning when
debt markets are tapped. Following Philip Ashton, Marc Doussard,
and Rachel Weber, we view financialization as a recursive process,
wherein individual transactions and bond offerings are moments in
a longer chain of state transformation.[26] Through this process, local governments simultaneously acquire additional powers and new
risk exposures. A framework that examines the intersection of these
powers and exposures avoids an either-or analysis that sees states or
markets as always dominating the other.

Debt instruments empower local governments by, at least in
the near term, advancing their specific policy goals. For example,
variable-rate debt provides municipalities with access to debt at
lower costs. Large-scale construction projects underwritten by such
debt enhance the capacity of municipalities to deliver on the promise of deficit spending, thereby satisfying residents, public-sector
personnel, construction workers, and voters.

Along with these powers, financial instruments produce new exposures in their transactions. Even though lengthy contracts and
underwriting guidelines are intended to protect taxpayer interests
in the event of a crisis, not all contingencies are included in the
terms of these agreements. When credit ratings change suddenly or
when transaction costs mount because of the complexity involved
in negotiating the deals, managing the fallout from these instruments can become challenging.

The Case of the Chicago Public Schools

The case of CPS, the second largest school district in the United States, illustrates the reasons why so many local governments use structured finance (as opposed to conventional debt or tax hikes) to pay for infrastructure (as opposed to other spending priorities). It also reveals the powers and exposures that accompany such choices. We base our analysis of CPS' financial status between 1990 and 2015 on a review of bond prospectuses, operating and capital budgets, comprehensive annual financial reports, news articles, and legislation as well as interviews with key decision makers.

The Promise of Local Control

The roots of CPS' policy financialization can be found during the devolutionary 1990s. From 1980 until 1995, the State of Illinois effectively managed the finances of Chicago's schools through the Illinois School Finance Authority ("Authority"), a body created in 1980.[27] The Authority had statutory powers over CPS' budget and was given the power to issue up to $500 million in bonds to stave off what many believed to be imminent fiscal collapse.[28] In 1995 state lawmakers devolved control over CPS into the hands of the Chicago mayor, Richard M. Daley, who became responsible for appointing all members to the school board and hiring for the newly created position of chief executive officer (CEO). As in New York City and Washington, D.C., "mayoral control" over a large urban school district was viewed as an important achievement that would allow the mayor to oversee major reforms to reverse trends of chronic underperformance. Proponents believed that having a single locus of accountability and sustained leadership would lead to improved quality.[29] In the letter accompanying CPS' first budget under mayoral control, CEO Paul Vallas referred to the budget as "a blueprint for a revolution."

Like many state governments, however, Illinois devolved responsibility to lower levels of government without providing adequate funding to cover operating, capital, and pension expenses.[30] Chastising the state for not contributing adequate resources became a mantra for both CPS and the city, but these actors also recognized that they were fighting an uphill battle and needed to devise their own strategies for raising funds. "Now is the time for the State of Illinois to accept its constitutional obligation to provide adequate funding to educate all children in this state," wrote Vallas, while touting CPS' own fiscal discipline.[31] Juxtaposing a reformed CPS against an irresponsible state government, CEO Vallas sought to signal to the municipal bond market that his district was a safe investment.

Making this case convincingly was difficult given the constraints on CPS' fiscal capacity. Key among these constraints was its inability to raise property taxes. Specifically, Illinois' Property Tax Extension Limitation Law (PTELL) curtailed CPS' ability to raise property tax revenue beyond the rate of inflation without a voter referendum.[32]

Similarly, the city's use of TIF to underwrite infrastructure and economic development prevented the school district from levying its tax rate on any incremental increase in property values in TIF districts.[33] Property tax revenues generated within a TIF district are unavailable to overlapping jurisdictions such as schools for the life span of the district. These taxing bodies must wait until the end of the life of the district—twenty-three years in Illinois—to levy taxes on the growth in the tax base within the TIF. The city went on a TIF spree in the late 1990s, designating almost 60 new districts between 1997 and 2000. If CPS had been able to tax all the appreciation in the city's roughly 150 TIF districts between 1995 and 2010, it would have generated up to an additional $2.2 billion in cumulative revenue.[34]

To make devolution more palatable, the State of Illinois put in place a regulatory apparatus to allow local governments greater access to debt markets. In 1988 lawmakers passed the Illinois Local Government Debt Reform Act, which gave municipalities the right to issue new types of debt. In the act, lawmakers expressed that it would be in the best interests of Illinois residents for local governments to have supplemental authority to issue "alternative bonds." Alternative bonds are general obligation bonds that can be paid for with any revenue source.[35] Further, local governments were granted permission to issue such bonds through "backdoor referenda"—that is, without voter approval. Under mayoral control, CPS was thus able to have more fiscal flexibility to increase its outstanding debt without public input.

In the law that returned CPS to mayoral control, state lawmakers provided the school district with another concession: the ability to forgo regular payments into its pension system, the Chicago Teachers' Pension Fund (CTPF).[36] Instead of contributing to the CTPF, CPS used property tax revenues for other line items in its budget.[37] CPS' contributions to the CTPF were supposed to increase in 1999, but in 1997 lawmakers changed funding requirements, which effectively reduced CPS' contributions to the pension fund.[38] As a result, CPS contributed almost no revenue to the CTPF between 1995 and 2010—even though current employees were accruing benefits.[39]

The school district's budget flexibility also increased when the state moved from a system whereby it allocated aid for specific line items to one based on block grants that could be used at CPS' discretion.[40] Such a move was immediately recognized as a positive development by the bond market. Standard & Poor's "cited Illinois lawmakers' willingness to give the new management team flexibility in spending state aid payments" as one of the reasons for upgrading CPS' credit rating.[41] CPS used this state aid as well as other funding streams, such as surplus TIF revenues allocated by city hall, to service its growing debt burden.

The Virtuous Cycle of Debt and Capital Spending

When Mayor Daley took over the schools in 1995, he inherited facilities that were in terrible condition. The district's CEO argued that executing a massive capital improvement plan was necessary because its old and deteriorated buildings made learning difficult. Several exposés of poor school quality had embarrassed officials and outraged parents and students. For example, a study by the U.S. Government Accountability Office (GAO) found that Chicago had been underfunding its school facilities budget—about 30 percent to 40 percent of needed repairs had been deferred annually for decades.[42] The GAO report quotes officials stating that $2.9 billion (nominal dollars) was needed just to repair existing schools, let alone construct new ones.

Pressing capital needs were clearly an incentive to borrow. However, the district's capital program became increasingly ambitious because bonded debt was easier to access when it funded brick-and-mortar investments. In contrast, credit rating agencies and institutional investors viewed the use of bonds to finance operating expenses, such as staff costs and programming, skeptically.[43] Gene Saffold, a director in Smith Barney's public finance department who would later serve on the Chicago Board of Education and as Mayor Daley's chief financial officer, stated, "These are capital expenditures . . . improvements that have long-term benefits and will create long-term assets, and we see no problem financing them with debt."[44] Linking its bond issuances to rehabbing and constructing schools helped CPS court the rating agencies, and thus gain access to financial markets. Underwriting capital expenses became CPS' main priority in the late 1990s, displacing other spending priorities.

Empowering a mayor already popular with the financial sector improved the school district's bond ratings. Daley had come into office in 1989, just as the city was entering a real estate–driven recession. In order to pull Chicago out of that crisis, his administration played an activist role by subsidizing an ever-flowing stream of new development. The city laid the groundwork for a building boom by using a panoply of policy instruments that only the public sector could deploy: taxation and spending on infrastructure, land-use regulation, and subsidies to developers and tenants.[45] He also sought out new legal powers to control government agencies and overlapping taxing districts, such as CPS, that could aid or obstruct this wave of building.

The decision to vest authority over the schools in the mayor's office was received warmly by the bond rating agencies and investors. For example, "Joseph O'Keefe [of Standard & Poor's], Warren "Bo" Daniels [a Goldman Sachs vice president], and others said Mayor Daley's increased role in the schools was important" to CPS' recent bond rating upgrades.[46] The year after control was formally handed over to Mayor Daley, all three of the major rating agencies raised their credit ratings for CPS. The district issued its first alternative bond in April 1996, which, officials noted, was only possible because it had "recently achieved investment grade ratings for the first time in twenty years."[47]

Table 8.1. Chicago Public Schools' capital plans and bond ratings, 1995–2002

CPS Fiscal Year	1995	1996	1997	1998	1999	2000	2001	2002
Capital Improvement Plans ($ Billions)	$0.60	$0.81	$1.40	$1.40	$2.00	$2.50	$3.00	$4.0
Standard & Poor's Rating Services	BBB–	**BBB**	**A–**	A–	A–	**A+**	A+	A+
Moody's Investor Services	Ba	**Baa**	**Baa1**	Baa1	**A3**	A3	**A2**	A2
Fitch Ratings	No Rating	**BBB**	**BBB+**	**A–**	A–	**A**	A	A

Note: Ratings in bold indicate a credit rating upgrade. The credit ratings correspond to CPS' fiscal year, which begins July 1 and ends June 30—that is, it spans two calendar years. Some of the rating changes correspond to CPS fiscal years, which differ from the applicable calendar year.

In almost immediate response to those upgrades, CPS increased its multiyear capital plans from an estimated $600 million to $806 million.[48] This pattern continued throughout the late 1990s and early 2000s, as rating agencies increased CPS' credit rating a total of eleven times between 1995 and 2002 (see Table 8.1).[49] As the cost of borrowing decreased, the size and scope of CPS' capital plans jumped from $600 million in 1995 to $4 billion by 2002.

When challenged about the size of its capital program at a time when it struggled to pay its operating costs, such as teacher salaries, CPS deflected blame to the state. Ultimately, however, the district had to repay debt service from the same revenue base used for its operating budget: state aid, property taxes, and the Personal Property Replacement Tax. So while CPS blamed constraints on its operating budget on the state, the district itself exacerbated the problem of operating shortfalls by diverting revenues to pay debt service on its capital program. The numerous credit rating upgrades and the swelling of CPS' capital improvement program are noteworthy because while CPS acquired new flexibilities in allocating revenues, its underlying fiscal structure—e.g., its capped property tax revenues—remained largely unchanged and oriented toward perpetual deficits.

Exotic Instruments

Like many other local governments, CPS turned to new debt issuances despite its worsening financial condition. However, few gravitated toward ARSs in the same way that CPS did.

In May 2003, the Illinois General Assembly passed legislation to specifically authorize variable-rate debt, such as ARSs.[50] A report on that legislation noted that "many units of local government are seeking more financial flexibility with their bonds because they are confronted with budget shortages."[51] Between 2000 and 2007, CPS issued twenty-seven different bond series, of which four were ARSs.[52] ARSs accounted for $990 million or a third (32 percent) of the total bond debt issued by CPS during that time. This was three times that of the municipal market as a whole (where ARS represented approximately 10 percent of the market at its peak in 2004).[53]

CPS' attraction to these instruments was partly due to the fact that ARSs had successfully lowered local governments' borrowing costs in the recent past. It was also due to the proximity of key decision makers in CPS and city hall to the financial sector, which gave them a level of familiarity with these sophisticated instruments infrequently used by other local governments. As early as 2000, a vice president of municipal finance at Goldman Sachs asked to meet with CPS officials about the possibility of the district issuing ARSs.[54] David Vitale, the chief administrative officer of CPS from 2003 to 2006, was in charge of overseeing the school district's borrowing strategy. Vitale, as well as several other high-level administrators and Board of Education members, came out of investment banking and had prior exposure to the use of ARSs. The law firms and boutique underwriting shops that advised CPS (e.g., Chapman & Cutler, Kirkpatrick Pettis, and A.C. Advisory) had been exposed to ARSs through their other dealings with public and private issuers across the country. Because banks are the initial broker-dealers for the bonds, they, too, played a critical intermediating role. For example, for the 2007A Series (CPS' final ARS), Bank of America was both a broker-dealer for the bond issuance and counterparty on one of the swaps connected to that bond.

Despite their expanded use by local governments, concerns with ARSs were becoming apparent by the mid-2000s. Pricewaterhouse-Coopers and other major accounting firms stated in February 2005 "that corporations should, in general, classify ARSs as 'investments' rather than 'cash equivalents' in financial reports."[55] That change in financial-reporting classification signaled that these beacons of risk management did not view ARSs as liquid investments—that is, assets with maturities of three months or less. The reclassification led some financial advisors to counsel investors to reduce or eliminate ARS holdings.[56] The accounting reclassification reduced the attractiveness of ARSs for some investors.[57] At the same time, investment banks—the same ones that acted as broker-dealers for the issuances and that stood to make millions in fees—were stealthily purchasing large amounts of ARS debt, thereby preventing auction failures and keeping the market afloat.[58]

In August 2007, CPS issued three bond series totaling $467.42 million, one of which was an ARS. Since investment banks were propping up the ARS market, it may not have been clear to CPS just how fragile the market was.[59] Around the same time (2006–7), the Securities and Exchange Commission (SEC) reached settlements with financial institutions selling ARS for alleged violations.[60] Of the six broker-dealers involved in the sale of CPS' 2007 ARS, four were firms that had to pay penalties because of the SEC settlements.[61] These same firms continued marketing ARSs to potential issuers as late as 2007.[62]

The 2007 bonds were a refunding and reissuance of previous debt and were intended to reduce CPS' debt service and fund school construction projects. However, almost immediately after CPS issued its last ARS, there were widespread auction failures, causing the interest rates CPS paid to soar.[63] Market wide, there were more than sixty auction failures in August and September of that same year as the major investment banks, facing their own crises, had to withdraw from the ARS market. Further, as insurers began to be downgraded, the value of ARSs also decreased.[64] In May 2008 CPS refinanced all its outstanding ARS debt into three new bond series, two of which were variable-rate debt paired with interest-rate swaps.

Powers

CPS' foray into ARSs paired with interest-rate swaps made some sense given the unpopularity of raising property taxes, lack of access to other sources of revenue, and perceived cost effectiveness of that form of debt. However, its increasingly ambitious capital plans, egged on by the bond rating agencies and other stakeholders, also fueled its pursuit of these instruments. Maintaining centralized political control and easy access to financial markets has meant that mayors can initiate pet building projects that win them votes while pushing the costs into the future so that they are someone else's problem.

For example, proceeds from the 2007 ARS issuance were meant to finance CPS' portion of Mayor Daley's Modern Schools across Chicago (MSAC) initiative.[65] Daley unveiled MSAC, a $1.1 billion plan to construct twenty-four new schools and renovate three existing ones, during his reelection bid.[66] The city pledged $666 million using bonds backed by TIF revenues, and CPS was responsible for the remaining portion. In other municipalities, schools protested the use of TIF, but in Chicago, the jurisdiction with the most to lose from TIF, CPS was effectively run by the mayor. To compensate the school district for diverting property tax revenues away from it (or, at the least, restricting its ability to levy its tax rate on the appreciation in TIF districts), the mayor authorized the use of TIF funds to pay for the construction of new public school buildings through the MSAC program.[67] CPS' 2007 bonds filled in the gap so that the city (through the Public Building Commission) could construct new schools.

Exposures

While financialization provides local governments with new powers, it also places local governments and their ability to control the bond ratings and transfer payments at the center of a fragile architecture of interlinked financial obligations and contingencies that is shot through with risks. Novel municipal securities were initially framed as financial marvels, able to reconcile the disjuncture between ballooning expenditure needs and increasingly scarce revenues. The financial crisis, particularly the collapse of the auction-rate market, interrupted that fantasy. Taking stock of the aftermath, the Federal Reserve Bank of Chicago noted:

> Auction rate securities represented an ingenious attempt to square a particular financial circle: to create a funding instrument that appears long term from the borrower's perspective but short-term from the lender's perspective. *We now see what should have been obvious before: Such an arrangement is impossible.*[68]

When the auction-rate market collapsed in February 2008, CPS had 32 percent of its outstanding debt in ARSs. For this reason, the collapse had far more serious implications for the district's fiscal health than for other school districts and cities. In the wake of the 2007–9 recession, CPS began to issue debt to pay for day-to-day operating expenses. Its outstanding debt increased from $4.5 billion in 2007 to $6.5 billion in 2014.[69] Although it created some short-term relief, this indebtedness only pushed the district's structural deficits into the future. Cognizant of this fact, the credit rating agencies downgraded CPS in 2011 for the first time since it had been returned to mayoral control in 1995. The three major rating agencies went on to downgrade CPS' credit rating multiple times between 2011 and 2015; Moody's alone downgraded CPS eight times during that period.

The downgrades affected CPS' debt payments. Although it no longer has ARSs in its portfolio, CPS nevertheless had $1.14 billion in variable-rate debt at the end of fiscal year 2014, and six of its nine variable-rate bonds were paired with swaps.[70] Furthermore, because CPS' credit rating dipped below designated thresholds, the counterparties to the swaps had the option to terminate them.[71] Out of the four ARSs, CPS refinanced two of them as fixed-rate debt, paying millions of dollars in new underwriting charges. Credit-enhancement providers also raised their fees in response to the downgrade.[72] Instead of suing the banks or petitioning the SEC

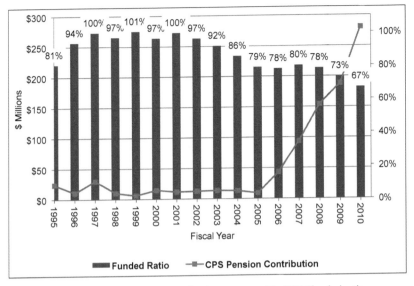

Figure 8.2. CPS annual pension contribution compared to CTPF funded ratio. Employee contributions and investment returns secured the fund's relative fiscal health between 1996 and 2003.

to recover losses, CPS paid $20 million to terminate the associated swap contracts.[73] The *Chicago Tribune* estimated that CPS will end up paying a total of $100 million more on the ARSs, swaps, and associated refinancing than if the district had just issued fixed-rate debt in the first instance.[74]

Compounding this difficult situation, the habitual underfunding of the teachers' pension fund came back to haunt CPS at exactly the wrong moment. State law allowed CPS to contribute nothing to its pension fund as long as the pension fund's funded ratio was at least 90 percent (the lower the funded ratio, the higher the contribution CPS has to make to its pension fund). In 2005 the funded ratio dipped below 90 percent, which meant that CPS had to start contributing to it per state statute. Figure 8.2 shows CPS' annual pension contributions to CTPF between 1995 and 2010.[75] Because reducing pension liabilities by cutting benefits was not an option, Daley's successor, Mayor Rahm Emanuel, and CPS demanded that the State of Illinois, not CPS, pay the required pension contributions.[76]

Revenue for debt-service payments, penalties, and pension contributions has to come from somewhere. Unfortunately, austerity measures have been the state's and city's response. In 2013 Chicago made national headlines when it was announced that forty-nine public schools were going to be closed in a single year. Although the school closures were initially presented as a necessary, cost-saving measure, the Board of Education largely framed that policy decision as a means of "rightsizing" the district and closing underutilized schools.[77] It then announced rounds of layoffs, including special education teachers, to close its budget gap.[78] The ultimate cost of CPS' precarious finances appears to be disproportionately displaced onto already vulnerable populations who depend upon the public school system.

Another response by the city has been to pit interest groups against each other and obscure the complex consequences of using financial instruments. Cities often focus on popular targets in the crosshairs of austerity debates—namely, public-employee unions. Instead of highlighting the instruments themselves or the factors that led to their adoption, the City of Chicago has blamed the Chicago Teacher's Union and a population of "difficult-to-serve" students for CPS' fiscal woes.[79] Shifting the blame to others masks the roles the city, CPS, investment banks, and credit rating agencies have all played in creating this fraught situation.

While risky financing techniques are not the only cause of CPS' fiscal problems, turning public assets into vehicles for financial accumulation intensifies pressure to protect repayment streams and asset values. The City of Chicago has chosen to take the side of the bondholders, who possess the legal protections that taxpayers lack, in hopes that it will not be barred from future access to the ever-important debt markets.

Conclusion

Chicago's experience with ARSs paired with interest-rate swaps illustrates the complex construction of public entities as financial subjects. While CPS was something of an outlier among school districts (although districts in Philadelphia and Denver adopted similar financial-management strategies), its behavior was not so unusual for local governments in general. Since the early 1990s, state and local governments in the United States and increasingly around the world have taken on record amounts of debt to finance operations and infrastructure (although levels stayed constant relative to total revenue).[80] They have moved from relying on general obligation bonds with fixed rates to variable-rate instruments to less-seasoned securities paired with derivatives.

When the interest rates local governments pay are set, reset, and indexed to the value of other assets and trades, governments are exposed to more volatility in global markets. This volatility came to a head with the financial crisis and, specifically, the collapse of the auction-rate market. Several local governments—from the City of Detroit to Jefferson County, Alabama, to transit authorities in San Francisco and New York City—have experienced collateral calls and terminations of their interest-rate swaps, which have triggered billions in penalties and costs.

An additional concern with the increasing financialization of urban policy is that it threatens to further remove political questions from the public sphere and widen the gulf between citizens and decision makers. As assets are collateralized and revenue streams are sold to different private entities, taxpayers have less oversight or control over their money. Few understand the mechanics of these instruments, let alone the sources of risk that might threaten repayment schemes. Immediately following the financial crisis, there was a sustained interest in protecting local governments and taxpayers, but this initially robust regulatory response has narrowed to increasing transparency and regulating the advisors promoting such instruments. The enabling and encouragement of high amounts of local government debt by both public and private actors leading up to the financial crisis have received little attention in comparison.

Our chapter seeks to fill in this gap. We have demonstrated how local governments such as CPS were both under pressure and legally enabled to take on "nontraditional" forms of debt in response to austerity and devolutionary measures imposed by state legislatures. Through their advisors and private-sector connections, local governments encountered investment banks overeager to purchase whatever they could issue and compliant credit rating agencies. The positive reception by investors and the apparent success of these strategies in lowering interest rates emboldened local governments to aim high with expensive capital plans. Understanding the structural and political drivers of risk-taking by the public sector is vital to understanding how local governance becomes financialized, as the fallout from extreme indebtedness has only reinforced these motivations in the postcrisis years.

Notes

1. Greta Krippner, "The Financialization of the American Economy," *Socio-Economic Review* 3, no. 2 (2005): 173–208; Rachel Weber, "Selling City Futures: The Financialization of Urban Redevelopment Policy," *Economic Geography* 86, no. 3 (2010): 251–74.

2. See, for example, Jason Hackworth, "Local Autonomy, Bond-Rating Agencies and Neoliberal Urbanism in the United States," *International Journal of Urban and Regional Research* 26, no. 4 (2002): 707–25.

3. Weber, "Selling City Futures," 251–74; Philip Ashton, Marc Doussard, and Rachel Weber, "Reconstituting the State: City Powers and Exposures in Chicago's Infrastructure Leases," *Urban Studies* 53, no. 7 (2014): 1384–1400.

4. Brett Christophers, "The Limits to Financialization," *Dialogues in Human Geography* 5, no. 2 (2015): 183–200.

5. Merton H. Miller, "Financial Innovation: The Last Twenty Years and the Next," *Journal of Financial and Quantitative Analysis* 21, no. 4 (1986): 459–71.

6. Christin Sgarlata Chung, "Municipal Securities: The Crisis of State and Local Government Indebtedness, Systemic Costs of Low Default Rates, and Opportunities for Reform," *Cardozo Law Review* 34 (2013): 1455–538.

7. Between 2000 and 2004 alone, new issuances more than tripled. See Craig Johnson, Martin Luby, and Tima Moldogaziev, "Lessons Learned from the Birth, Growth and Collapse of the Municipal Auction Rate Securities (MARS) Market," in *State and Local Financial Instruments Policy Changes and Management* (Northampton, Mass.: Edward Elgar, 2014), 147–68.

8. Johnson, Luby, and Moldogaziev, 149.

9. Johnson, Luby, and Moldogaziev, 149.

10. Eric Chu, Craig Underwood, Thomas Fox, Jon McMahon, Roger Davis, Stephen Spitz, Albert Simons III, and George Wolf, "Interest Rate Swaps and Their Application to Tax-Exempt Financing," in *The Handbook of Municipal Bonds*, ed. Sylvan Feldstein and Frank Fabozzi (Hoboken, N.J.: John Wiley & Sons, 2008), 299–344.

11. Chu et al., 155–59.

12. Chu et al., 147–68. A put feature allows an investor to liquidate a security, demanding payment from the issuer at a stated time before the final stated maturity of the bond; see Neil O'Hara, *The Fundamentals of Municipal Bonds*, 6th ed. (Hoboken, N.J.: John Wiley & Sons, 2012), 276.

13. W. Bartley Hildreth and C. Kurt Zorn, "The Evolution of the State and Local Government Municipal Debt Market over the Past Quarter Century," *Public Budgeting & Finance* 25, no. 4s (2005): 127–53.

14. Hildreth and Zorn, 152. The bond insurance lulled "investors and issuers to sleep as to the full risks inherent and explicitly stated in their [Auction Rate Security] debt indentures."

15. Johnson, Luby, and Moldogaziev, "Lessons Learned," 150.

16. We address this issue in more detail in Amanda Kass, Martin J. Luby, and Rachel Weber, "Taking a Risk: Explaining the Use of Complex Debt Finance by the Chicago Public Schools," *Urban Affairs Review* 55, no. 4 (2019): 1035–69.

17. Matt Taibbi, "The Great American Bubble Machine," *Rolling Stone*, April 5, 2010, www.rollingstone.com/politics/news/the-great-american-bubble-machine-20100405.

18. Daniel Coq-Huelva, "Urbanisation and Financialisation in the Context of a Rescaling State: The Case of Spain," *Antipode* 45, no. 5 (2013): 1213–31.

19. Jamie Peck, "Pushing Austerity: State Failure, Municipal Bankruptcy and the Crises of Fiscal Federalism in the USA," *Cambridge Journal of Regions, Economy and Society* 7, no. 1 (2014): 17–44.

20. Hackworth, "Local Autonomy, Bond-Rating Agencies," 707–25.

21. Susan Clarke and Gary Gaile, *The Work of Cities* (Minneapolis: University of Minnesota Press, 1998); Sara Hinkley and Rachel Weber. "Incentives and Austerity: How Did the Great Recession Affect Municipal Economic Development Policy?" Urban Affairs Review (2020): 1078087420964254.

22. Jason Hackworth, *The Neoliberal City: Governance, Ideology, and Development in American Urbanism* (Ithaca, N.Y.: Cornell University Press, 2007); Shaun French, Andrew Leyshon, and Thomas Wainwright, "Financializing Space, Spacing Financialization," *Progress in Human Geography* 35, no. 6 (2011): 798–819.

23. O'Hara, *Fundamentals of Municipal Bonds*.

24. Weber, "Selling City Futures," 251–74.

25. Weber, "Selling City Futures," 251–74.

26. Ashton, Doussard, and Weber, "Reconstituting the State."

27. The School Finance Authority was created via Public Act 81–1221.

28. Charles Mount, "Jenner Urges OK of Finance Panel," *Chicago Tribune*, February 20, 1980.

29. Jeffrey R. Henig and Wilbur C. Rich, *Mayors in the Middle: Politics,*

Race, and Mayoral Control of Urban Schools (Princeton, N.J.: Princeton University Press, 2004); Frederick M. Hess, "Looking for Leadership: Assessing the Case for Mayoral Control of Urban School Systems," *American Journal of Education* 114, no. 3 (2008): 219–45.

30. Public education in Illinois is primarily financed by local property tax revenues. State school aid as a portion of total primary and secondary school spending is among the lowest in the country. See Casey Banas and Daniel Egler, "Byrne School Bailout: Raise Tax, Bond Power," *Chicago Tribune*, December 8, 1979; Michael Klonsky, "GOP Clears Field, Daley Runs with the Ball," *Catalyst Chicago*, September 1, 1995; and Lorraine Forte, "New Law Lets Board Shift Money to Balance Budget," *Catalyst Chicago*, September 7, 1995.

31. Chicago Public Schools, *Final Budget, School Year 1995–1996* (Chicago, August 14, 1995).

32. PTELL limits the property tax extensions of non-home-rule governments to the lesser of 5 percent or the increase in the national Consumer Price Index for the preceding year. CPS can raise property tax revenue beyond the PTELL limit only through a referendum.

33. A local government designates a TIF district for improvement and subsidizes developers to make improvements there. As property values in the district rise and taxes there increase, the local government uses the incremental growth in tax revenues to pay off the initial and ongoing development expenditures.

34. This analysis does not distinguish between increments that would have occurred "but for" the use of TIF and increments that would not have materialized without TIF—so represents the outer limit of possible opportunity costs for CPS. See Bob Bruno and Alison Dickson Quesada, *Tax Increment Financing and Chicago Public Schools: A New Approach to Comprehending a Complex Relationship* (University of Illinois Labor Education Program White Paper, December 2011).

35. The legislation defines alternative bonds as "bonds issued in lieu of revenue bonds" so that the financed project does not have to generate the revenue necessary to pay off the bond.

36. This was part of Public Act 89–15. In Illinois, state law dictates the amount of money local governments have to contribute annually to public pension systems.

37. Forte, "New Law Lets Board."

38. The relevant law is Public Act 90–548.

39. Administrators in CPS recognized that they were taking a calculated risk; eventually the CTPF's funded ratio would dip below 90 percent, and the district would have to begin contributing to it (see *CPS Tentative Budget 1998–9*).

40. Andre Ward, "S&P Upgrades Chicago Schools to A-Minus," *The Bond Buyer*, April 8, 1997.

41. Ward, "S&P Upgrades Chicago Schools."

42. GAO, *School Facilities: Condition of America's Schools* (February 1995).

43. Before the return to mayoral control, the Illinois School Finance Authority issued $427 million in bonds to cover operating expenses; see Cris Carmody, "Chicago School Officials Craft Capital Plan; $175 Million in Debt Proposed," *The Bond Buyer*, April 14, 1995. Prior to the issuance, Moody's vice president stated, "Selling bonds to meet operating expenses doesn't quite fit that bill"; see April Hattori, "Bonds May Not Be Best Bet for Chicago Schools, Rating Officials Say," *The Bond Buyer*, July 14, 1993.

44. Carmody, "Chicago School Officials."

45. Rachel Weber, *From Boom to Bubble: How Finance Built the New Chicago* (Chicago: University of Chicago Press, 2015).

46. Andrew Ward, "Chicago Schools' $500 Million Offering Gets a Welcome Yawn," *The Bond Buyer*, April 23, 1997.

47. Chicago Public Schools, *Tentative Budget, School Year 1996–1997* (Chicago, June 1996).

48. The Tentative Budget 1996–7 states, "Due to the ratings boost, CPS was able to finance its $806 million capital improvement plan."

49. In 1997 all three rating agencies again boosted CPS' credit rating, stating that those increases were connected to mayoral control being made permanent.

50. Sponsors of the legislation portrayed the change as a technicality that clarified existing law. Interestingly, CPS issued its first auction-rate security prior to the passage of that legislation in February 2003 (Illinois House transcript, May 31, 2003; Illinois Senate transcript, March 26, 2003; Illinois Senate floor debate, March 26, 2003).

51. Jason Grotto and Heather Gillers, "Risky Bonds Prove Costly for Chicago Public Schools," *Chicago Tribune*, November 7, 2014.

52. It issued two in 2003, one in 2004, and the last in 2007. This figure only shows that the bonded debt is from the Outstanding Debt as of the June 2007 schedule (CPS' Official Statement for the Series 2009A bond, which includes debt for the 2007A and 2007BC Series). Chicago Public Schools, *Official Statement: Unlimited Tax General Obligation Refunding Bonds (Dedicated Revenue), Series 2009A* (Chicago, March 11, 2009).

53. This figure was calculated using the Outstanding Debt as of the June 2007 schedule contained in CPS' Official Statement for the Series 2009A bond (CPS, "Series 2009A," A-34), including the debt for the 2007A and 2007BC Series. Total variable-rate debt accounted for 57 percent of debt issued during this time.

54. Grotto and Gillers, "Risky Bonds."

55. Andrew D. Austin, *Auction-Rate Securities*, Congressional Research Service (Washington, D.C., 2012), 7.

56. Austin, 7.

57. Austin, 7.

58. Johnson, Luby, and Moldogaziev, "Lessons Learned," 147–68.

59. CPS was likely aware of the role banks were playing in the auctions, given that the official statement for the 2007A Series notes SEC settlements with broker/dealers about disclosing their involvement in auctions; see CPS, *Unlimited Tax General Obligation Refunding Bonds (Dedicated Revenues), Series 2007A* (Chicago, August 24, 2007): 18–19. Further, in light of the SEC's probes, Cook County "scrapped their bond sales in the auction market" in June 2004; see Lance Pan, "Forecasting a Perfect Storm: New Developments Aggravate the Potential Fall of the Auction Rate Securities Market" (Capital Advisors Group, 2005).

60. Austin, "Auction Rate Securities."

61. Bank of America, Merrill Lynch, Morgan Stanley, and RBC Capital Markets all paid penalties.

62. Grotto and Gillers, "Risky Bonds Prove Costly."

63. Johnson, Luby, and Moldogaziev, "Lessons Learned," 147–68.

64. Johnson, Luby, and Moldogaziev, 147–68.

65. Yvette Shields, "Chicago Schools $210M Deal the First of Three," *The Bond Buyer*, July 30, 2007.

66. Mayor Emanuel initiated a program that required every school to have a functioning playground. This politically popular move, intended to soften his image after closing almost fifty schools in 2013, came at the expense of investing to upgrade and maintain existing buildings.

67. To make the payments, city officials "ported" revenues from TIF districts across the city, even from those that did not receive new school buildings. Fran Spielman, "Side Deals Seals $1 Billion School Building Plan," *Chicago Sun-Times*, December 12, 2006.

68. Emphasis added, Johnson, Luby, and Moldogaziev, "Lessons Learned," 165.

69. Chicago Public Schools. *Comprehensive Annual Financial Report, for the Year ended June 30, 2014* (Chicago, 2015); Chicago Public Schools, *Official Statement: Unlimited Tax General Obligation Bonds (Dedicated Alternative Revenues), Series 2015CE* (Chicago, April 21, 2015).

70. As of June 30, 2014 (CPS, "Comprehensive Annual Financial Report"), variable-rate debt accounted for 18.4 percent of CPS' total outstanding debt of $6.18 billion.

71. As of 2015, none of the counterparties had terminated the swaps.

72. Saqib Bhatti and Carrie Sloan, *Our Kind of Town: A Financial Plan that Puts Chicago's Communities First* (Refund America Project and the Roosevelt Institute, March 24, 2015).

73. Heather Gillers and Jason Grotto, "How the Tribune Analyzed CPS' Bond Deals," *Chicago Tribune*, November 7, 2014.

74. Gillers and Grotto, "How the Tribune Analyzed CPS' Bond Deals."

75. CTPF actuarial reports do not separate pension contributions by their revenue sources, so the CPS pension contributions in Figure 8.2 include those also made from federal funds.

76. The state's constitution prevents reductions in public pension benefits.

77. Linda Lutton and Becky Vevea, "Chicago Proposes Closing 53 Elementary Schools, Firing Staff at Another 6," 91.5 WBEZ FM, March 21, 2013.

78. Heather Cherone, "CPS Announces Special Education Cuts, but Questions Remain," *DNAinfo Chicago*, September 28, 2015.

79. Alana Baum, "Commentary: I Support Chicago Teachers—But Not Their Union," *Chicago Tribune*, December 6, 2015.

80. Ronald Fisher and Robert Wassmer, "The Issuance of State and Local Debt during the United States Great Recession," *National Tax Journal* 67, no. 1 (2014): 113–50.

Part IV

Bringing the Public State Back In

9

Building the Public City, Privately

David C. Perry and Mary Donoghue

> The impasse is deep: Americans' appetite for government
> services exceeds their willingness to be taxed.
>
> —Robert J. Samuelson, *Washington Post*

Building the public city, privately, in the United States is part of everyday urban life and politics. While 40 percent of U.S. bridges overall were in need of repair in 1994, today in the 102 most populated metropolitan areas, this number is a bit over 15 percent.[1] We have seen a great shift in the devolution of infrastructure services from the federal government to the state and local levels, but without the fiscal wherewithal to pay for such increased service demands we have seen a concomitant rise in commodification and privatization. In short, in political and economic terms, the Columbia University public administrator Steven Cohen suggests, "just at the time when government is needed most to build twenty-first century sustainable infrastructure, citizens at the local level are least interested in paying for new infrastructure through taxes."[2] This condition makes Samuelson's observation, now two decades old, even more prescient—devolution of policy to the local level makes Americans even more demanding of public infrastructure in the twenty-first century and, it seems, equally unwilling to pay the taxes necessary to provide the new and sustainable public works.[3] At the same time, this process includes services as proximate as today's pothole fillings and as futuristic as tomorrow's next bridge or dam. It also revisits that most fundamental of questions in liberal-democratic and devolutionary American politics: Who's going to pay? No one likes potholes and almost everyone is intrigued by the possibilities of a technical and innovative future, but such convergence of concern and interest breaks down when it comes time to pay the bill or increase the taxes with which to pay the bill.

Hence, the growing number of potholes in the street is just as likely to be the result of lack of funds for maintenance as it is to be the result of inclement weather. And while there is a growing consensus that every household can benefit from the services generated by fiber optics and broadband, the debate over ownership and finance (between cable companies, telephone companies, and the state) is actually drifting away as the *public* nature of universal access and citizen rights is replaced by the *individualistic* ownership and administration claims of private firms. Infrastructure policy has changed with the transformed role of the state in the political-economic production of policy, starting with the public–private notions of infrastructure.[4] This chapter does two things: (1) it first discusses the changing significance of "internal improvements" to public works; (2) it then examines the subsequent fiscal move toward commodification and privatization.

Public-Infrastructure Policy

In the early nineteenth century, the federal government tried, without success, to build a national program of "internal improvements." But a federal politics of public infrastructure, or building even a national highway system (à la Albert Gallatin), fell victim to regional and even presidential (in this case, Andrew Jackson's) opposition. From Albert Gallatin's description of internal improvements early in the nineteenth century to Herbert Muschamp's claims for (privatized) infrastructure near the end of the twentieth, and even to past-President Clinton's unfulfilled promise to inaugurate a state-directed multibillion-dollar program to "rebuild America," it is hard in this "age of Trump" to find a more impassioned or purposive policy discourse than that concerning public works.[5]

Yet, for all this heady discussion, public infrastructure is often taken for granted. When roads, bridges, waste disposal sites, and water systems work best, they are noticed least or not at all. And when attention is finally focused on "infrastructure" (usually in response to systemic failure or severe and continued congestion) the "real damage has already been done."[6] This reactive, postcrisis pattern has certainly been the case for most of the past four decades, with one national study after another describing a litany of decayed and deteriorating conditions plaguing the nation's public facilities.[7]

It is both the seminal role that public works play in social formation and their ubiquitous influence in our everyday lives that make it all the more urgent that we grasp the political forces behind infrastructure policy. Public works, or infrastructure, whether public or privatized, are at the very heart of the physical, technological, and fiscal foundations of the American city now and in the future; or, as urban designer William Morris puts it, "Infrastructure is the safety net of the social system."[8] Put bluntly, when the "infrastructure" of a city fails, the entire city as well as our individual daily existence can be dramatically changed. Therefore, understanding the politics, not just the engineering, of infrastructure is important.

Public Works

At the local level, the actual process of building public works was and is a problematic one. The rapid rate of nineteenth-century urbanization in the United States created conditions that overwhelmed many attempts to deal with such problems.[9] The increase in the number and population of cities in the nineteenth century created unprecedented levels of disease, congestion, and fires. Yet historian Letty Anderson found significant lags in the time it took cities to mount concerted attacks on such conditions. First, there was a lag between the appearance of the problem (i.e., disease or fires) and the perception of its true significance. A second lag occurred between the time it took to mobilize people to respond to the problem and the discovery of a perceived solution (for example, the installation of citywide water systems). Third, Anderson suggests there was always a delay while cities tried to come up with plans to "minimize the uncertainty of the results."[10] Anderson found that these three time lags were reduced as more cities found out that others had applied similarly acceptable solutions to similar problems. Josef Konvitz suggests this pattern of urban intransigence occurred almost every time cities attempted to employ new technologies to meet new issues of internal improvement.[11] He found that "ideas and techniques in city building did not evolve as rapidly as the economic, demographic and social aspects of urbanization. City builders, anxious to exploit the opportunities urban growth provided, mastered the design and construction of specialized, utilitarian building types (many of an unprecedented scale or functional purpose) by applying already proven techniques to labor, land and capital."[12] Put another way, even after it became clear that new infrastructure systems would help with conditions of rapid urbanization and stimulate economic growth, cities would take years to determine the right approach and even longer to decide on how to pay for the system.[13] The relationship of water systems and water treatment to the control of disease was fully established by the late 1880s.[14] However, water treatment, sewers, and sewage treatment did not become an everyday fact of life until well into the twentieth century.[15]

In the absence of any clear federal role in the late nineteenth century, this pragmatic and temporized approach to public works delivery was all the more understandable given the scale of the projects and the costs of production. The introduction of large-scale networked sewage systems, for example, demanded large-scale financial investments and geographically broad networks of pipes and pumps that spread across municipal boundaries. Their installation could be politically perilous in that while these technologies could remove sewerage from one municipality, they might have deleterious downstream effects for a neighboring community. More broadly, "the various characteristics of sewerage technology, such as its capital intensiveness and its planning requirements, as well as the fact that its effective operation bore little relationship to municipal boundaries, required a number of institutional adaptations and innovations. These involved planning innovations for large-scale public works, [and] developing methods to raise capital funds."[16] By the 1940s the technological networks promised by nineteenth-century reformers were finally in place: sewers, water systems, tracks, and electrical and telephone wires crisscrossed the city providing services at a level that was inconceivable in the 1890s.[17]

Along with the technology and the physical networks, however, other features of building the public city were also in place. The scale of public works in the twentieth century far exceeded any dreams in the nineteenth century and with scale came issues of government and finance. Building the public city in the twentieth century introduced substantial new issues of governmental relations. The magnitude of the demands for new highways and utility systems, the reemergence of the federal government, and the creation of local public authorities and special purpose governments served as three of the cornerstones of service delivery. The final cornerstone of policy formation was finance—not only did the new technologies of public works portend substantial changes in the environment; they also caused substantial increases in public debt.

Public Infrastructure

Few terms have undergone such dramatically altered connotations as the word *infrastructure*. Early on in the last century, *infrastructure* was essentially a military term used to describe the permanent fixtures of military installations—the base camps and airstrips or fixed ports that when taken together formed the systems of defensive and offensive warfare. The historian Bruce Seeley suggests that it was economists who first extended the term's usage, including, for example, those features of a society that W. W. Rostow once labeled "social overhead capital."[18] By this, Rostow and others meant the capital invested in roads, utility systems, communications, education, health, and other governmental facilities as the foundation for economic development. However, it was not until the 1980s that *infrastructure* replaced *public works* as the term most commonly used to describe the physical artifacts and what Tarr and Dupuy have called the "technological sinews" of contemporary social formations.[19] Today the notion of infrastructure has come to include "almost every support system in modern industrial society, public or private. Infrastructure is said to include not only roads and sewers but national transportation grids, communication systems, media, housing, education, computer networks, and fiber-optic "information superhighways."[20] Or as Muschamp concludes, *infrastructure* is "shorthand for the structural underpinnings of the public realm"— and, of course much of the private realm too.[21]

Josef Konvitz combines the definitions of Seeley and Muschamp, when he concludes approvingly that, "unlike public works, which it subsumes, the term infrastructure is at once a description of physical assets and of their economic, social and political role."[22] And of these three roles, the role most often stressed is the economic one. Most recent descriptions of infrastructure, whether they be ones describing the uses of public projects or ones assessing conditions of physical decay and fiscal distress, include some measure of its sufficiency to meet "future economic growth and development."[23] In this sense, what Thomas Jefferson and George Washington called "internal improvements" or, later on, what engineers, reformers, and Franklin D. Roosevelt called "public works" are today described as infrastructure: the technologies and their structural and spatial applications that serve as the support systems of market society.

The term *public* was added to *infrastructure* as a way of referring to the mixture of public- and private-sector activities that go into the definition, design, finance, operation, and maintenance of these "support systems." What separates the notion of *public infrastructure* from the earlier terms *internal improvements* and *public works* is its inclusiveness and its emphasis on systems of support. Earlier discussions concentrated on the "improvements"—the highway itself, or the canal itself, as part of the support system. And the same can be said of public works. In 1984, Triborough Bridge and Tunnel Authority executive secretary Harold Blake noted the oddity of hearing public works described as infrastructure. What Blake was referring to was the incremental political practice at the local level that, for much of this century, placed less emphasis on describing public works as systems and more on the bridges or highway networks as projects. But ultimately the term *public infrastructure*, understood as the "technological systems, with each road, bridge and drainpipe closely linked to an intricate . . . delicate . . . network of supporting elements"[24] is a far more complete description than *public works* or the nineteenth-century term *internal improvements*.

Ironically, then, while the primacy of the relationship of these fragile technological systems to growth and development has a long-standing currency in America, there is a similarly lengthy history of American reluctance to pay for public works at the national, state, or local levels.[25] For features of the public realm so technologically fragile and potentially capable of breaking down, it is surprising how little time, money, and effort are employed in rehabilitation, maintenance, and upkeep. This contrary combination of the accepted importance of public infrastructure and the lack of stable finance and maintenance policies to support it forms much of the dynamic basis of the politics of public infrastructure.

Infrastructure

In the past two decades, the word *public* has been detached from *infrastructure*, leaving the term alone as the preferred usage. Rhetorically, this seems like a simple linguistic shift. Politically, though, the way in which policy makers and other officials discuss infrastructure can change the way it is viewed and defined, as we saw in the expanding systemic definition from *public works* to *public infrastructure*. There are potential implications that relate to the role of the public in infrastructure—the "public," linguistically, has been removed at this point. So, potentially, infrastructure is no longer considered a "public good" or a civic right. It instead can become a privilege or a commodity that one pays to use. We must consider this, if only because of the timing of the change. In the past decade or so, more states and municipalities are removing themselves from increasing parts of the service provision and infrastructure administration process. Particularly since the recession of 2008, city governments have had to scramble to find ways to finance infrastructure maintenance without going bankrupt. The public, at this moment, is for an increasing number of key infrastructure networks removed from both the collective discourse and the provision of public infrastructure.

Aside from arguing over the definition of *infrastructure*, it is important to remember the historical conception of "public" in public works and infrastructure. "Public" is generally considered to be the domain of the state. Public works are provided for collective consumption. Everyone, regardless of his or her status, is said to have access, at least nominally, both to public provisions, such as the sewer system and sidewalks, and to public facilities, such as public schools and libraries. That said, quality may vary spatially—that is, one may have *access* to a public school in the neighborhood, but that school may not be of the same quality as one on the other side of town. So, defining what is *public* is about *access*, not necessarily about *quality*. Public works have varying significances and importance on the provision side and the use side. States and municipalities, historically, relied on the public collectively, through taxes or other collected revenue, to finance the grid that creates modern society and allows for the maintenance of public health, safety, and convenience. The public, in turn, relies on the state to provide these aforementioned pieces of infrastructure that are often overlooked and taken for granted. In short, when *public* is removed from the term *public infrastructure* or *public works*, its social significance changes.

Financing

While the importance of the state provision of resources is a key part of this discussion, the crux of the argument is financing mechanisms. All projects, deemed vital or not, face one of the key questions we started this essay with: Who pays? There are a variety of reasons for this, starting with the fact that, in the United States, there has always been a lack of a clear federal public works policy. Provision of public works and the construction of public infrastructure have generally been left to individual states. Over time, more and more of the infrastructure burden has devolved to the municipalities. This suggests the continuing devolution of state authority. Even so, states nearly bankrupted themselves in the 1800s undertaking massive projects such as railroads and dams. After that, state legislatures set limits on the amount of public debt the state could take out at one time, requiring a referendum process for individual projects. This worked for the twenty-four states allowing them, but the lingering question of who pays—combined with the general individualistic reluctance to raise taxes—required new financing schemes: from general obligation bonds and, then, revenue bonds in the nineteenth century to special districts and public authorities in the twentieth century and other localizing methods of service delivery, maintenance, and administration (more recently).[26] These evolving methods have come to be the main ways in which many states and municipalities finance a substantial share of infrastructure development, administration, and maintenance.

These methods are substantially the ways in which officials, faced with almost two centuries of increasing local and state devolution, have built the city through the "backdoor" of public financing. After states were banned by the legislatures from forming debt without referenda or raised taxes, they turned to cities as an initial backdoor debt financing mechanism. Initially, localities could engage in debt formation for infrastructure building without having to gain public support. These devolutionary policy changes strengthened urban governance, but they required an enormous amount of capital, which led to increased localized debt formation and the need for new financing mechanisms that could allow cities to avoid default. Localities, facing possible taxpayer revolt, moved from general obligation debt to particularized revenue bonds, where the debt would be paid by the users—the "public" was no longer a part of public works.

Another method of infrastructure financing is the public authority, which gained immense popularity during the second half of the twentieth century. By as early as 1990, more than two-thirds ($601.9 billions) of local debt was secured through newly created special agencies or through public authorities; hence, a thematic focus of this volume. Public authorities today are used to financing new projects separately from the general state or local budget. The public authority became an increasingly popular mechanism for debt financing. Public authorities and their special district cousins were especially praised for their efficiency, proper modes of debt formation, and lack of taxation. In 1953 they were praised by the Council of State Governments for their extraconstitutionality—basically, for being a backdoor financing mechanism.[27] That they became a permanent fixture in urban policy is expressly against their initial purpose, but their efficiency and popularity made it impossible to get rid of them. Robert Moses is seen as perfecting the use of public authorities in New York State to build projects such as the Triborough Bridge. When he was asked to speak on the occasion of the fifth anniversary of the bridge, he spoke about the emergence of the Triborough Bridge Authority as a new debt-formation device and not about the bridge's engineering wonders.[28]

The use of public authorities and revenue bonds is indicative of a larger change in the theory of public works. As devolution caused municipalities to take on more of the burden of infrastructure building and with traditional debt formation and financing mechanisms having fallen out of favor, municipalities have had to come up with more creative ways to pay for expected public works. This leads to the concept of the commodification of public works and public infrastructure. Infrastructure becomes less a public good and more an available service that one must seek out and pay for. Examples include everything from parking meters to tolls on roads and bridges to infrastructure fees on water and electrical services.

Building the Public City, Privately

We want to begin this discussion with the argument that the processes of commodification and privatization, while closely linked, are distinct entities. Commodification of public services has been around for decades, existing since the time of revenues and user fees. Toll roads are a fact of life in American travel, and bridge, tunnel, and parking fees are nothing new either. The planning scholar Philip Ashton and his colleagues helped us make the distinction between commodification and privatization when they found that "existing assets that charged user fees took a longer time to privatize than new, non-tolled facilities."[29]

Let us go further and suggest that the concept of privatization exists on a different scale from that of commodification. Instead of capturing revenues through use, privatization gets revenue through the sale or lease of *ownership*, so a governing body both receives money from the deal and relieves themselves of the tasks of administration and maintenance of the piece of infrastructure sold. Of course, privately owned infrastructure is also commodified. The Chicago Skyway is owned by a private firm and charges tolls based on use. So commodified infrastructure is not necessarily private, but privatized infrastructure is generally commodified as well.

Changes in Revenue Structure

Sources of infrastructure financing have changed dramatically in the past several decades. A study by Michael A. Pagano and David Perry in 2008 found that municipal governments came to rely more on user fees and charges than on taxes, overall.[30] By 2016 the magnitude was highly significant.[31]

As the data in this chart suggest, over time, user charges and fees have become an increasingly popular mechanism of infrastructure revenue generation. These charges are easier for services that benefit someone personally, such as membership in a recreation or fitness center, than for something that benefits the society as a whole, such as water and sewer systems. Additionally, new technologies make it easier to impose user fees. For example, with improved tracking methods, municipalities are able to better monitor water usage and could develop easier methods of putting tolls on roads.[32] Some things, though, are still nearly impossible to place under a fee-for-use system, and therefore their financing has to come out of a government's general revenue account or through a specific tax. One example of this is a city's sidewalks. A city cannot reasonably place a charge on sidewalk use, or be certain that the only people using the sidewalk are those who pay taxes. However, there is only so much taxation that the general public will abide. So municipal governments turn to the use of specific taxes on certain business activities or on special events.

Take the city of Chicago, for example. From its website, it is possible to view a list of existing taxes and for whom each tax applies. These include, among others, an airport departure tax, applying to any business that operates ground transportation from the O'Hare or Midway airports, and an electricity infrastructure maintenance fee, which is imposed on companies delivering electricity to customers. As the city puts it, the fee is "compensation for the privilege of using public rights of way."[33] These examples help to explain the ways in which cities must get creative in order to capture enough revenue to maintain existing services and provide more infrastructure in an increasingly devolutionary governmental climate.

Privatization

Financialization and valorization indicate a reorientation in the urban from supportive government to governance and increased market-based and consumer-oriented practices, as described earlier in the discussion of a fee-based revenue structure. Some scholars argue that these processes are also related to the larger push toward privatization.[34] Privatization of city services, as some see it, is the "natural" outcome of current urban policy and the continued commodification of public works.[35] But where commodification involves a shift toward extracting revenue through the use of a service or piece of infrastructure as a means of paying for the construction and maintenance of a particular piece of infrastructure, privatization takes the administration and maintenance of an infrastructure project or public service completely out of the hands of the municipality and places it under the control of a private company. This can be done through a long-term lease or an outright sale. Long-term leases, though, complicate the idea of privatization somewhat, as will be discussed later.

The move to privatization is not a direct line from commodification, however. Ashton and his colleagues found that infrastructure projects that had not yet been commodified were often among the first to be privatized.[36] This is possibly because commodified projects were seen to be still bringing in some kind of revenue to the city, rather than seen as total "money pits." After turning to commodification, municipalities started to use privatization to try to "plug" holes in their budgets—just as they did with commodification processes in the first place. They were attempting to get out from under the sinking ship of aging infrastructure. As Ashton and his colleagues put it, "Leasing these assets was viewed as a last-ditch effort to correct their poor physical and financial performance through the introduction of market discipline."[37] However, there is no guarantee that this move to a private company takeover will improve much less maintain the current levels of service. In fact, a privatization strategy has the potential to create *new* budget and service holes in, for example, the transportation network or system, such that patching roads falls privy to *different*, privatized, owners.

An important consideration, however, is whether the long-term leases contained in some privatization ventures truly represent privatization, or simply a further form of advanced commodification. In short, the private company is simply leasing the infrastructure from the municipality—producing an "arm's-length agreement" where the government could, theoretically, regain ownership of the piece of infrastructure, if deemed necessary. So perhaps there are some safeguards built into this system that have not yet been explored at length. Therefore, the processes of private management and changes in administrative control suggest that the boundaries between "public" and "private," when it comes to municipal services, may not be as distinct as previously thought.

Private, Public, and in Between

But in spite of this, private ownership or administration is seen as a big fiscal plus, institutionally, because it allows city governments to fill gaps in their budgets and relieve themselves of the burden of infrastructure maintenance, without the political liability of raising taxes. From a provider side, the only thing that is changing is who is in charge and the impact on their budget. It can be seen as a better deal for everyone, as taxpayer money is no longer required for upkeep. If city governments can make room in their budgets by selling or leasing one or more of their infrastructure assets, they can dedicate their money to other areas that are perhaps less of a drain on resources. The long-standing American resistance to increased taxation, and the desire to maintain a placid public, makes this a near ideal solution to budget shortfalls.

Commodification and privatization have mixed effects for municipal governments and the long-term implications are yet to be seen. Ashton found that bidders were willing to pay more than the initial asking price for things such as the parking meters and the Skyway toll road, both in Chicago, but the long-term value of leasing these things may not have been as lucrative to governments as it initially seems.[38] There is a massive influx in revenue at the start of the lease, but management companies are able to make significant profits off the lease's administration. Part of this is due to the levels of information available to both parties in the deal-making process. Companies are able to use data on ridership, usage rates, and other things one can track from an existing piece of infrastructure. Municipalities, on the other hand, do not have the financial expertise or forecasting mechanisms to see how the deal will work out for them in the future, because it is impossible to know the future.

Privatization has become commonplace, especially after the recession of 2008, which left municipalities hurting for revenue even more than they were before.[39] But privatization raises some important concerns about infrastructure maintenance and changes to urban governance. Another issue raised by Ashton and his colleagues is that investors use their advanced financial knowledge to make deals that look good upfront but are potentially damaging to a city's overall financial health.[40] This is because "they increase the investor's indebtedness, require higher annual revenues to cover costs, and potentially encumber the public sector with responsibilities to creditors and counterparties should purchasers default on the concession agreement."[41] So privatization creates new financing issues despite being seen as an early fiscal panacea for infrastructure issues. Privatization also raises issues for urban governance more broadly, as we will see in the next section.

Finally, commodification and privatization raise concerns about the rights of citizens as the pieces of infrastructure they interact with on a day-to-day basis are further privatized. This raises questions, more generally, with regard to the "right to the city" and who has access to municipal services.[42] Services may become more selective by charging higher user fees, thereby limiting access to a nominally public good. The "right to the city," then, becomes less a citizen's political right than a consumer's economic right. This seemingly minor distinction can mean a world of difference from a user's point of view. In some ways, commodification can be seen as taking formerly public goods and moving them closer to privatization. These once-public goods and services, then, become less about collective rights of urbanness and more about individual consumption or membership. This can also be seen in the rise of private spaces, such as gated communities that exist within a wider municipality, as detailed in Evan McKenzie's *Privatopia: Homeowner Associations and the Rise of Residential Private Government.*[43]

Urban Governance

Privatization is part of a larger shift in the economic foundation of cities everywhere in the world. But even with such a shift to global entrepreneurialism, the question remains: Why have so many cities, globally, chosen market-oriented policies as the basis for a political-economic model of governance? The answer, for geographer and political economist David Harvey, is a shift from govern-mental "managerialism to entrepreneurialism."[44] Harvey, among several scholars, argues that this is due to the very real risk of capi-tal mobility.[45] Cities believe that they must do all they can to keep businesses within city limits. It is easier than ever for a business to move to a new location—taking its tax payments and employment opportunities along with it. Jason Hackworth offers another possi-ble explanation for this move to entrepreneurialism and privatiza-tion. Hackworth says it is "the result of an institutionally regulated and policed disciplining of localities"—a marketized urban political economy and a state that supports this marketization.[46]

One thing that all these scholars will agree on is that urban poli-tics, and the resultant processual governance that privatization creates, have changed focus in recent decades. One of the key con-testations defining urban politics has become the entrepreneurial competition between localities—instead of working to better the city for the citizens, officials are now focused on building a "global city" that appeals to outsiders and business interests—one that could attract more investment.[47] The debate is more closely related to choice, and few would argue that neoliberalism has not changed the way cities operate and plan. Harvey, for one, says that this accel-eration in interurban competition is a natural process under capital-ism. Further, he argues that entrepreneurial urbanism or full-bore privatization is a reaction to the increasingly distressed (infrastruc-tural) condition of cities in the 1980s.

A decreased tax base, and the decline of central or federal sup-port, has left U.S. cities in a pinch. Having already commodified public services and utilities, but needing more assistance, cities have been forced to look anew for another means of getting and maintaining a fiscal base for infrastructure development. As long ago as 1985 a colloquium of business leaders, policy makers, and academics from major world cities took it as standard wisdom that they could improve cities by attracting new enterprises.[48] The process of attracting and retaining business development defined the shift from what Harvey termed "the managerial approach," which would subsidize or even take over struggling businesses, to "the entrepreneurial approach," which would attempt to lure new investment with infrastructure improvements, tax breaks, and other attractions.[49] As we have seen in the three decades since that colloquium, many cities, worldwide, have adopted "the entrepreneurial" or privatization model as the latest version of "post-commodification" financialization.

Hackworth, however, would argue that this "entrepreneurial" approach to urbanism is less a "natural choice" that is the result of advanced capitalism than it is the result of institutional regulation and policing.[50] This regulation model rewards those who follow a devolutionary, antitax, neoliberal policy path and punishes those who diverge from that path, making it difficult to utilize alternative forms of urban development and politics. Globally, these regulation and policing mechanisms operate through the World Bank and the International Monetary Fund. More particularly, in the "developed" world, the regulation mechanisms are generally U.S.- or U.K.-based bond-rating agencies, such as Moody's and Standard & Poor's. In most of the rest of the developing world, the World Bank and International Monetary Fund, for example, require global urban debtors to follow their protocols or face sanctions, and the bond-rating agencies can give localities lower ratings, if the agencies do not agree with their practices. Using Jason Hackworth's framework, municipalities must promote economic growth above other municipal issues or face serious repercussions, which makes it difficult to undertake any sort of development project or improvement.[51] Public infrastructure historian Alberta Sbragia would agree, saying that elected officials "often have relatively little control over the capital infrastructure that shapes a city and the opportunities enjoyed by its residents."[52]

With the continued proliferation of public authorities, special districts, and Community Improvement Districts, the increased need to come up with yet another mode of financing short of raising taxes in the United States has led to new forms of privatization or entrepreneurialism. In this search, municipal governments have become further decentralized—turning to new modes of public–private partnerships or municipal process or governance. This is especially the case when considering privately owned or entrepreneurial pieces of the infrastructure grid. This raises both challenges and opportunities for urban governments. Municipalities must now come up with unusual and often opaque (to voters) financing mechanisms, as discussed in chapter 8. One by now familiar example is cities that are using "payments in lieu of taxes," or PILOTs, to gain revenue from universities and other tax-exempt organizations. More important are the implications that infrastructure privatization has for citizens. As pieces of the city are broken apart and sold to separate buyers, the devolutionary state further removes itself from accountability to the public. Public goods are no longer seen as a right, but rather as a service—available for purchase by the well-heeled consumer. Privatization does not just affect infrastructure; it changes the definition of "public" in the city. The rise of subdivisions, gated communities, and homeowners' associations further the support of government(s) and change the structure of governance in the city. The new networks of advancing privatization leave little in the way of accountability. In the end, therefore, it can be unclear exactly who is responsible for the maintenance of public assets, the construction of new infrastructure, and more in this age of increasing privatization. What is clear is that urban infrastructure privatization is an evolving process that gained popularity as municipalities struggled to both fill gaps in their budget and maintain an expected level of service provision. Building the "public city" has become an increasingly "private" activity.

Notes

1. Transportation for America, *The Fix We're in For: The State of Our Nation's Busiest Bridges* (Washington, D.C., October 2013), http://t4america .org/maps-tools/bridges/metros.

2. Steven Cohen "Paying for Infrastructure," *Huffington Post*, December 28, 2016.

3. Robert Samuelson, "We Need Higher Taxes," *Washington Post*, August 27, 2017.

4. Cohen, "Paying for Infrastructure."

5. Albert Gallatin, "Report on Roads, Canals, Harbors, and Rivers" (1808), https://bit.ly/2HTygMs.

6. National Council on Public Works Improvements, *Fragile Foundations: A Report on America's Public Works* (Washington, D.C.: Government Printing Office, 1988).

7. Pat Choate and Susan Walters, *America in Ruins: The Decaying Infrastructure* (Durham, N.C.: Duke University Press, 1981); U.S. Congress, Office of Technology Assessment, *Rebuilding the Foundations: Report on State and Local Public Works Financing and Management* (Washington, D.C.: Government Printing Office, 1990), https://bit.ly/2JYsOnX.

8. Quoted in Herbert Muschamp, "Architecture View: Two for the Roads, A Vision of Urban Design," *New York Times*, February 13, 1994.

9. Letty Anderson, "Fire and Disease: The Development of Water Supply Systems in New England 1870–1900," in *Technology and the Rise of the Networked City in Europe and America*, ed. Joel A. Tarr and Gabriel Dupuy (Philadelphia: Temple University Press, 1988), 141–42.

10. Anderson, 141–42.

11. Josef W. Konvitz, *The Urban Millennium: The City-Building Process from the Early Middle Ages to the Present* (Carbondale: Southern Illinois University Press, 1985).

12. Konvitz, 101.

13. Konvitz, 103.

14. Konvitz, 108.

15. Konvitz, 112.

16. Letty Anderson, "Hard Choices: Supplying Water to New England Towns," *Journal of Interdisciplinary History* 15, no. 2 (1984): 211–34.

17. Anderson, 211–34.

18. Bruce E. Seeley, "The Saga of American Infrastructure: A Republic Bound Together," *Wilson Quarterly* 17 (Winter 1993): 18–39.

19. Tarr and Dupuy, *Technology and the Rise of the Networked City*, 152.

20. Seeley, "Saga of American Infrastructure," 30.

21. Muschamp, "Architecture View."

22. Konvitz, *The Urban Millennium*, 129.

23. Office of Technology Assessment, *Rebuilding the Foundations: State and Local Public Works Financing and Management* (Washington, D.C.: Government Printing Office, 1990); Pat Choate and Susan Walter, *America in Ruins: Decay of Infrastructure* (Durham, N.C.: Duke University Press, 1983).

24. Seeley, "Saga of American Infrastructure," 20.

25. See David C. Perry, ed. *Building the Public City: The Politics, Governance and Finance of Public Infrastructure* (London: Sage, 1995).

26. John G. Matsusaka, "Initiative and Referendum," in *Encyclopedia of Public Choice*, ed. Charles K. Rowley and Friedrich Schneider (Kluwer: Academic Publishers, 2004), 2.

27. Perry, "Building the City Through the Back Door: The Politics of Debt, Law, Infrastructure," in Rowley and Schneider, 1–20.

28. Perry, 20.

29. Philip Ashton, Marc Doussard, and Rachel Weber, "The Financial Engineering of Infrastructure Privatization: What Are Public Assets Worth to Private Investors?" *Journal of the American Planning Association* 78, no. 3 (2012): 300–312.

30. Michael A. Pagano and David Perry, "Financing Infrastructure in the 21st Century City," *Public Works Management & Policy* 13, no. 1 (2008): 22–38.

31. Lincoln Land Institute, "Cities Increasing Reliance on Fees as Other Revenues Fall" (May 7, 2015), https://bit.ly/2JzwnEo; Michael A. Pagano, "Why All Those New Fees Your City Is Charging Are Likely Permanent," CityLab, October 17, 2012, https://bit.ly/2E6VRW1.

32. Pagano and Perry, "Financing Infrastructure in the 21st Century City," 27.

33. City of Chicago, Revenue Department, Tax Policy Division, "Information Bulletin: Electricity Use Tax & Infrastructure Maintenance Fee," 1998, https://bit.ly/2IkvSxB; City of Chicago, Department of Finance, Tax Collection and Enforcement, "Tax List," 2015, https://bit.ly/1tzCUB4.

34. David Harvey, A Brief History of Neoliberalism (New York: Oxford University Press, 2007).

35. Harvey, 12.

36. Ashton, Doussard, Weber, "Financial Engineering of Infrastructure," 302.

37. Ashton, Doussard, Weber, 302.

38. Ashton, Doussard, Weber, 301.

39. Ashton, Doussard, Weber, 302.

40. Ashton, Doussard, Weber, 304.

41. Ashton, Doussard, Weber, 304–5.

42. Henri Lefebvre, "The Right to the City," in Writings on Cities, trans. and ed. Eleonore Kofman and Elizabeth Lebas (Hoboken: Wiley-Blackwell, 1996); David Harvey, "The Right to the City," in The City Reader, 6th ed., ed. Richard T. LeGates and Frederic Stout (London: Routledge, 2015), 23–40.

43. Evan McKenzie, Privatopia: Homeowner Associations and the Rise of Residential Private Government (New Haven, Conn.: Yale University Press, 1994).

44. Harvey, "Right to the City," 29.

45. Jamie Peck, "Geography and Public Policy: Constructions of Neoliberalism," Progress in Human Geography 28, no. 3 (2004): 392–405.

46. Jason Hackworth, Neoliberal City: Governance, Ideology, Development in American Urbanism (Ithaca, N.Y.: Cornell University Press, 2007).

47. David Harvey, "From Managerialism to Entrepreneurialism: The Transformation in Urban Governance in Late Capitalism," Geografiska Annaler 71B, no. 1 (1989): 3–17.

48. Harvey, 6.

49. Harvey, 12.

50. Hackworth, Neoliberal City.

51. Hackworth, 111.

52. Gail Radford, The Rise of the Public Authority: Statebuilding and Economic Development in Twentieth-Century America (Chicago: University of Chicago Press, 2013), 155.

Conclusion

The Fate of the Public Realm

Dennis R. Judd, Evan McKenzie, and Alba Alexander

The political scientist Adam Przeworski referred to a style of democracy that he calls "contra-majoritarian," by which he meant the subjecting of "decisions of the majority to control by an unelected body . . . or to remove some aspects of policy . . . from the control of majorities."[1] The institutional arrangements that govern America's urban regions have become "contra-majoritarian" by reducing what E. E. Schattschneider called the "scope of conflict."[2] In the case of the region-wide port and development authorities that began in the 1920s, reformers were motivated by the desire to insulate professional expertise from the patronage systems presided over by party organizations. These institutions served as the template for the countless variations on the public authority and special district that have evolved in the years before and just after World War II, during the urban renewal era of the 1950s and the Great Society programs of the 1960s, and in the 1970s and beyond when mayors and public officials searched about for new ways to raise capital for inner-city redevelopment projects. The privatization of housing and urban development was motivated by a similar impulse. By the twenty-first century, the institutional architecture of urban regions had been utterly transformed.[3]

The essays in this volume have traced the consequences of this decades-long process. James M. Smith demonstrated that the rise of the Metropolitan Pier and Exposition Authority in Chicago reduced the scope for citizen influence by moving most major development decisions in the city behind nearly impenetrable institutional walls. As Smith noted, Chicago is not peculiar in this regard; in other cities, as well, the institutional capacity and financial resources necessary for ambitious undertakings have been moved beyond the confines of municipal government.[4] Smith's study shows that even well-insulated quasi-public authorities sometimes respond to public pressures, but only when major controversies break into the open.[5]

Evan McKenzie shows that multipurpose special districts have become a common mechanism for moving municipal affairs out of the public realm and behind closed doors. These multipurpose special districts are able to fund a range of services and build infrastructure by issuing revenue bonds, which are then repaid through taxes imposed on residents who reside within special districts. In McKenzie's view, this arrangement is problematic because these districts operate under an astonishingly large assortment of names and their governance and powers are opaque and often ambiguously defined. For the average citizen, they are virtually invisible.

Peter Eisinger's essay on Detroit's 2013 bankruptcy provides a glimpse into just how fast municipal authority can be curbed when political and economic elites feel threatened by popular control. In exchange for delivering Detroit from bankruptcy, state officials and investors demanded that the city transfer much of its authority to regional, state, and nonprofit bodies. Private money began flowing into new developments in the downtown and into a few neighborhoods, but the city's elected officials and their supporters were elbowed to the sidelines. The Detroit case poses troubling questions about local democracy and accountability, all the more so because the black majority that had governed the city was effectively forced to transfer its political influence to political actors outside the city and to even more distant financial institutions. As Eisinger points out, Detroit's example has not yet been replicated in other cities, but inner-city residents who live elsewhere may not find this fact to be especially reassuring.

Special authorities take many forms. Steven P. Erie, Scott A. MacKenzie, and Jameson W. Doig point out that the American federal system "gives states and local governments wide latitude in structuring the governance of transportation systems and thereby enables citizens to determine where to place their trust." In the case of New York, a huge and sprawling, politically powerful and resource-rich multipurpose bistate authority has built and administered the region's transportation networks; in Los Angeles, by contrast, multiple single-purpose local agencies with close ties to municipal governments emerged. The authors argue that New York's regional approach has created a separate realm dominated by professional staffs who forge connections with powerful political leaders. By contrast, a multitude of constituencies have been able to influence transportation policies in Los Angeles. Despite these very different structures, however, special authorities in both contexts have been careful to maintain broad support through "careful stewardship of their reputations and active cultivation of supporters." Above all, the success of these public authorities "in carrying out [their] projects on time and without scandal marginalized opposition."

In their essay, Ellen Dannin and Douglas Cantor argue that private actors and public institutions have always been involved in the construction of water systems, and sometimes their relationship has resulted in an awkward dance. Dissatisfaction with water quality and availability sometimes has led to full or partial privatization; in other cases, reformers have successfully pressed for full public control. Public–private partnerships have often been employed as a solution, but the contracts associated with them have provoked controversy because they guarantee compensation to savvy private contractors and leave individual citizens liable for any failings. Recently, according to Dannin and Cantor, a middle ground has been found.

Public–public partnerships (PUPs) have emerged to provide urban water services in both developed and developing countries. These entities, which keep financial arrangements in-house, involve some combination of local, state, national, and nonprofit organizations.[6] There are several types of collaborations, defined by the specific objectives or mandates that established the PUPs. Evaluations of water PUPs (numbering more than 130 in at least seventy countries) confirm that their benefits include "improved service delivery capacity at [a] lower cost" than is offered in public–private partnerships; greater user participation in decision-making and service delivery; and extended areas of service to the previously unserved.[7] PUPs also align with the wider objective of reviving the city as a publicly controlled, rather than a private and exclusionary, entity.[8]

In the British case, Alba Alexander finds that reducing the state's size leads not to, and probably was never intended to lead to, less public intervention but rather to a recrafting of relationships between public and private sectors in the latter's favor. Recently, however, the Labour Party has successfully promoted a realistic political alternative. Despite the 2019 Brexit-induced defeat, the Labour Party still offers a popular program to deprivatize utilities and transport, revive public housing, restore at least some taxes on the wealthy, and extend public oversight over an economy that has generated ever steeper inequality for decades.[9] With the collapse in 2018 of a major U.K. construction firm, and the huge negative knock-on effects, much of the mainstream and highly conservative British press has come to the conclusion that public–private partnerships may no longer be the policy solutions they were purported to be.[10] As a result, these partnerships, which began under Margaret Thatcher's government, have been on the wane of late.[11]

Shu Wang and Rebecca Hendrick's essay in this volume offers a perceptive case study revealing how fiscal crises drive the constant search for seemingly neutral and nonpolitical solutions to local problems. As they point out, this search has been going on since the recessions of the 1970s. The Great Recession of 2008–9 introduced a new normal: local officials now thoroughly understand that a large share of urban infrastructure and public services will be financed privately by users, and not as much by taxes. Special assessments (SAs) have become one of the popular instruments for this purpose. SAs normally take the form of additional, and usually temporary, property taxes levied against individual property parcels contained within a designated area. Such a system constitutes, in effect, a privatized marketplace for public goods, one that replaces an overall public agenda with short-term, highly specific and targeted costs and benefits. The attraction of SAs is that they appear to be merely technical and nonpolitical instruments of urban finance, but their effect is to move questions about the larger public good out of the public arena entirely.

Rachel Weber, Amanda Kass, and Sara Hinkley analyze the widespread use of variable-rate debt instruments by local governments to build infrastructure. The authors particularly focus on the case of the Chicago Public Schools (CPS) and its use of auction-rate securities and interest-rate swaps during the 2000s. For school districts and other local governments, the municipal-securities market filled a critical funding vacuum left in the wake of the state and federal cutbacks that began in the 1980s. With access to debt at initially lower costs, proceeds from debt allowed the CPS to pay down past debts, fund current operations, and invest in capital projects. Along with these powers, however, exotic financial instruments exposed the schools, and the city of Chicago, to the risks inherent in global capital markets and entailed new sets of legal liabilities, costs, and institutional compromises that posed considerable risk to taxpayers and local residents, and practically no risk at all for the firms providing the credit.

The full meaning of the case studies presented in this volume can be fully appreciated only within a larger historical context. In their essay, David C. Perry and Mary Donoghue trace the trajectory of infrastructure policy in the United States, which has moved from a nineteenth- and early twentieth-century emphasis on public infrastructure projects undertaken by states and local governments to the creation of special authorities and special districts. In recent decades, the particular institutional form has become less and less relevant because all of them tend to rely on financing methods that commodify and privatize infrastructure and services. Whatever the institutional arrangement may be, creative financing schemes are used to bring together allegedly tax-averse public officials, private actors, and financial institutions into a closed realm of consultation, cooperation, and negotiation.[12] There are few if any realistic alternatives to this model because the system "rewards those who follow a devolutionary, antitax, neoliberal policy path and punishes those who diverge from that path." This model has now become truly ubiquitous, and even international, as can be seen with the crucial role of the World Bank, the International Monetary Fund, and, in the European Union, the European Bank. At all levels of government, a constellation of specialized institutions facilitates bargaining and cooperation within a closed system. The impact on urban politics has been truly profound; because the "pieces of the city are broken apart and sold to separate buyers, the devolutionary state further removes itself from accountability to the public."[13]

Bringing the Political Back into the Local State

The shrinking role of the municipality in the governance of America's urban regions has sharply reduced the ability of local residents to influence some of the most important decisions that affect their lives. In our introductory essay, we made reference to "shadow governments" that operate mostly out of sight and out of mind. The essays in this volume open a partial window onto that world. A wide range of institutional arrangements—both formal and informal—constitute the playing field of urban development in the contemporary era. As we have seen, a dizzying variety of public authorities and special districts have been proliferating for decades. The conversion of public assets into sources of private profit has become a common remedy for the fiscal problems facing local governments. Creative financing schemes have become the norm. Privatizations in municipal life vary according to the degree they shift accountability and ownership away from public control.[14] Cities strapped for resources to cover budget shortfalls have sought to sell or lease public infrastructure or land, outsource services, and engage in public–private partnerships.[15] Cash infusions for struggling municipalities have entailed transfers of public assets, such as land, parking meters, toll roads, and airports, to private direction. Cities also may cease providing a public service and subsidize private provision of it instead, as with prisons, schools, and general maintenance contracts.[16]

For scholars, studying "urban politics" once meant a focus on city governments, but we are now aware that the net must be cast much wider in an era when mobile capital, quasi-governmental authorities (local, regional, public/private), and the privatization of the public sphere has become the norm. Although the movement away from democratic governance may now seem irresistible, a space for change remains. Kimberly Morgan and Ann Shola Orloff have recently noted, "Although many once advocated shrinking public sectors so as to liberate markets, many policymakers now believe that building up states and improving their 'quality' (e.g., governance) is vital for economic development or political stability."[17] Inducing the local state to achieve more inclusive decision-making and collective social protections (beyond a status quo of austerity) will require both political will and institutional design.[18] In some cases private-sector contracts, especially in the provision of water and energy, have been replaced by full public-sector control.[19] A few years ago the Baltimore City Council approved a charter amendment that prohibits the sale or lease of government-owned water-supply and sewer systems.[20] The Northampton, Massachusetts, City Council made it illegal for the city's water to be "sold, leased or transferred into private ownership."[21] The city of Atlanta ended the largest water-privatization deal with United Water only four years into a twenty-year deal because of "poor service, fraudulent billing, and poor water quality."[22] Winter Park, Florida, assumed responsibility for the provision of electricity.[23] For years, Boulder, Colorado, was embroiled in a protracted battle with Xcel Energy Inc. to create a city-owned electric utility, a measure approved in 2011 by Boulder voters on the condition that the new utility meet or exceed existing rates and service.[24] Chattanooga, Tennessee, was not successful in taking over ownership of its water supply, but the failed attempt illustrates what can happen when citizens become aroused. Despite these examples, however, any effort to achieve reform on other than a case-by-case basis would meet with formidable obstacles. The most important of these is the chronic fiscal problems faced by local governments.

The most obvious—and perhaps only—way to remove the fiscal straightjacket imposed on municipalities would entail some degree of assistance from the states or the federal government. A 2016 Chicago Council on Global Affairs panel conceded that cities cannot be a force for greater equity "without national-level financial and policy support." Absent that aid, the dilemma remains that "cities must ensure the wealthy pay more taxes to fund and protect inclusion, but this may well drive them out of the city . . . a prospect about which . . . cities are generally "terrified."[25] Within their regions, cities are engaged in a constant competition for taxpayers and businesses. This circumstance makes cities loath to raise taxes for social programs; in addition, it tempts, or forces them, to find ways of offloading some of their responsibilities onto quasi-governmental or nonpublic institutions. Changing this fact would require serious rethinking on a national scale.[26]

It is possible that some help may come from the Democratic administration that won the presidency in 2020. Large infrastructure and energy projects funded through a "Green New Deal," "Second New Deal," "New New Deal," and "New Deal for the 21st Century, could provide a big boost for cities and, potentially, change the institutional structure of urban development in the U.S."[27] The task would be to design institutions that "elicit identification, interest, mobilization, [and] solidarity . . . which then have a recursive element, so that participation leads to a virtuous circle of more trust, more solidarity, more active mobilization in favor of normatively attractive values, which then, if they work actually to improve people's lives, can generate further support."[28] The politics supporting such a transformation are hard to foresee, but it is not impossible.

In the meantime, those seeking to open new spaces for democratic engagement would be well served to seek more practical and less ambitious reforms. First, it is essential that shadow governments of all kinds be exposed to the light of day. Systems characterized by transparency are corrigible; those that are not are extremely difficult to change. As it now stands, the multitude of special authorities and special districts that exist in urban regions are mostly hidden behind an impenetrable curtain. It is time to pull it back. All quasi-public governing units should be required to record their presence in a public statewide registry, follow standardized governance procedures, abide by open meetings and open reporting statutes, and conform to freedom-of-information statutes. All essential documents pertaining to the operation of such entities—such as budgets, proposals, plans, meeting minutes, rules of operation, and biographies of board and staff members—should be public and posted on the web. It should be as easy for the media and interested citizens to discover what quasi-public governments are up to as it is for them to follow the deliberations of city councils and municipal departments.

Second, it should be difficult, not easy, to bring quasi-governmental units into existence. States should put into place mechanisms that carefully govern the process by which special authorities and districts are created. Since 1963 every county in California has had a Local Agency Formation Commission that has the power to approve, establish, reorganize, and, in some cases, dissolve, special districts and even municipalities. State and local governments should scrutinize proposals to create such entities to ensure that they remain transparent, accountable, and well managed.

Third, where there are elections for the boards of special authorities and districts, state law should prohibit property-based voting (such as one acre, one vote) and instead impose the principle of one person, one vote. Twenty-first-century democracy, rather than some archaic version of democracy inherited from the nineteenth century, must be the guiding standard.

It is time to expand the spaces for local democratic governance in America's urban regions by expanding the reach of municipal governance. In this way the metropolis can, once again, become a domain for a healthy and expansive democratic politics.

Notes

1. Adam Przeworski, *Why Bother with Elections?* (Cambridge, U.K.: Polity Press, 2018).

2. "The size of the constituencies being mobilized, the inclusiveness or exclusiveness of the conflicts people expect to develop have a bearing on all theories about how politics is or should be organized . . . Nearly all theories about politics have something to do with the question of who can get in to the fight and who is to be excluded." E. E. Schattschneider, *The Semisovereign People: A Realist's View of Democracy in America* (New York: Holt, 1961), 20.

3. Naomi Klein, *The Shock Doctrine: The Rise of Disaster Capitalism* (New York: Henry Holt, 2007); Philip Mirowski, *Never Let a Serious Crisis Go to Waste* (London: Verso, 2014); Bernard Harcourt, *The Illusion of Free Markets: Punishment and the Myth of Natural Order* (Cambridge, Mass.: Harvard University Press, 2012); Wendy Brown, *Undoing the Demos* (New York: Zone Books, 2015).

4. This point is echoed by Philip Ashton, Marc Doussard, and Rachel Weber, "Reconstituting the State: City Powers and Exposures in Chicago's Infrastructure Leases," *Urban Studies* 53, no. 7 (May 2016): 1384–1400. They argue that "infrastructure leases require a mobilisation and reconfiguration of state powers."

5. Ryan Smith, "The End of Rahm Emanual's Rule Means the Center May No Longer Hold in Chicago," *Chicago Reader*, September 5, 2018.

6. See Gemma Boag and David A. McDonald, "A Critical Review of Public-Public Partnerships in Water Services," *Water Alternatives* 3, no. 1 (February 2010): 1–25.

7. Boag and McDonald, 13.

8. Gerald E. Frug, "The City: Private or Public?" (LSE Cities Working Papers, London School of Economics and Political Science, March 13, 2017), https://bit.ly/2s2H3kM.

9. Toby Helm, "Labour Gains Three-Point Lead as May's Brexit Plan Hits Buffers," *The Guardian*, November 17, 2018.

10. Kimiko Freytas-Kamura, "Collapse of Construction Giant Rattles the Government," *New York Times*, January 15, 2018.

11. For example, the Labour Party has reversed its previous policy since the 1990s, promoting private-finance initiatives. See the following comment by the Labour Party deputy leader. John McDonnell, "The Carillion Scandal Must Bury the Rip-Off PFI Dogma for Good," *The Guardian*, January 16, 2018.

12. This attribution of antitax sentiment is "at odds with the evidence." The reality is that "most Americans are willing to pay taxes to fund concrete pragmatic programs targeted to jobs and wages, educational opportunity, and protection against illness and deprivation that rob Americans of their chance to make their way in the world." Benjamin Page and Lawrence Jacobs, *Class War: What Americans Really Think about Inequality* (Chicago: University of Chicago Press, 2009), 23. See also Vanessa S. Williamson, *Read My Lips: Why Americans Are Proud to Pay Taxes* (Princeton, N.J.: Princeton University Press, 2017). On why some taxes are "more protest-prone than others," see Isaac William Martin and Nadav Gabay, "Tax Policy and Tax Protest in 20 Rich Democracies, 1980–2010," *British Journal of Sociology* 69, no. 3 (September 2018): 647–69.

13. Perry and Donoghue, "Building the Public City, Privately," in this volume, 263.

14. Paul Starr, "The Meaning of Privatization," *Yale Law and Policy Review* 6 (1988): 6–41.

15. Emanuel S. Savas, *Privatization and Public-Private Partnerships* (New York: Congressional Quarterly, 1999).

16. Philip Mattera and Mafruza Khan with Greg LeRoy and Kate Davis, *Jail Breaks: Economic Development Subsidies Given to Private Prisons* (Washington, D.C.: Good Jobs First, 2001), https://osf.to/1WsiGDO; Josh Cunningham, *Comprehensive School Choice Policy* (Washington, D.C.: National Conference of State Legislatures, 2013).

17. Kimberly J. Morgan and Ann Shola Orloff, introduction to *The Many*

Hands of the State: Theorizing Political Authority and Social Control, ed. Kimberly J. Morgan and Ann Shola Orloff (New York: Cambridge University Press, 2017), 1.

18. "We cannot assume, automatically, that the local generates more robust and meaningful participation. We should ask about the conditions that determine whether central or local participation is more likely to generate practical and normative solutions that are highly desirable, including enhanced patterns of participation. Presently, we do not have good enough answers." Ira Katznelson, "Democracy After the Welfare State: An Interview," in *Democracy and the Welfare State: The Two Wests in the Age of Austerity*, ed. Alice Kessler-Harris and Maurizio Vaudagna (New York: Columbia University Press, 2018), 97.

19. Soren Becker, Ross Beveridge, and Matthias Naumann, "Remunicipalization in German Cities: Contesting Neo-Liberalism and Reimagining Urban Governance," *Space and Polity* 19, no. 1 (2015): 76–90; Diane Cardwell, "Cities Weigh Taking Over from Private Utilities," *New York Times*, March 13, 2013; Joyce Valdovinos, "The Remunicipalization of Parisian Water Services: New Challenges for Local Authorities and Policy Implications," *Water International* 37, no. 2 (2012): 107–20; Mildred E. Warner and Amir Hefetz, "Insourcing and Outsourcing: The Dynamics of Privatization Among U.S. Municipalities, 2002–2007," *Journal of the American Planning Association* 78, no. 3 (2012): 313–27; Laura Macdonald and Arne Ruckert, eds., *Post-neoliberalism in the Americas* (New York: Palgrave, 2009).

20. Carey L. Biron, "Baltimore Votes to Become First Large U.S. City to Ban Water Privatization," Reuters (website), November 7, 2018, https://reut .rs/2R1G2IJ.

21. Lucas Ropek, "Northampton City Council Votes to Ban Privatization of the City's Water System," MassLive (website), May 5, 2016, https:// bit.ly/2BR21rh.

22. Craig Cox, "Atlanta Ends Failed Water Privatization Deal," Utne (website), January 2003, https://bit.ly/2TnDr8H; Douglas Jehl, "As Cities Move to Privatize Water, Atlanta Steps Back," *New York Times*, February 10, 2003.

23. Steve Lemongello, "Ten Years Later, Winter Park Celebrates Break from Private Utility," *Orlando Sentinel*, June 8, 2015; Associated Press, "TRA Accepts Chattanooga Water Settlement," September 20, 2000.

24. Jensen Werley, "City Council Approves Agreements with Xcel in Boulder Municipalization," BizWest (website), September 21, 2018, https:// bit.ly/2EYCBfs.

25. Michael Tiboris, "The Two Cities: Inequality in Global Cities," Chicago Council on Global Relations (website), June 14, 2016, https://bit .ly/2ZvYXMl.

26. See Margaret Weir and Jessica Schimer, "America's Two Worlds of Welfare: Subnational Institutions and Social Assistance in Metropolitan America," *Perspectives on Politics* 16, no. 2 (June 2018): 380–99.

27. Harold Meyerson, "Elizabeth Warren Proposes a Second New Deal," *American Prospect*, August 17, 2018, 1–5; "L.A. Need Its Own Green New Deal, City Council Says," MyNewsLA (website), April 16, 2019, https://bit.ly/2VqzS67; Nate Homan, "Mayor DeBlasio Rolls Out New York City's Green New Deal," Metro.US (website), April 22, 2019, https://bit.ly/2voSO6w; Fred Block, "Crisis and Renewal: The Outlines of a Twenty-First Century New Deal," *Socio-Economic Review* 9, no. 1 (January 2011): 31–57; Edward B. Barbier, *A Global Green New Deal: Rethinking the Economic Recovery* (Cambridge, U.K.: Cambridge University Press and United Nations Environment Programme, 2010); Theda Skocpol and Lawrence R. Jacobs, eds., *Reaching for a New Deal: Ambitious Governance, Economic Meltdown, and Polarized Politics in Obama's First Two Years* (New York: Russell Sage Foundation, 2011).

28. Ira Katznelson, "Democracy after the Welfare State: An Interview," in *Democracy and Welfare State: The Two Wests in the Age of Austerity*, ed. Alice Kessler-Harris and Maurizio Vaudagna (New York: Columbia University Press, 2018), 82–104. Also, for sympathetic critiques of the New Deal, see Katznelson, *Fear Itself: The New Deal and the Origins of Our Times* (New York: Liveright, 2014); and Nancy Rose, *Put to Work: The WPA and Public Employment in the Great Depression* (New York: Monthly Review Press, 2007).

Contributors

Alba Alexander is clinical associate professor of political science at the University of Illinois at Chicago and author of *Playing Fair: The Politics of Tax Reform in the U.S.* (forthcoming).

Douglas Cantor is lecturer in political science at California State University and Loyola Marymount University. He is a doctoral candidate in political science at the University of Illinois at Chicago.

Ellen Dannin is retired from the Dickinson Law School of Pennsylvania State University, where she was the Fannie Weiss Distinguished Faculty Scholar and professor of law. Her most recent book is *Taking Back the Workers' Law: How to Fight the Assault on Labor Rights*.

Jameson W. Doig was professor emeritus of politics and public affairs at Princeton University and visiting research professor of government at Dartmouth College. He is author of *Empire on the Hudson: Entrepreneurial Vision and Political Power at the Port of New York Authority*.

Mary Donoghue is a project analyst at Full Circle Communities, Inc., in Chicago.

Peter Eisinger is Henry Cohen Professor Emeritus of Urban Affairs at the Milano School of International Affairs, Management, and Urban Policy at the New School. Among his numerous publications is *The Rise of the Entrepreneurial State: State and Local Economic Development Policy in the United States*.

Steven P. Erie is professor emeritus of political science and director emeritus of the Urban Studies and Planning Program at the University of California, San Diego. He is coauthor of *Paradise Plundered: Fiscal Crisis and Governance Failures in San Diego* and the author of three books.

Rebecca Hendrick is professor of public administration at the University of Illinois at Chicago. She is author of *Managing the Fiscal Metropolis: The Financial Policies, Practices, and Health of Suburban Municipalities.*

Sara Hinkley is lecturer in city and regional planning at the University of California, Berkeley, where she is also policy research specialist at the Center for Labor Research and Education.

Dennis R. Judd is professor emeritus of political science at the University of Illinois at Chicago. He is coauthor of *Building the City of Spectacle: Mayor Richard M. Daley and the Remaking of Chicago.*

Amanda Kass is associate director of the Government Finance Research Center and doctoral candidate in urban planning and policy at the University of Illinois at Chicago.

Scott A. MacKenzie is associate professor of political science at the University of California, Davis, and coauthor of *Paradise Plundered: Fiscal Crisis and Governance Failures in San Diego.*

Evan McKenzie is professor of political science at the University of Illinois at Chicago. His most recent book is *Beyond Privatopia: Rethinking Residential Private Government.*

David C. Perry is professor emeritus of urban planning and policy and former director of the Great Cities Institute, University of Illinois at Chicago. The latest of his eleven books is *The University as Urban Anchor.*

James M. Smith is associate professor of political science at the University of Indiana South Bend.

Shu Wang is assistant professor of agriculture, food, and resource economics at Michigan State University.

Rachel Weber is professor of urban planning and policy at the University of Illinois at Chicago and author of *From Boom to Bubble: How Finance Built the New Chicago.*

Index

Page numbers in italic refer to figures.

(continued from page ii)

VOLUME 22
The Fragmented Politics of Urban Preservation: Beijing, Chicago, and Paris
Yue Zhang

VOLUME 21
Turkish Berlin: Integration Policy and Urban Space
Annika Marlen Hinze

VOLUME 20
Struggling Giants: City-Region Governance in London,
New York, Paris, and Tokyo
Paul Kantor, Christian Lefèvre, Asato Saito, H. V. Savitch, and Andy
Thornley

VOLUME 19
Does Local Government Matter? How Urban Policies Shape Civic Engagement
Elaine B. Sharp

VOLUME 18
Justice and the American Metropolis
Clarissa Rile Hayward and Todd Swanstrom, Editors

VOLUME 17
Mobile Urbanism: Cities and Policymaking in the Global Age
Eugene McCann and Kevin Ward, Editors

VOLUME 16
Seeking Spatial Justice
Edward W. Soja

VOLUME 15
Shanghai Rising: State Power and Local Transformations
in a Global Megacity
Xiangming Chen, Editor

VOLUME 14
A World of Gangs: Armed Young Men and Gangsta Culture
John M. Hagedorn

VOLUME 13
El Paso: Local Frontiers at a Global Crossroads
Victor M. Ortíz-González

VOLUME 12
Remaking New York: Primitive Globalization and the
Politics of Urban Community
William Sites